Teacher Education through Open and Distance Learning

How can open and distance learning and information and communications technology (ICT) provide us with more – and better – teachers?

Open and distance learning is increasingly used in teacher education in developing and industrialized countries. It has the potential to strengthen and expand the teaching profession of the twenty-first century and to help achieve the target of education for all by 2015. *Teacher Education through Open and Distance Learning* examines the case for using open and distance learning and ICT to train our educators. It describes and analyses the ways in which these methods and technologies are used for:

- Initial teacher training and continuing professional development
- Training principals and school managers
- Training those who provide non-formal adult and community education
- Communities of practice and sharing of knowledge and ideas within the teaching profession

It also discusses the policy-making, management, technology, costing, evaluation and quality assurance aspects of this work.

Teacher Education through Open and Distance Learning draws on wide-ranging and international experience to summarize the strengths and weaknesses of new approaches to the education of teachers. It offers invaluable guidance to policymakers, planners, headteachers and teachers.

Bernadette Robinson is an independent consultant on teacher education and distance education, and Special Professor of Comparative Education at the University of Nottingham. **Colin Latchem**, now a consultant in open learning, was formerly Head of the Teaching Learning Group at Curtin University of Technology, Australia, and President of the Open and Distance Learning Association of Australia.

World review of distance education and open learning
A Commonwealth of Learning series
Series editor: Hilary Perraton

Higher Education through Open and Distance Learning
World review of distance education and open learning: Volume I
Edited by Keith Harry

Basic Education at a Distance
World review of distance education and open learning: Volume 2
Edited by Chris Yates and Jo Bradley

Teacher Education through Open and Distance Learning
World review of distance education and open learning: Volume 3
Edited by Bernadette Robinson and Colin Latchem

Editorial advisory group

Maureen O'Neill	President, International Development Research Centre, Canada (chair)
Professor Uma Coomaraswamy	Vice-Chancellor, Open University of Sri Lanka
Sir John Daniel	Assistant Director General, UNESCO
Dato' Professor Gajaraj Dhanarajan	President, Commonwealth of Learning
Dr Linda Harasim	CEO TeleLearning Research Network, Simon Fraser University
Dr John Middleton	Director, Global Learning, World Bank Institute
Dr Hilary Perraton	Director, International Research Foundation for Open Learning (secretary)
Professor Deryck Schreuder	Vice-Chancellor, University of Western Australia
Frances van Wyk	Director, Namibia College of Open Learning

The World review of distance education and open learning is published on behalf of the Commonwealth of Learning.

The Commonwealth of Learning is an international organization established by Commonwealth governments in 1988. Its purpose is to create and widen opportunities for learning, through Commonwealth co-operation in distance education and open learning. It works closely with governments, colleges and universities with the overall aim of strengthening the capacities of Commonwealth member countries in developing the human resources required for their economic and social development.

Teacher Education through Open and Distance Learning

World review of distance education
and open learning: Volume 3

Edited by Bernadette Robinson
and Colin Latchem

London and New York

THE COMMONWEALTH *of* LEARNING

First published 2003 by RoutledgeFalmer
11 New Fetter Lane, London EC4P 4EE

Simultaneously published in the USA and Canada
by RoutledgeFalmer
29 West 35th Street, New York, NY 10001

RoutledgeFalmer is an imprint of the Taylor & Francis Group

Typeset in 10/12pt Palatino by
Graphicraft Limited, Hong Kong
Printed and bound in Great Britain by MPG books Ltd, Bodmin, Cornwall

British Library Cataloguing in Publication Data
A catalogue record for this book is available
from the British Library

Library of Congress Cataloging in Publication Data
A catalog record for this book has been requested

ISBN 0-415-36955-X (hbk)
ISBN 0-415-36956-8 (pbk)

Contents

Figures

Tables

Boxes

Contributors

Mohammad Aslam is a Professor and former Director of the School of Continuing Education, Indira Gandhi National Open University, India. He is Director of the Panchayati Raj Project.

Tony Bush is Professor of International and Comparative Education at the University of Reading. He was previously Professor of Educational Management and founding Director of the Educational Management Development Unit at the University of Leicester.

Chai Hon-Chan is a World Bank consultant and former World Bank Education Senior Evaluation Officer responsible for education investment projects in the Asia and Pacific Region, Eastern Africa, Middle East and West Indies. He was also Professor of Sociological Studies in Education and Dean of Education, University of Malaysia.

Richard Charron is Secretary-General of the Association francophone internationale des directeurs d'établissements scolaires (AFIDES) (International Association of Francophone School Administrators).

Betty Collis is Shell Professor of Network Learning, University of Twente, the Netherlands.

Helen Craig is a senior education specialist working at the International Institute for Educational Planning (IIEP). Her current responsibilities include the professional development of teachers and the impact of HIV/AIDS on education systems.

Charles Joyner is Director of International Programs, Continuing Studies and Distance Education at Simon Fraser University in Vancouver, British Columbia. Before joining Simon Fraser University in 1999, he served as a teacher education and human resources development specialist on long-term assignments in Kenya, the Philippines, Malaysia, Thailand, Pakistan and China.

Insung Jung is Associate Professor, Department of Educational Technology and Director of the Multimedia Education Center, Ewha Woman's University, South Korea.

Adrian Kirkwood is Head of the Programme on Learner Use of Media at the British Open University. He has wide experience of course development, from planning to evaluation, and has provided advice on developing open and distance learning materials in a range of contexts. He is editor of the international *Journal of Educational Media*.

Colin Latchem was formerly Head of the Teaching Learning Group, Curtin University of Technology, Perth and President of the Open and Distance Learning Association of Australia. He consults in open learning, mainly in Australia, South-east Asia and the Caribbean and researches and writes on educational matters.

Bob Moon is Professor of Education at the Open University, and a former head teacher. He was responsible for designing and implementing the university's first postgraduate certificate of education programme.

Hena Mukherjee is Lead Education Specialist in the South Asia Human Development Unit of the World Bank and a former Chief Programme Officer in the Education Programme of the Commonwealth Secretariat. She is also Associate Professor in Social Foundations, Faculty of Education, University of Malaysia.

João Batista Oliveira is an educational consultant, based in Brazil, and a former staff member of the World Bank and the International Labour Organisation.

François Orivel is Professor, Institut de Recherche sur l'Economie de l'Education, Université de Bourgogne, France.

Hilary Perraton was, at the time of writing, Director of the International Research Foundation for Open Learning (IRFOL). He is a former member of the Commonwealth Secretariat with long experience in international education and distance learning.

Charles Potter is former Deputy Director of the Centre for Continuing Education, University of the Witwatersrand, Johannesburg and head of the centre's evaluation unit. He is currently Associate Professor and Coordinator, Research Psychology Programme, School of Human and Community Development, University of the Witwatersrand.

Bernadette Robinson is an independent consultant on teacher education and distance education for governments, institutions and international agencies such as the World Bank, UNESCO, UNDP and UNICEF. Formerly in the School of Education at the British Open University, she is now Special Professor of Comparative Education, School of Continuing Education, University of Nottingham and a Research Associate of IRFOL.

Foreword

Some 60 million teachers are currently in the education workforce throughout the world. In order to meet the targets agreed upon by the 180 delegates who in 2000 participated in the Education For All forum in Dakar, Senegal, a further 15 million teachers will be required between now and the year 2010. These figures do not include the replacements that will be needed for teachers absent from classrooms, young teachers dying or incapacitated by the HIV/AIDS scourge, early retirement and migration to other vocations. The worldwide challenge to train, retrain and continuously refresh the skills and knowledge of nations' education workforce is both enormous and urgent. Apart from relying on traditional ways of providing this training and retraining, governments and all other parties interested in the health of global education need to explore other methods of teacher education and training. One option is the application of distance education in order to deliver teacher training much more aggressively.

The chapters contained in this third volume of the World Review of Distance Education and Open Learning consider the experience, strengths, weaknesses, challenges, costs and effectiveness of teacher training by distance education. The chapters also consider policy issues and management challenges that governments and institutions encounter in using distance education. Although distance education itself is getting much more widely used in the delivery of liberal arts, sciences, business and computing and continuing professional studies, its use in teacher training is sporadic and often poorly resourced, especially in the developing nations of the world where it can provide maximum benefits.

The Commonwealth of Learning (COL), which has been co-sponsoring the World Review is committed to promoting wider use of distance education generally, and in teacher training, particularly. In two large regions, South Asia and Sub-Saharan Africa, the need for in-service training of under-qualified or untrained teachers is especially pressing. Not surprisingly, these two regions are also home to the most educationally deprived populations in the world. Not too long ago, policy secretaries of education from 17 Sub-Saharan African countries met under the aegis of a COL-sponsored dialogue in Namibia. Every one of them pleaded for access to more information and knowledge on how they could put in place effective, efficient, well-functioning and well-managed distance education systems to support their teacher-training efforts. This book responds to their pleas in a number of ways. We are confident that this volume of collected works from some of the leaders in the field will add not only to their knowledge but also to that of many others concerned with teacher education.

On behalf of the Commonwealth of Learning, I wish to record our sincere appreciation to the editorial team that worked very hard in putting this publication together. We also wish to record our thanks to our publishers RoutledgeFalmer for supporting us in this venture.

Gajaraj Dhanarajan
President and CEO
Commonwealth of Learning

Acknowledgments

The editors wish to acknowledge the assistance received from the Commonwealth of Learning and its editorial advisory group in the development of the plan of the book.

Work on this book has been carried out in parallel with research activity by the International Research Foundation for Open Learning on the use of open and distance learning for teachers. This was funded by UNESCO and by the Department for International Development (DFID), under a project that was funded as part of DFID's knowledge and research strategy, 'Researching the Issues 2000'. We are grateful to both agencies for being able to use material developed within those projects. It has fed into the book generally and is reflected, in particular, in material in chapters 2 and 5. We are also grateful to Hilary Perraton for permission to reproduce Table 11.2 in Chapter 11.

Chapter 1

Teacher education

Challenge and change

Bernadette Robinson and Colin Latchem

There is increasing and strong interest among governments, institutions, international agencies and teachers themselves in the use of open and distance education methods and technologies for initial training and continuing professional development for teachers. The last decade has seen considerable growth in the number and diversity of distance education programmes, the integration of distance education with traditional provision and new initiatives using information and communication technologies (ICT). These trends are prompted by the need to meet teacher shortages, the demand for more continuing education for teachers in a changing world, the shift of attention from quantity to quality by policy-makers and planners, the introduction of new teacher education standards as countries progress, the new opportunities afforded by ICT, a search for improved training approaches and the imperative of finding new ways of using scarce resources.

International agencies, such as the World Bank, UNESCO, the Asian Development Bank, and the Commonwealth of Learning, and donors, such as the Department for International Development, UK; the Canadian International Development Agency (CIDA) and AusAid (among many others), are giving new emphasis to distance education in their policies and plans for teacher education. Distance education is appearing more often as an option in the strategic planning of governments and traditional teacher training institutions (universities and colleges).

As a result, policy-makers and planners at several levels (international, national, provincial and institutional) are in need of up-to-date information about the use of open and distance learning for teacher education and some guidance in its application. Such information can be difficult to find because reports of experience are scattered over many sources, often in the grey literature of project reports or institutional documents, or are unpublished or dated or restricted to the level of description.

To provide an up-to-date resource, this book addresses a range of planning and implementation issues in the use of open and distance learning, taking an international perspective. It draws on the international expertise and experience of professional planners and practitioners who describe and analyse experience in the use of open and distance learning approaches and technologies for teacher training and professional development. From their review of experience and research so far, they provide some guidance for policy-makers, planners and implementers of distance education programmes, showing how such programmes may replace, complement, extend, enhance, transform or combine with more traditional forms of face-to-face, institution-based provision. They also offer cautions in drawing lessons from experience.

THE PROBLEMS OF TEACHER EDUCATION

Our starting point for drawing those lessons is within teacher education. Open and distance learning programmes for teachers do not exist in isolation from the complex web of issues, policies and resource decisions that in any country affects teaching and teacher education. The decision to use open and distance learning, its purpose, content and the form it takes are situated within this broader environment and shaped by the agendas operating there. Open and distance education is more than an alternative delivery system and its concerns are more than operational ones. Its planning and use soon confront fundamental issues in teacher training and development: for example, how to achieve effective integration of theory with practice, or what model of 'ideal teacher' or theories of learning should underpin programmes and practices, or what kinds of teacher development result in better pupil learning. The extent to which planners of open and distance education engage with or neglect these kinds of issues affects the quality of the provision.

The importance of teachers in determining the quality of education is emphasized in many international reports (for example, Delors *et al.* 1996; UNESCO 1998; UNICEF 1999; UNESCO 2000a; European Commission 2000; OECD 2001). Yet attention to teacher education has tended to lag behind changes in other parts of the education system:

> Scarce resources have frequently been used for expanding systems with insufficient attention to quality improvement in areas such as teacher training and materials development.
>
> (UNESCO 2000a: 17)

Most countries still have targets to reach in providing sufficient numbers of appropriately qualified teachers or in improving the quality of their teaching force (and what counts as 'quality' changes too). This presents a formidable challenge in terms of human resource development, both logistically and financially. But the issues go beyond training alone. In synthesizing findings from the *Education for All 2000 Assessment*, the UNESCO (2000b: 57) report concludes that in some countries and especially in the European region, employers' organisations are calling for a radical restructuring of salaries, performance pay, short-term contracts . . . and more exacting standards for entry into the profession.

So the quality of teachers and teaching is affected by two related aspects: the conditions of teachers in a changing environment and their training and professional development. In this chapter we examine both of these since they provide the context in which open and distance teacher education and training are embedded.

A CONTEXT OF CHANGE

In many countries, teacher education sits uneasily in a context of rapid educational change, driven by:

- a concern to make lifelong learning a reality and to equip a country for global economic competition;
- increasing government intervention and control alongside greater decentralization;
- growing use of 'quality' to regulate education and increase accountability;
- attempts to use limited resources differently;
- the growing prominence of information and communication technologies (ICT) and high expectations of the roles they will play in education;
- greater attention among policy-makers and planners to international comparisons and standards in education;
- emerging national standards for teacher qualifications;
- curriculum reform;
- changing views of learning, from transmission models of teaching to constructivist models of learning;
- a shift of emphasis from inputs to outcomes in judging the quality and effectiveness of education systems.

Societies expect a great deal from their education systems. National governments and international organizations continue to set new goals: gender parity by 2005 and universal basic education by 2015; lifelong learning; inclusive education; education for peace, democracy and social cohesion; HIV/AIDS education; learners who are self-managing and independent, skilled in critical thinking and problem solving, and equipped with life skills; and learners competent in the use of ICT. These goals run alongside a persistent demand for education for economic purposes, leading to the criticism that 'Education is now seen as a branch of economic policy rather than a mix of social, economic and cultural policy' (Marginson 1993: 56).

As key agents in these changes, teachers face high expectations:

> Teachers become still more critical to the success of schooling as expectations about quality increase. Responses to these pressures will often result in teachers having to operate in new organisational structures, in close collaboration with colleagues and through networks, facilitating learning and overseeing individual development.
>
> (OECD 2001: 140)

Teachers face a widening range of demands everywhere, for example,

> Teachers throughout Europe are experiencing an unprecedented transition in their role and status and demands on them are becoming increasingly multi-faceted. . . . Many teachers do not have the training or experience to cope with this changing role.
>
> (European Commission 2000: 40)

Unfortunately, the high expectations and growing demands on teachers tend to run in parallel with low status, low pay and poor working conditions: 'teachers are at the heart of the education revolution, but many feel under siege . . . their diminished status is a worldwide phenomenon' (UNICEF 1999: 39).

In 1991, the situation of teachers had reached what the International Labour Organisation described as 'an intolerably low point', because working conditions had declined in all but a few countries (UNESCO 1998: 38). A decade later, the problems persist. Many qualified teachers leave teaching for more attractive careers, new graduates are not attracted to teaching, and recruitment into teacher training draws lower-qualified entrants as teaching becomes an occupation of last resort. Though many countries see a need to improve their teacher training, better training alone will not result in a teaching force of good quality.

TEACHERS

At least 1 per cent of the world's population works as teachers in the formal education system alone (in OECD countries[1] about 3 per cent

1 OECD countries (30 in June 2001): Australia, Austria, Belgium, Canada, Czech Republic, Denmark, Finland, France, Germany, Greece, Hungary, Iceland, Ireland, Italy, Japan, Korea, Luxemburg, Mexico, Netherlands, New Zealand, Norway, Poland, Portugal, Spain, Sweden, Switzerland, Turkey, United Kingdom, USA, Slovak Republic.

of the labour force is teachers). Two-thirds of the world's teachers live in developing countries (UNESCO 1996). Between 1970 and 1988, the total number of teachers employed in formal education increased from 25.5 to 44.1 million and by the mid-1990s it reached 60 million. For governments and societies, this represents a huge task of human resource development.

Within this occupational group, there is considerable diversity. Teachers vary in:

- the number of years of education received and the levels attained;
- the nature and amount of training completed and the kind of assessment made of their competence to teach;
- average age, social status, location (urban or rural) and income levels in relation to annual Gross Domestic Product (GDP) and to other professions;
- their skills as adult and independent learners;
- their beliefs and models of 'ideal teacher';
- their levels of motivation to teach well and to develop professionally;
- their access to information and communication technologies (ICT) and learning resources (teachers' journals, books on teaching, professional associations, newsletters);
- their opportunities for professional development and support;
- the number of days per year and hours per day they work, and the proportion of working time spent teaching;
- the extent to which teaching is combined with a second job;
- the time taken to progress up the salary scale from minimum to maximum (for example eight years in New Zealand but forty-two in Spain);
- their degree of choice over placement in their first post or transfer to another school;
- the way they perceive teaching – as a stepping stone to other kinds of work or as a career for life.

Professionals and 'para-professionals'

Are teachers members of a profession? An intergovernmental conference on the status of teachers recommended that:

> Teaching should be regarded as a profession: it is a form of public service which requires of teachers expert knowledge and specialist skills, acquired and maintained through rigorous continuing study; it calls also for a sense of personal and corporate responsibility for the education and welfare of pupils in their charge.
>
> (UNESCO and ILO 1966, recommendation 6)

However, the status of teaching continues to be disputed. Some argue that it cannot be a profession because of the sheer size of the teacher population, the diversity of qualification within it and its categorization in some countries as 'government work' (with accompanying low status). The use of strike action, absenteeism and teachers' withdrawal of labour in pay bargaining are also seen as 'non-professional'. There are gaps, wider in some countries than others, between teachers and other professionals:

> In some respects, teaching sits uneasily alongside professions such as medicine, law, or architecture. Teachers, for instance, are not self-employed, in most countries they do not have their own professional association that oversees a standard of good practice, nor generally do they have high status or higher salaries.
>
> (Calderhead 1994: 83)

In some countries the feminization of teaching as an occupation, especially at the primary level, has been linked to low status and pay for teachers.

The educational level on entry to teaching varies widely. Though the Recommendations Concerning the Status of Teachers (UNESCO and ILO 1966) proposed the completion of secondary education as a minimum entry standard, this has not yet been achieved worldwide. A typical primary school teacher in one country may have a master's degree and postgraduate teacher training and teach in a well-resourced school with small classes, good pay, a well-defined career path, and access to a choice of staff development opportunities and professional communities of teachers. In another, a primary teacher may have completed primary education only, be untrained as a teacher, have two jobs (teaching plus farming, trading or private tutoring) in order to earn a living wage, teach in a poorly resourced school in a remote area with little job security, salary paid months late, no career ladder in teaching and little opportunity for professional development.

The use of 'para-professionals' has grown with the expansion of education and the growth of community-supported initiatives to widen educational access and relevance. Para-professionals have also appeared as a second layer of teaching staff to enable qualified teachers to concentrate on selected aspects of their professional role or to compensate for teacher shortages. While the employment of para-professionals is often resisted by teachers' unions, they have been used successfully in a number of basic education projects, for example, the Bangladesh Rural Advancement Committee (BRAC) programme (Ahmed *et al.* 1993; Rugh and Bossett 1998), the Meghpal experiment in tribal areas of India (Barpanda 1999), rehabilitating child soldiers in Liberia and establishing community village schools in Mali (DFID 2000). These programmes show that with careful selection, some basic training and ongoing support, para-professional teachers can be effective in the roles designed for them. Some have gone on to achieve required teacher qualifications.

For some countries, unqualified teachers have been a necessity. China's considerable achievements in the expansion of universal basic education in the last two decades result in part from the use of unqualified *minban* (community-paid) teachers, though these have now been phased out as planning goals start to shift from quantity to quality. Some have achieved qualifications through distance education and joined the government-paid (*gongban*) teaching force.

SUPPLY, DEMAND AND ATTRITION

Many of the issues about the quality of teachers and teacher training are linked to problems of supply and demand, shaped by specific circumstances. While some countries have too few qualified and trained teachers, others have too many. For example, in Russia there is an over-supply, and the number of trained teachers is growing three times as fast as the number of students, because of inefficiencies in the system, (Canning *et al.* 1999). In some countries shortages and inefficiencies coexist. For example, in India in the mid-1990s, 28 per cent of schools had only one teacher for every three to four classes (ActionAid 1996), while in some places large numbers of posts remained unfilled because of bureaucratic delays or malpractices even though qualified teachers were available (Mankad 1999; Kaul 1999). Other countries face severe shortages. In some African countries (for example, Malawi and Ghana) current demand for teachers far exceeds the output capacity of the teachers' colleges.

Teacher shortages may exist throughout an educational system or be confined to particular ethnic or gender groups, specialist subjects, or rural or geographical areas (rural, mountainous, island, remote or poor urban). Shortages can also refer to teachers who have the required academic qualifications but lack professional training. For example, in the United States in the mid-1990s, over 12 per cent of newly appointed teachers had no formal training and a further 15 per cent failed to meet state standards fully (National Commission on Teaching and America's Future 1996). In Uruguay, 70 per cent of secondary teachers had not completed teacher training courses (UNESCO 1998). In both developing and industrialized countries teacher shortages may be masked because, although there are enough qualified teachers overall, they teach subjects they are neither qualified nor trained for (especially mathematics, science, art and music).

Several factors contribute to the problems of teacher supply:

- the rapid expansion of educational systems to provide basic schooling (more children in schools for longer);
- outflows through retirement being greater than the inflows of new recruits (mainly though not exclusively in industrialized countries);
- the coexistence of general skill shortages outside education, offering teachers more attractive options;
- the inability of economies to finance the levels of teachers' pay or conditions needed to make teaching more attractive;
- inefficiencies in the utilization of trained teachers;
- the length of time required before positive effects appear from any government intervention to increase supply;
- sudden political decisions which ignore human resource implications (for example, unexpected declarations of universal primary or secondary education or the removal of school fees);
- the loss of trained teachers through HIV/AIDS, expected to reach 10 per cent of teachers in the worst affected countries by 2006.

Teacher shortages so far have led to large classes, the appointment of unqualified teachers with lower levels of education, reduced school hours for pupils, temporary suspension of classes or subjects and an increase in teachers' workloads where they cover for teacherless classes. One OECD (2001) report predicts an alarming 'meltdown scenario' where standards decline and inequalities widen if present trends continue. Attempts to solve problems of shortages have included searches for new untapped sources of potential teachers, a relaxation of entry qualifications to training, emergency training schemes, increased use of substitute or paraprofessional teachers, experiments with technology as a teacher substitute or supplement, and the creation of alternative (and often innovative) routes to qualified teacher status. Some of these are stop-gap measures, others are longer-term.

Teacher attrition

Teacher attrition (the loss of teachers from teaching) has become a major problem in some countries, both developing and industrialized. Teachers leave teaching to seek better pay and conditions and improved career prospects elsewhere. For example, in Canada in the 1990s, only 75 per cent of newly qualified teachers took up posts as teachers and 25–30 per cent of these left teaching within their first five years (*Canadian Teacher* 2001). In the United Kingdom (with a total teaching force of about 430,000) around 26,700 people completed teacher training in 1998 but only 19,120 (72 per cent) were still teaching one year later (*TES* 4.5.2001: 3). In the

United States, the national average attrition rate among first-year teachers is 40 per cent (Jambor *et al.* 1997; Russell and McPherson 2001). This means that a teacher's professional life may be short and raises questions for planners about the returns to investment in training.

Could the use of incentives retain teachers for longer? It is not clear. The issue of teacher incentives is complicated and research shows that

> However well planned, non-monetary teacher incentives will rarely be effective in the absence of adequate pay, benefits and working conditions: non-monetary benefits are a complement, not a substitute for monetary benefits.
>
> (Kemmerer and Windham 1997: 197)

Few education systems have effective incentive systems and some incentives have only short-term effects (Kemmerer 1993). Good induction programmes may achieve more. A 50-state survey in the United States showed that induction programmes reduced the attrition rate of new teachers (Darling-Hammond 2000). One programme reports a 10 per cent attrition rate instead of the 40 per cent average (Jambor *et al.* 1997).

Teachers are increasingly being recruited to teach in countries other than their own. For example, Guyana (a small, poor country in South America, using donor-funded distance education programmes to upgrade its underqualified teachers) has lost many of its better and newly qualified teachers to other Anglophone countries in the Caribbean, North America and Africa (Botswana). In May 2001, New York City's Board of Education sent teams to the Caribbean to recruit 8,000 teachers for the city's poorly performing public schools at a salary at least four times that of teachers in Caribbean countries. At the same time, the United Kingdom recruited teachers from the United States and many other countries to help solve its problems of teacher supply. These few examples illustrate the increasing mobility of teachers in what is now an international labour market.

So far we have examined some macro-level issues. In the next section we turn to teacher education and training.

THE SEARCH FOR EFFECTIVE TEACHER EDUCATION AND TRAINING

The education and training of teachers was identified as one of sixteen indicators of quality in school education (European Commission 2000) but there is uncertainty about what constitutes effective training and teaching:

> The paucity of models of learning to teach, and lack of systematic data on such central issues as teaching competences and mentoring, highlight the lack of a sound empirical base from which to develop teacher education.
>
> (Bennett *et al*. 1993: 220)

Programmes vary in curricula, length, standards, levels, location (school-based or institution-based), accreditation, funding and the balance between professional or pedagogical and academic subject components.

Before going any further, we need to clarify our use of 'training'. Though 'teacher training' and 'teacher education' are often used interchangeably, many teacher-educators consider teacher training too narrow a term to describe the range of professional and personal learning experienced and criticize it as indicating a behaviourist approach. Teacher training is also used to refer to the professional studies or pedagogic part of teacher preparation and development. Teacher education, on the other hand, is seen as encompassing the whole process of teacher preparation in academic subjects, pedagogy and personal development. However, 'teacher education' and 'training' are difficult to disentangle because

> learning to teach involves being able to reason about one's actions, being able to justify particular strategies, understanding the subject matter, children and their ways of learning, and having a conception of the purposes of education and the ways in which schools operate in order to promote education.
>
> (Calderhead and Shorrock 1997: 192)

In this chapter we use 'teacher training' to mean far more than narrow skills training.

In some countries, teacher quality is defined mainly by level of qualification and the idea that a highly qualified teacher can be a poor one is alien. Subject knowledge is essential and influences what and how teachers choose to teach, but by itself it is insufficient for effective teaching and learning. To be effective, a teacher needs a combination of knowledge and skills: in academic subjects, school curricula, pedagogy, child development, communication, classroom management, creation and use of learning resources, assessment of learning and monitoring of individual progress. Research shows that teacher ability, teacher education and teacher experience are consistently related to pupil achievement (Greenwald *et al*. 1996) and that three critical determinants of effective teaching are knowledge of the subject matter, pedagogical skills and motivation to teach (World Bank 1990). A growing body of research also reveals the importance of teachers' beliefs in shaping what and how they teach and their attitudes to teaching in general.

A major challenge for teacher educators is to find ways of integrating the different elements that come under the label of 'teacher education' into a coherent whole.

Reconceptualizing teacher preparation and development

The need to reconceptualize teacher preparation and development as a 'whole career' is repeatedly voiced yet difficult to achieve for several reasons: the conflicting views of stakeholders; the multiple sources of control and funding; competing demands for resources and entrenched imbalances in the allocation of funding; adherence to traditional training models; widespread neglect of the induction phase; and inadequate policies.

Teachers' development has three main phases: initial preparation, induction to teaching and continuing professional development. The first two are sequential in most countries but in some, teaching experience may precede initial training or, in the case of school-based training, may be simultaneous. Each phase has different needs for training and support. Although there is agreement that important qualitative differences exist in the thinking of novice and expert teachers (Chi et al. 1986; Calderhead and Robson 1991), the planning for teacher preparation, induction and development sometimes takes little account of them. Research has indicated some identifiable stages in the process of becoming a teacher and different models have been constructed (for example, Berliner's (1994) five-stage model of novice, advanced beginner, competent performer, proficient performer and expert teacher). While models like Berliner's have been criticized as too linear and neat (unlike messy reality) or not having the right number of stages, at least they provide a principled basis for planning – an element often missing. Out of such models, some countries are experimenting with competency-based national standards for different stages of a teacher's career. In some cases, a statutory framework is being established (see Table 1.1 for an example).

Preparing teachers: initial teacher training

Initial teacher training most often takes the form of full-time residential pre-service programmes in teachers' colleges (post-secondary) or universities or, in some developing countries, secondary-level 'normal' teacher training schools. Initial qualifications may also be available to serving unqualified teachers through distance education or 'out of school' programmes during vacations or on release from schools for extended periods of time.

The professional studies or pedagogical components of initial teacher training programmes can be either consecutive or concurrent with academic subject study. In some countries, such as the United Kingdom

Table 1.1 Career stages and standards for teachers in the United Kingdom

Stage of career in schools	National Standards (government initiative)
Headteacher	National standards for headteachers National professional qualification for headships Leadership programme for serving headteachers
Newly appointed headteacher	'Headlamp' programme, to be taken within two years of appointment (entitlement to grant for it)
Aspiring headteacher Deputy headteacher	National professional qualification for headships a prerequisite for appointment to headships
Positions of leadership (middle management) • Head of department • Subject co-ordinator • Key-stage co-ordinator • Head of a year-group (several classes) • Head of special educational needs	National standards and professional qualifications for subject leaders

National professional standards for special educational needs co-ordinators |
Expert classroom practitioner (for excellent teachers wanting to remain classroom practioners but also with a role in disseminating good practice)	Advanced skills teacher (licence), national standards
Practitioner	Three distinct areas for development: 1 Identified national priorities 2 School development priorities Both funded through the government Department for Education and Employment's Standards Fund and New Opportunities Fund. 3 Individual development needs identified through annual appraisal Upgrading of degrees financed mainly by individual teachers
Beginning teacher. Career entry profile (identifies individual teacher's strengths and needs for development)	Qualified teacher status (national standards) Statutory induction year
Trainee	Initial teacher training (national standards)

Source: Teacher Training Agency 1998

> **Box 1.1   Variation in initial teacher training programmes in Europe**
>
> A study of initial teacher training programmes for lower general secondary teaching in thirty European countries shows wide variation in two respects: the duration of courses overall and the balance of time between study of academic subjects and pedagogy or practical training.
>
> Programme length varied from three years (Belgium) to seven (Luxembourg). The average length of programme was four to five years. In eight countries, programmes took five years to complete; in fourteen countries, four years.
>
> The amount of time spent on pedagogic or practical training within programmes varied too, from less than a year (Ireland, Poland, Romania and Slovenia) to almost four years (Germany). As a proportion of total programme time, this varied from a sixth to two-thirds. The study notes that the balance of time given to the teaching of subject knowledge and to pedagogy and practical training was a matter of concern to all countries in the study.
>
> Source: European Commission 2000: 41

and New Zealand, both models exist. For primary and lower secondary training, the concurrent model of pre-service training predominates while for upper secondary, the consecutive model is more common (OECD 2001). The consecutive model offers more potential for cost savings and flexibility in meeting fluctuating demand. The length of programmes and balance of academic subject study with pedagogy varies (see Box 1.1). Internationally, the duration of teacher preparation programme ranges from 100 hours to several years.

Initial teacher training is often criticized for its inadequacy in preparing students for teaching. Part of the criticism may be attributed to the unrealistic expectation that initial training can produce a fully fledged teacher, but part may relate to the form of preparation provided. There is surprising adherence to the traditional residential college-based model of initial training. This is costly yet continues to be the only route to qualified teacher status in some countries. However, the last decade has seen the introduction of more alternative routes to qualification, such as school-based training, mixed-mode programmes combining formal campus-based study with lengthy periods in schools, accelerated training programmes, mobile training programmes and distance education. A problematic feature of initial teacher training is the school experience component (also referred to as teaching practice or the practicum). Much debate focuses on this: its duration, purpose, value, logistics, management, assessment practices, quality assurance, costs and the co-ordination of different partners involved (headteachers, supervising teachers, mentors, tutors, local government administrators, colleges or universities).

The amount of school experience provided through traditional college-based programmes is limited by the finances available, competing demands on trainer time and the value placed on it. School-based training may resolve some of these problems but raises new ones: the adequacy of the supervisors and mentors; the capacity of school staff to provide a breadth of input beyond the narrow practices of one school; the demands on school staff; the availability of support materials; and relationships among partners (universities, teachers' colleges, schools and local administrators). Despite the problems, the school experience component of initial teacher training is growing in importance though its role in the assessment and accreditation of student-teachers varies widely.

Support for beginning teachers: the induction phase

Research shows that successful induction programmes can set expectations, encourage good practice, assign appropriate teaching responsibilities (and appropriate schools) for novices, provide mentoring support and collaborative teaching opportunities, and engender more positive experiences and a higher commitment to teaching. Investment in induction for beginning teachers, together with better teacher placement policies, has the potential to reduce attrition rates since some of the costs of induction and mentoring can be offset by reduced attrition rates. It may also improve teacher quality, since without it,

> There is little hope for future professional development if the beginner takes early flight or becomes socialized into the teaching profession as one who works in isolated and unreflective practice.
>
> (Russell and McPherson 2001: 9)

Yet induction into teaching is the most neglected phase of a teacher's professional development. Most countries operate on the principle of 'sink or swim' and any efforts towards deliberate and supportive induction for beginning teachers are often left to the initiative of individual headteachers and the prevailing school culture. To institute induction programmes, there needs to be clear policy guidance, a reorganization of school practices, the institution of formal obligations, appropriate funding, training for headteachers and mentors, support materials and opportunities for interaction with peers. In some cases, induction is tied

---

Box 1.2   Induction for beginning teachers in New Zealand

Beginning teachers in New Zealand are not eligible to become fully registered until they have completed at least two years of satisfactory classroom experience. An 'advice and guidance' programme is available to them during these two years. The induction programme includes several elements: provision of learning resources; structured personal support from other teachers; a programme of visiting and observing experienced teachers; meetings with other staff; appraisals of progress; and a written record of the induction programme experiences. To enable this to happen, schools with beginning teachers receive additional teacher help each week, freeing the required time for the new teachers or the senior staff working with them.

Source: Darling-Hammond and Cobb 1995: viii

---

to teacher licensing (successful completion earns a teaching licence). An example of an induction programme is given in Box 1.2.

Continuing professional development

Learning to teach is a process which occurs unevenly over time and requires ongoing support and resources to meet a range of needs. The initiation of professional development comes from several sources:

- central government in orienting teachers to curriculum or examination changes and in upgrading qualification levels;
- provincial or state governments in upgrading qualification levels or selecting priorities for improvement;
- district education authorities for locally identified priorities or local interpretation of policies;
- donor-funded projects;
- professional teachers' associations in developing subject teaching (such as mathematics or science), or sometimes teachers' unions;
- school or community level groups in the implementation of school improvement plans;
- individual teachers aiming to improve their qualifications or career prospects or just wanting to be a better teacher.

Budgets for continuing professional development are often small and earmarked by a ministry of education or government department for particular purposes, with little left to finance local choices. Staff development for teachers is much less than that in corporate contexts. Little (1992: 178) describes it as:

> a low intensity enterprise. It occupies little of teachers' time, squeezed along the margins of teachers' ordinary work. It requires little of teachers by way of intellectual struggle or emotional commitment. It takes only the most superficial account of teachers' histories or present circumstances.

It all too often takes the form of single events, isolated and decontextualized from a teacher's own circumstances, on topics chosen by district or provincial administrators. Many of the decisions about the what, who, when, how and why of continuing professional development are still made in administrators' offices (national and provincial), a long way from the teachers for whom it is intended.

Access to professional development opportunities varies widely. About 40 per cent of teachers in France and Korea participate annually in professional development (UNESCO 1998) and about a third of teachers in Denmark and the Netherlands. A few countries, like Brazil, offer teachers a wide range of provision while in others teachers may participate in a week's in-service course once every five years at most. Continuing professional development may be wholly voluntary, left to the motivation of individual teacher or, less commonly, be mandatory. In China the amount of continuing professional development is legislated by central government and every teacher is required to undertake a fixed number of hours (currently seventy-two) of professional development a year. In some countries teachers have entitlements to staff development (see Box 1.3 for an example), in others not.

Once access is gained, what then makes professional development effective? This question is under-researched but one set of guiding principles is given in Box 1.4. In addition, research shows that teachers'

Box 1.3   Entitlement to retraining in the Samara region of Russia

During Russia's transition to a market economy, Samara, a region (*oblast*) on the lower Volga, used its strong economic position to initiate new professional development opportunities for teachers. Samara had 32,000 teachers, 92 per cent of them female with an average age of thirty-five.

Samara introduced a system of vouchers for teacher retraining and continuing development. These entitled individual teachers to 240 hours of training every five years (the federal norm for in-service retraining was 140 hours every five years). The vouchers could be used for different subjects and teachers could choose the courses (the type of course and where to take it, at a pedagogical university or some other approved institution).

The voucher system was innovative in providing teachers with choice and some control in a formerly highly centralized system. It gave teachers the responsibility and resources for meeting their own needs though the provision on offer was all out-of-school and institution-based. It is not yet apparent what the impact of this will be on individual teachers' career development or on the schools where they teach. Nor is it clear whether the higher education institutions competing to attract voucher-students will pay greater attention to the teachers' expressed needs in designing their programmes.

Source: Canning et al. 1999: 57–62

Box 1.4   Principles for professional development

These principles or guidelines for professional development were developed by the American Federation of Teachers and intended to result in programmes that made a difference (since much professional development does not).
   Professional development should

1   Ensure depth of content knowledge.
2   Provide a strong foundation in the pedagogy of particular disciplines.
3   Provide more general knowledge about teaching and learning processes, and about schools as institutions.
4   Reflect the best available research.
5   Contribute to measurable achievements in student learning.
6   Expect teachers to be intellectually engaged with ideas and resources.
7   Provide sufficient time, support and resources to enable teachers to master new content and pedagogy and integrate these into their practice.
8   Be designed by representatives of those who participate in it, in co-operation with experts in the field.
9   Take a variety of forms and not be limited to what has always been done.

Source: American Federation of Teachers 1995

contributions to their own staff development may be greater when institutional priorities are balanced with individually initiated development, when the rewards and incentives are clear and varied and when the school has a culture of continuous improvement (Little 1992). In general, teachers need access to information resources, interaction with peers (either in person or via ICT), constructive assistance in self-appraisal or school review and pathways to further qualifications. The commitment of planners and managers to supporting and financing these options is essential. Innovatory ways of meeting some of these needs can be found in later chapters of this book.

Preparing teachers for curriculum change and innovation

Despite consistent research findings that teachers play a central role in the effective implementation of school and curriculum change (Stein and Wang 1988), the preparation of teachers for this role receives far less attention than it should. As far back as 1977, Fullan and Pomfret compiled evidence to show that teacher development and the successful implementation of change were related and involved changes in the practices, beliefs and understanding of teachers. The relationship of teacher development to educational change

> is not just a matter of better implementation of selected innovations (though it includes this) but more basically a change in the profession of teaching, and in the institutions in which teachers are training and in which they work. Teacher development is thus tantamount to transforming educational institutions.
>
> (Fullan and Hargreaves 1992: 6)

However, central planners often minimize teachers' participation in the process or neglect to cultivate the ownership of changes, involving them too little or too late (see Box 1.5).

Two important elements in achieving change and improvement in teaching are teacher educators and headteachers. Teacher educators are frequently a neglected contingent. In some countries they are remote from schools on the one hand and policy formation on the other. They may also be unused to researching their own practice. Some teacher educators have never taught in schools and primary teacher trainers may only have taught in secondary schools. There may be few professional development options open to them, other than further formal study in their subject specialisms (though this is often needed too). This lack of professional development and support for teacher educators may lead them to be a conservative force in any change or innovation. Finally, college

Box 1.5 Preparing teachers for curriculum change in Paraguay

In 1992, the Government of Paraguay decided to change the primary school curriculum. New programmes were designed, emphasizing processes of cognitive development. The preparation of teachers took the form of nine-day orientation meetings, each attended by hundreds of teachers from the same grades in neighbouring schools. The training was sequenced to deal with one grade each year (first grade teachers in 1993, second grade in 1994, and so on), to match the sequence of curriculum introduction to schools. New textbooks were provided at these meetings.

How did the teachers rate this kind of training? Teachers said it provided them with very limited motivation to attempt to teach differently. After the nine-day meeting, it left them to their own devices, especially if they were the only teacher for a particular grade in a school with no other similar teachers with whom they could discuss their experiences, difficulties and achievements. This was a particular problem for first-grade teachers, the first group in the training programme. As a 'single event' form of preparation, it offered no further opportunities for teachers to develop deeper understanding and skills. The teachers rejected this form of training because it 'assumed that teachers had no history, no prior knowledge, and that they were not part of a system where roles are constructed in interaction with peers and principles' (p. 475).

Source: Villegas-Reimers and Reimers 1996

resources (libraries, computers, Internet access, funds for travelling to schools, consumables for learning materials production) may be severely restricted, limiting what teacher trainers can do.

Research shows a close correlation between the quality of teaching, learning and school leadership. Yet in some countries teachers are appointed to headships without any training. However, greater decentralization and accountability are leading to more training for headteachers and those aspiring to these positions. Training for both post-holders and aspirants is now a requirement in some countries (see Table 1.1) though the provision for it is often too limited.

COSTS AND FUNDING

In many countries investment in teacher education is concentrated on initial teacher training. The cost of preparing a teacher can be surprisingly high. Where the secondary-level curriculum is taught in teacher training 'normal' schools, the cost can be seven times that of students in general secondary schools (World Bank 1990). If the costs per qualified teacher are high (as in residential pre-service college courses) any significant expansion of numbers may be unaffordable. A current issue relates to investment in training. If three to five years is the span of time that the majority of teachers take to become fully functioning professional teachers (Berliner 2000, 1994; Hatton and Smith 1995; Schempp et al. 1998) and if large proportions of teachers in some countries leave teaching within the first three to five years, then questions arise about the returns on investment in training and the most efficient use of resources. In general, the shorter the teacher's working life as a teacher, the more expensive the per capita cost of pre-service training, especially for concurrent forms of general education and professional training. The quality of this sector of the teaching force may be lower too, since teachers are only in the process of becoming competent in their first years of teaching.

There has been a growing acceptance that initial teacher training is not the end-point of a teacher's development but only the beginning. Despite this, the distribution of resources does not sufficiently reflect this. It is difficult to determine what the expenditure levels for professional development are because of its different sources of funding, from national government, provincial and district authorities, special projects and teachers themselves. Nonetheless, evidence available shows that expenditure on teachers' professional development tends to be small, usually 1 per cent or less of a national or provincial (or state) education budget (compared to an average of 6 per cent by corporate employers). By itself, this is inadequate to meet the wide range and volume of needs. However, where governments have aimed to raise national standards, funding for continuing professional development has been increased. In addition, new initiatives have come from the non-governmental or private sector, as illustrated by the Brazilian A-Plus television series, which provides daily programmes for teachers and a support network (Perraton et al. 2001) A challenge for planners is to find ways of increasing the provision at affordable cost. However, the resource issue is also a political one because resources represent power and privilege.

The political dimension of teacher education

Though crucial to understanding teacher education, the political dimension is often ignored. A country's policies in teacher education are influenced by local circumstances, national dynamics and international interventions, often interacting in complex ways. This means that the discourses embodied in teacher education are not neutral or descriptive (Popkewitz 1995). Strategic questions such as who should provide teacher education, for whom, for how long, of what kind, to what standard and at what cost, tend to be addressed largely in terms of academic, professional and technical issues but they have a political dimension too (Ginsburg and Lindsay 1995). These issues also affect decisions about the adoption and use of distance education for teacher education, as its history shows.

CONCLUSIONS

Several conclusions and implications for teacher training and professional development can be drawn from this chapter.

- Teachers and their training are repeatedly affirmed as key elements in the provision of good quality education. But training alone cannot provide good quality teachers if poor conditions, low pay and status create a climate where teaching is an occupation of last resort, entrants are of low quality and teachers lack motivation to perform well or invest time and effort in professional development. Teacher training is but one element in a complex system.
- The changing patterns of teacher employment raise questions about the nature of teacher training systems, the assumptions on which they operate, notions of what constitutes the life-span of a teacher's career, the deployment of training resources and the cost-benefit of different training models.
- The planning of teacher training and development needs to be tied more effectively into issues of supply, demand and retention. Traditional training forms and practices may lack the capacity to be sufficiently responsive to a changing environment.
- A solution frequently offered as a first response to perceived teacher shortages, especially in the absence of reliable data or careful analysis of the problem, is to train more teachers. Sometimes distance education is proposed as the means of doing this rapidly and on a large scale. This may be the wrong solution and compound the problems.
- The growing needs for professional development require more flexible forms of provision and more channels for reaching teachers, to offer them more access and choice.
- The increasing mobility of teachers is likely to require more attention in the future, together with portable qualifications, international accreditation and possibly course provision.
- While differences in teacher training and development exist between developing countries and between developing and industrialized countries, concerns increasingly converge.

QUESTIONS FOR OPEN AND DISTANCE EDUCATION

All this leads to some questions for planners of open and distance teacher education.

- What roles can open and distance education play in meeting some of the needs identified in this chapter? When is it an appropriate solution to a teacher training problem? What can distance education do that traditional kinds of provision cannot or what can it do better? What are its limitations?
- What strategic roles do planners assign to open and distance education in teacher training provision? What influences decisions to use it or not? What kind of enabling policy is needed for it?
- Can distance education offer a less costly but effective way of providing initial teacher training? In what circumstances? How can it use existing resources differently and to good effect?
- Can open and distance learning be sufficiently responsive to the rapidly changing needs of teacher education and training? Is it more or less responsive than traditional forms?
- Can open and distance learning support continuing professional development more widely, effectively and affordably than present patterns of provision? To what extent and how?
- If locally relevant and school-based professional development is thought to be the most effective, what role can large-scale standardized programmes of distance education play?
- Is open and distance learning capable of supporting the changes that take place in teachers' thinking and beliefs, from novice to expert teachers? Can it support the development of reflective practice or action research or whole-school development?
- Can teachers develop practical teaching skills through distance education? How can these be assessed on distance education courses? If this is a weak component in some traditional programmes, why should distance education be able to do it any better when the logistical problems may be greater?
- Can open and distance education reach remote and rural teachers more effectively than traditional means? How can it meet the needs of teachers using minority languages or where the infrastructure is weak?
- What can the various media, technologies and ICT contribute to teacher training? What comparative advantages do they have and at what cost? What kinds of considerations do planners need to take into account in making choices?
- Is open and distance learning effective in educating and training teachers?

- Is it cost-effective?
- What can evaluation and research studies on distance education tell us? What do we still need to research?

The following chapters will provide some answers to these questions in the light of international experience.

SUMMARY OF THE BOOK

In Chapters 1 and 2, Bernadette Robinson and Colin Latchem, the editors, set the context. In Chapter 1 they identify the changes and challenges facing teachers around the world and the implications of these for teacher education in general. They conclude with key questions about the role of open and distance education in meeting the challenges that arise for teacher education.

In Chapter 2, they review experience so far in using open and distance learning for teacher education, training and professional development. They provide a broad overview as an introduction to the field and as a background for the more specialized chapters which follow.

In Chapter 3, Chai Hon-Chan and Hena Mukherjee examine critical policy-making and planning issues in initiating distance education programmes for teachers and in integrating them into existing structures at national, regional and institutional levels. They identify strategic questions that planners need to ask in translating policy into practice when using distance education for teacher training.

Chapter 4, by Bob Moon and Bernadette Robinson, analyses and illustrates ways in which open and distance learning is used for initial teacher training. They examine key issues and problems in planning, developing and implementing such programmes, particularly the management of practical work and school experience.

In Chapter 5, Helen Craig and Hilary Perraton review the use of open and distance learning for continuing professional development. They examine its achievements and limitations and the factors that planners need to consider in developing and implementing such programmes.

Chapter 6, by Charles Potter and Mohammad Aslam, explores the training of tutors, teachers and group leaders in non-formal and community education in contexts of open and distance learning and highlight differences in the training models for teachers in formal and non-formal education.

Head teachers and senior teaching staff are critical to educational change and improvement in schools. In Chapter 7, Tony Bush and Richard Charron show why the status, role, knowledge and skills of such educational managers need to be improved and how open and distance learning can be used to develop leadership and management skills in both developed and developing countries.

Policy-makers, planners and practitioners are currently confronted with a sometimes perplexing range of options in media and technology. In Chapter 8, Adrian Kirkwood and Charles Joyner review the use of media and technologies (mainly other than ICT) for teacher education and development. They analyse the different functions that media can serve in teachers' learning and provide guidelines for planners and designers in selecting and using media.

In Chapter 9, Betty Collis and Insung Jung provide an analytic overview of how computers and computer communications (Internet and the World Wide Web) are being used for teachers' training and professional development. They review international experience so far and provide some guidelines for planners and practitioners.

A recurring question on the use of distance education for teacher education is 'Is it any good?' Chapter 10, by Bernadette Robinson, examines evaluation and quality in relation to this question. Issues and problems are examined and evaluation findings reviewed. Out of experience and research, some guidelines and an organizing framework are provided for evaluating distance education programmes for teachers.

The costs of distance education for teacher education are a major consideration but not always well understood or known. In Chapter 11, João Batista Oliveira and François Orivel provide a guide to costing, useful for both planners and providers. They show how the costs can be analysed and provide some conclusions from experience so far about the costs of distance education for teacher education.

Finally, in Chapter 12, the editors return to the questions posed in Chapter 1, about the value and roles of open and distance learning for teacher education. They draw some conclusions from the research and experience provided by the contributors to this book and offer some guidelines for policy-makers and planners. They conclude with the research agenda needed if a stronger base of evidence and research is to be built on the use of open and distance learning for teacher education.

REFERENCES

ActionAid (1996) *Education Sector Strategy Paper 1996–8*, Bangalore: ActionAid.

Ahmed, M., Chabbott, A., Joshhi, A. and Pande, R. (1993) *Primary Education for All: Learning from the BRAC Experience*, Washington, DC: Academy for Educational Development.

American Federation of Teachers (1995) *Principles for Professional Development*, Washington, DC: AFT.

Barpanda, N. (1999) 'Teacher empowerment strategies to ensure continuing involvement in the universalisation of elementary education', *DPEP Calling*, March, pp. 19–23.

Bennett, N., Carré. C. and Dunne, E. (1993) 'Learning to teach', in N. Bennett and C. Carré (eds) *Learning to Teach*, London: Routledge, pp. 211–220.

Berliner, D. (1994) 'Expertise: the wonder of exemplary performance', in J.N. Mangieri and C.C. Block (eds) *Creating Powerful Thinking in Teachers and Students*, Forth Worth, Tex.: Holt, Rinehart & Winston, pp. 1–43.

—— (2000) 'A personal response to those who bash teachers', *Journal of Teacher Education*. 51: 358–71.

Calderhead, J. (1994) 'Teaching as a professional activity', in A. Pollard and J. Bourne (eds) *Teaching and Learning in the Primary School*, London: Routledge, pp. 80–83.

Calderhead, J. and Robson, M. (1991) 'Images of teaching: student teachers' early conceptions of classroom practice', *Teaching and Teacher Education*, 7: 1–8.

Calderhead, J. and Shorrock, S.B. (1997) *Understanding Teacher Education*, London: Falmer.

Canadian Teacher (2001) <www.thecanadianteacher.com/article14.htm>

Canning, M., Moock, P. and Heleniak, T. (1999) *Reforming Education in the Regions of Russia*, Technical Paper no. 457, Washington, DC: World Bank.

Chi, M.T.U., Glaser, R.K. and Farr, M.N. (eds) (1986) *The Nature of Expertise*, Hillsdale, NJ: Erlbaum.

Darling-Hammond, L. (2000) 'Teacher quality and student achievement: a review of state policy evidence', *Education Policy Analysis Archives*, 8: 1–45.

Darling-Hammond, L. and Cobb, V.L. (eds) (1995) *Teacher Preparation and Professional Development in APEC Members: A Comparative Study*, Washington, DC: US Department of Education.

Delors, J., Amagi, I., Carneiro, R., Chung, F., Geremek, B., Gorham, W., Kornhauser, A., Manley, M., Quero, M.P., Savané, M-A., Singh, K., Stavenhagen, R., Suhr, M.W. and Nanzhao, Z. (1996) *Learning: The Treasure Within – Highlights*, Report to UNESCO of the International Commission on Education for the Twenty-First Century ('The Delors Report'), Paris: UNESCO.

DFID (Department for International Development) (2000) *Towards Responsive Schools: Supporting Better Schooling for Disadvantaged Children*, London: Department for International Development.

European Commission (2000) *European Report on Quality of School Education: Sixteen Quality Indicators*, Brussels: Directorate-General for Education and Culture, European Commission.

Fullan, M. and Hargreaves, A. (eds) (1992) *Teacher Development and Educational Change*, London: Falmer.

Fullan, M. and Pomfret, A. (1977) 'Research on curriculum and instruction implementation', *Review of Educational Research*, 47, 2: 335–97.

Ginsburg, M. and Lindsay, B. (eds) (1995) *The Political Dimension in Teacher Education: Comparative Perspectives on Policy Formation, Socialisation and Society*, London: Falmer.

Greenwald, R., Hedges, L. and Laine, R. (1996) 'The effect of school resources on student achievement', *Review of Educational Research*, 66, 3: 361–96.

Hatton, N.G. and Smith, D. (1995) 'Reflection in teacher education: towards definition and implementation', *Teaching and Teacher Education*, 11: 33–49.

Jambor, M., Patterson, J. and Jones, R. (1997) 'TEACH is for all new teachers', *Principal*, 77, 1: 36–8.

Kaul, S. (1999) 'Introducing transparency, merit and rationalisation in the recruitment and deployment of elementary education teachers', *DPEP Calling*, July–August, 7–9.

Kemmerer, F.N. (1993) 'Monitoring teacher incentive systems: a new use for the EMIS?' in D.W. Chapman and L.O. Mählck (eds) *From Data to Action: Information Systems in Educational Planning*, Paris and Oxford: International Institute for Educational Planning UNESCO and Pergamon Press, pp. 48–67.

Kemmerer, F.N. and Windham, D.F. (eds) (1997) *Incentives Analysis and Individual Decision Making in the Planning of Education*, Paris: International Institute for Educational Planning, UNESCO.

Little, J.W. (1992) 'Teacher development and educational change', in M. Fullan and A. Hargreaves (eds) *Teacher Development and Educational Change*, London: Falmer, pp. 170–93.

Mankad, S.C.G. (1999) 'Appointment of primary school teachers', *DPEP Calling*, July–August, pp. 45–7.

Marginson, S. (1993) *Education and Public Policy in Australia*, Cambridge: Cambridge University Press.

National Commission on Teaching and America's Future (1996) *What Matters Most: Teaching for America's Future*, Kutztown, Penn.: Kutztown Publishing.

Organisation for Economic Cooperation and Development (OECD) (2001) *Education Policy Analysis 2001*, Paris: Centre for Education Research and Innovation, OECD.

Perraton, H., Robinson, B. and Creed, C. (2001) *Teacher Education through Distance Learning: Technology, Curriculum, Evaluation, Cost*. Paris: UNESCO.

Popkewitz, T.S. (1995) 'Teacher education, reform and the politics of knowledge in the United States' in M. Ginsburg and B. Lindsay (eds) *The Political Dimension in Teacher Education: Comparative Perspectives on Policy Formation, Socialisation and Society*, London: Falmer, pp. 54–75.

Rugh, A. and Bossett, H. (1998) *Involving Communities: Participation in the Delivery of Education Programs*, Washington, DC: USAID/Project ABELL.

Russell, T. and McPherson, S. (2001) 'Indicators of success in teacher education: a review and analysis of teacher research', paper presented at the Pan-Canadian Education Research Agenda (PCERA) Symposium on Teacher Education and Educator Training, May 22–23, Université Laval, Quebec.

Schempp, P., Tan, S., Manross, D. and Fincher, M. (1998) 'Differences in novice and competent teachers' knowledge', *Teaching and Training: Theory and Practice*, 4: 9–20.

Stein, M.K. and Wang, M.C. (1988) 'Teacher development and school improvement: the process of teacher change', *Teaching and Teacher Education*, 4: 171–87.

Teacher Training Agency (TTA) (1998) *National Standards for Teachers*, London: TTA.

TES (*Times Educational Supplement*), 4 May 2001, <http://www.tes.co.uk/>

UNESCO (1996) *EFA (Education For All) 2000 Bulletin*, 23, April–June, Paris: UNESCO.

—— (1998) *World Education Report: Teachers and Teaching in a Changing World*, Paris: UNESCO.

—— (2000a) *The Dakar Framework for Action. Education for All: Meeting our Collective Commitments*, Paris: UNESCO.

—— (2000b) *Global Synthesis: Education for All 2000 Assessment*, Paris: UNESCO.

UNESCO and ILO (International Labour Organisation) (1966) *Recommendations Concerning the Status of Teachers: Special Intergovernmental Conference on the Status of Teachers*, Paris: UNESCO and ILO.

UNICEF (1999) *State of the World's Children*, New York: UNICEF.

Villegas-Reimers, E. and Reimers, F. (1996) 'Where are the 60 million teachers? The missing voice in educational reforms around the world', *Prospects*, xxvi, 3: 419–92.

World Bank (1990) *Primary Education: A World Bank Policy Paper*, Washington, DC: World Bank.

Chapter 2

Open and distance teacher education

Uses and models

Bernadette Robinson and Colin Latchem

Open and distance education for teacher education and training is not new. It has been used since at least the 1960s to solve the kinds of problems in teacher supply and quality identified in Chapter 1. What is new in recent years is the extent of its use and the variety of its applications, its growing presence in national and institutional strategic planning for teacher education, and the appearance of new information and communication technologies (ICT).

There are several reasons for this growth:

- the expansion in open and distance education in general and for professional training in many fields, and in the number of universities and institutions providing it;
- the pressure on governments and providers to seek more cost-effective ways of training and developing teachers;
- a gradual shifting upwards of the levels and standards of teacher qualifications as the attention of governments in many countries turns to quality as well as quantity within its teacher force, with a consequent need for upgrading programmes;
- the nature of the target group (teachers) which is, on the whole, likely to succeed at self-managed learning (though some teachers in developing countries have very low educational levels).

So how has open and distance education been used for teacher education? What kinds of needs has it met? What organizational models have been used? This chapter provides an overview of uses and models as a background for more detailed examination of different aspects in later chapters.

OPEN AND DISTANCE EDUCATION FOR TEACHERS

Distance education has been defined as an educational process in which teachers and learners are separated in space and/or time for some or all of the time of study and in which the learning materials take over some of the traditional role of the teacher. Learning materials play a central role, incorporating a variety of media and, in most systems, provision is made for students to interact with tutors and other students as a means of support. Many distance education programmes include some face-to-face contact, either at local centres or in weekend or residential schools, and the balance of time between face-to-face contact and self-study in programmes varies widely.

Open learning is an organized educational activity where learners also study by themselves for some or all of the time. It is based on a set of values in which constraints on study are minimized in terms of access, time, pace and method of study. Translated into concrete terms it means providing learners with access to learning resources, advice, support and, in many cases, assessment of learning. Distance education programmes may or may not incorporate some of the values which characterize open learning. Access to teacher education programmes is sometimes restricted by entrance qualifications or examinations and by the requirements of programmes of study for recognition by teacher accreditation authorities. *Virtual learning* or *e-learning* employs similar principles and methods but exploits the capabilities of the Internet and Web for providing access to learning materials and supporting two-way communication between individuals and groups. In some countries, 'distance education' has now become synonomous with the use of ICT. *Open and distance education* is an umbrella term which covers a variety of organizational arrangements to provide learning resources and opportunities (formal and non-formal, structured and unstructured, award-bearing or not). This flexibility is at the same time a strength, in terms of the adaptability of open and distance education to a variety of needs and situations, and a problem, in terms of definition.

Extent of use

Distance education for teacher education and training is widely used around the world, in both small and large countries and in a variety of contexts. In Latin America, some of the largest distance education programmes are for teacher training (Chacón 1999) and two-thirds of all post-secondary institutions offering distance education have provided teacher training courses. Most countries with a high population (Bangladesh, Brazil, China, Egypt, India, Indonesia, Mexico, Nigeria and Pakistan) make use of it, some heavily. Brazil, Nigeria, China and Indonesia all have very large-scale programmes of distance education for teacher training. In India there is a wide variety of distance education programmes for teachers and Pakistan and Bangladesh provide them too through their open universities. Only two of the nine countries (Mexico

Box 2.1   Video-conferencing for teacher education in Egypt

To provide in-service teacher education to more teachers more quickly, the Egyptian government set up a national video-conferencing network. This covered all provinces (governorates); by 2001, thirty-nine distance learning centres had been set up using high-speed fibre-optic connections or satellite delivery. The network accommodated about 5,000 participants at any one time and operated nine hours a day, with an average use of 2,664 hours a year. Teachers attended the centres where video-conference sessions provided a mixture of lectures and interaction with experts and other participants. Through this means a wide range of courses was provided for teachers, headteachers, school supervisors and inspectors.

By December 2000, 575,000 teachers and education personnel had participated in courses – ten times as many as the previous system of face-to-face training within the same timescale. Though having high initial costs (recovered in the first three years of operation), the cost of use was less than attendance at centralized in-service training events if more than 300 teachers participated, though more than if training events were held locally.

Source: Ministry of Education, Egypt 2001

and Egypt) make relatively little use of distance education for teacher training (Creed and Perraton 2001) though Egypt has established a video-conferencing system (see Box 2.1). In Africa, though there is still much scope and need for the further use of distance education, there are over 140 public and private institutions offering distance education programmes and between a half and three-quarters of these are for teacher training (World Bank 2001).

Some of the least populated countries are using distance education too: Mongolia has used it to reach teachers scattered over huge distances (Robinson 2001) and Canada for teachers in thinly populated areas (Burpee and Wilson 1995). In industrialized countries, a wide range of distance education programmes is available through distance teaching universities and, increasingly, through traditional universities, especially for higher level courses (diplomas and degrees). The establishment of ICT in schools, teacher training institutions and universities is expanding this provision and also prompting the use (and acceptance) of distance education in contexts where it had previously been little used for teacher education (see Box 2.2).

Box 2.2 The impetus of ICT in Korea

Although open education is not yet widely used for in-service training of Korea's 340,000 teachers, several teacher training institutions and centres have begun to use computer networks for it. With government support, several major initiatives have been launched in developing Internet-based distance teacher education programmes. However, distance or online training courses for teachers were not credited by the provincial administrative offices of education until 1997, when the Korean National Open University provided a distance teacher education programme on 'Introducing open education in primary schools: why and how?' In 1997 also, the ministries of education and information and communication funded a project to create a Cyber Teacher Training Centre <http://edunet.kmec.net> within a newly established Korea Multi-media Education Centre. Since then, teachers and institutions from all sixteen provinces have been able to access training materials and courses. Individual teachers' autonomy in selecting their own training courses based on personal need has increased.

Source: Jung 2001

The variety of distance education programmes on offer for teachers is wide. The International Centre for Distance Learning (ICDL) database <http://www-icdl.open.ac.uk> in 2001 listed over 1,000 distance education courses for teachers, trainers and non-formal adult educators. These covered a range of content, subject specialisms and levels of study for teachers in pre-school, primary, secondary, adult, further and higher education. Apart from programmes like these, designed specifically for teachers, many teachers (and would-be teachers) also study on other distance learning degree or diploma programmes, either to gain graduate status or entry to teaching, or to improve their subject knowledge and qualification levels, or to pursue specialist fields (such as teaching children with special needs or primary science or school management). In addition to structured formal courses (long and short) leading to accreditation, open and distance provision is used to support 'unstructured' or non-formal learning by teachers in their schools, local teachers' centres or homes.

Scale of programmes

The scale of programmes ranges from very large to very small. For example, China's extensive network of Radio and TV Universities provides teacher education on a massive scale (Ding 1999; Chen Xiangming 2000). Between 1987 and 1999, 717,300 primary and 552,000 secondary school teachers gained qualifications through this system (Perraton *et al.* 2001). In India, the planned annual enrolment on the Special Orientation Programme for Primary Teachers was 450,000 a year for four years (from 1994). In Nigeria 21,000 trainees graduated (1994) with a primary teaching qualification from the National Teachers Institute (a dedicated distance teaching college) – a number equivalent to the total admissions of the fifty-eight regular colleges of education in the country.

By contrast, the scale of programmes at the other end of the spectrum is small: Australia's Remote Area Teacher Education Programme (RATEP) had 36 students enrolled in 1999; Belize had 70 teachers enrolled on one distance teacher education programme in 1994, and 58 headteachers on another in 1997; and Guyana had 144 teachers enrolled in its Hinterland Teacher Training Project in 1994 (Creed 2001). Though economies of scale are one of the attractions of distance education for planners, scale is clearly not the only measure of value in the decision to use distance education: reaching otherwise inaccessible teachers is another.

A large proportion of the world's distance learners are teachers. They have been large groups in the student populations of open universities, for example, India's open universities (Mouli 1997; Harry and Khan 2000), Pakistan's Allama Iqbal Open University (Mussaret Anwar Sheikh 2001), the Bangladesh Open University (Islam and Haque 2001), Indonesia's Universitas Terbuka (Belawati 2001) and the United Kingdom's Open University (Prescott and Robinson 1993), among others. In Australia's dual mode universities too the situation is similar (Evans and Nation 1993). Teachers are, in one sense, a captive audience since their qualification requirements are set by government policy and alternatives for upgrading them often few. The use of distance education to upgrade the qualification levels of teachers has been widespread, in both industrialized and developing countries.

USES FOR TEACHER EDUCATION

Open and distance learning for teacher education has been used, with varying degrees of success, to serve the following purposes:

- to provide cost-effective teacher education and training;
- to reach remote and rural teachers and widen their access to learning opportunities and resources;
- to provide education and training (initial and continuing) on a large scale and within shorter time-scales than traditional forms (sometimes as emergency 'crash training' programmes);

- to recruit potential teachers from new untapped sources within a population;
- to serve widely dispersed groups of specialist teachers or managers, often a single individual in a school;
- to provide an affordable alternative to 'off-the-job' residential models of in-service training, either for initial training or continuing professional development, and to avoid depleting schools of staff by taking them out of service for training;
- to support school-based programmes of initial teacher training;
- to provide a route for unqualified graduate teachers to gain the required teaching licences or teaching qualifications while working, and for qualified teachers to upgrade their qualifications;
- to make scarce specialist expertise and resources available to large teacher populations who would not otherwise have access to them in their immediate environment;
- to increase the inflow of information and learning opportunities (formal and non-formal) for teachers in their work contexts;
- to deploy limited training funds and teachers' college facilities in different, more efficient and effective ways;
- to achieve better integration of theory with practice through on-the-job learning and reflection;
- to develop (through computer communications) communities of practice;
- to disseminate information widely and rapidly about curriculum change, new teaching approaches and new teaching standards.

Examples of all of these are given in later chapters of this book. Overall, open and distance education has been used to serve three broad categories of teacher education and training: initial training of unqualified teachers, continuing professional development, and curriculum reform (see Table 2.1).

The balance of emphasis among these has shifted over time and differed according to context. The extent of continuing professional development is greater in developed countries, while developing countries still struggle to establish a minimally qualified teaching force. However, problems in teacher supply have resulted in the use of distance education for initial teacher training in the United Kingdom and for teacher licensing in the United States (in California). Within the category of continuing education, non-formal provision is increasing as perceptions change about teachers' professional needs, shifting from the norm of 'one-off' occasional week-long courses at long intervals to ongoing access to information, learning resources and peer interaction. The use of open and distance learning approaches as a strategy for curriculum reform and change management is still relatively small (and neglected)

Table 2.1 Three categories of open and distance education use for teacher education and training

Category	Examples
1 Initial training of unqualified teachers	
• Concurrent Academic subject and professional studies and practical training for unqualified teachers	Malawi Integrated In-service Teacher Education Programme (MIITEP) ('sandwich' or 'integrated' mixed-mode programme, distance education combined with periods in college) National Teachers Institute, Nigeria
• Consecutive Professional studies and practical training for untrained teachers with qualifications in academic subjects (at varying levels in different countries, from Matriculation/Secondary Certificate to university degrees)	UK Open University Postgraduate Certificate of Education India, Indira Gandhi National Open University (IGNOU) and National Centre for Educational Research and Training (NCERT), Diploma in Primary Education
2 Continuing professional development	
• Upgrading qualification programmes for under-qualified teachers or for career progression	Chinese Central Radio and Television University (CCRTVU), China, upgrading primary teachers to teach in junior secondary schools (to diploma level) UK Open University, upgrading bachelors' graduates to masters' degrees India, IGNOU: BEd degree for teachers with a bachelor's degree in academic subjects and two years' teaching experience Vietnam: English Language Teacher Training Project (ELTTP): training for junior-secondary school teachers of English as a foreign language
• Specialist subject training	USA Teletechnet Program, Old Dominion University, Virginia, specialist qualifications for teachers of children with special needs
• Refresher and updating programmes	Turkey, Anadolu University Open Education Faculty (now Open University): updating subject knowledge and completing degree qualification for teachers who had not completed university degrees

- Preparation for roles, in school management or as a teacher trainer or resource-centre co-ordinator

  Egypt, Ministry of Education: video-conferencing network providing short programmes for teachers, headteachers, school supervisors and inspectors
  Israel, OFEK, Open University of Israel, an educational network, funded by the Ministry of Education, of 41 sites, providing interactive programmes (one-way video, two-way audio) for primary and secondary teachers on a variety of topics
  Belize, Teacher Training College: professional development for primary school principals
  China, CCTRVU: qualification programmes for teachers aiming to teach in the normal (secondary level) teacher training schools
  UK, National College of School Leadership: provision of resources, courses and contact with a community of headteachers
  Burkina Faso: training for school headteachers
  India, Bombay Television Centre: 'Hints for Teachers'
  Brazil, TV-Futura: television as a launchpad for teacher activities
  Malaysia: self-access resources for teachers to improve their English language skills
  UK, Scottish Virtual Teachers Centre: access through ICT to a range of continuing education resources for teachers
  Canadian School Administrators' Technology Integration Resource (SATIR-RITAS) (www.satir-risat.org)

- Non-formal education

3 Curriculum reform

- Training and preparation for changes in the curriculum and teaching approaches

  Mongolia: UNICEF primary teachers' programme to prepare for child-centred teaching and new teaching approaches
  Korea, Comprehensive Teacher Training Institute and Korean National University of Education: to prepare headteachers and teachers for a reform of kindergarten education

- Dissemination of information and guidelines

  UK, dissemination of information about a new secondary school leaving examination (GCSE) through the Open University

- Retraining teachers

  UK Open University: conversion courses to retrain teachers of biology and chemistry to teach physics

Box 2.3 An alternative to the use of a cascade approach in India

Tele-SOPT is part of the Special Orientation Programme for Primary School Teachers (SOPT) in India. It was an experiment (1996–7) in two states, Karnataka and Madhya Pradesh, in using interactive technology for providing information and in-service training for untrained and under-trained primary teachers (on multi-grade teaching, language skills, environmental sciences, blackboard use and teaching pedagogy of mathematics among other topics). Tele-SOPT was launched as a direct result of the inadequacies of the cascade approach in the SOPT programme, which had used a four-tier model of 50 master trainers, 500 key resource staff and 10,000 resource persons who then trained 1.8 million teachers. The problems with this cascade model were typical of those found elsewhere: dilution of information quality with progression down the levels, an inadequate number of suitable resource persons locally, slowness in reaching all teachers and difficulties in covering large territories and teachers in remote areas. With Tele-SOPT, the use of one-way video transmission by satellite to local centres and interaction through telephone and fax put teachers in direct contact with specialist educators. Compared to the face-to-face equivalent provision, Tele-SOPT was more effective in terms of participants' involvement and amount and quality of interaction, and cost less. As a result, the approach was used more widely for other programmes.

Source: Creed 2001

and the employment of often ineffective cascade methods of information dissemination persists (see Box 2.3 for an alternative).

ORGANIZATIONAL MODELS

The organizational models of distance education for teacher education vary and are shaped by their contexts of policy, infrastructure, purpose and teacher education systems. In some countries, several models coexist. The types of organizational models and providers of programmes are given in Table 2.2. It is not possible, as Perraton (1993) concluded in his review of twelve case studies, to rank structures in order of effectiveness. However, each model has its strengths and limitations.

The open universities offer several benefits and have proved to be a sustainable way of providing teacher education at a distance. They have

Table 2.2 Organizational models and providers of distance education for teachers

Organizational models	Examples
1 Universities Distance teaching or open universities	Bangladesh Open University China TV Teachers College, China Central Radio and Television University Indira Gandhi National Open University, India Open University of Hong Kong Open University, United Kingdom University of South Africa (UNISA) Open University of Sri Lanka Universitas Terbuka, Indonesia (and many others)
Conventional universities with distance teaching capacity • dual mode *(institutions providing traditional courses and distance education courses, sometimes equivalent versions of the on-campus course)*	University of Zambia Universidad Javeriana, Colombia Universidad de la Frontera, Chile Monterrey Institute of Technology and Higher Education, Mexico Many UK, Australian and Canadian universities Universities of Hué and Can Tho, Vietnam University of Malawi University of London Institute of Education higher degrees programme

• mixed mode
  (programme studied through a combination of on-campus and self-study periods)
  'Virtual' universities
	Cyber Teacher Training Centre and the Open Cyber University, Korea

2 Colleges of education (teachers' colleges) Public colleges with distance education capacity	Belize Teacher Training College Institut Perguruan Darul Aman, Malaysia National Teachers' Institute, Nigeria
Public colleges dedicated to distance education	
Private distance education colleges	South Africa: Promat College, Success College, Lyceum

Table 2.2 (continued)

	Organizational models	*Examples*
3	Consortia Of private and public agencies	TV-Futura, Brazil Continuing Science Education via Television (Constel), Philippines
	Of institutions, with or without ministries or provincial departments of education	Australia: Remote Areas Teacher Education Programme (RATEP), Queensland Department of Education, James Cook University and Far North Queensland Institute of Technical and Further Education
4	Non-governmental organizations	South Africa: Open Learning Systems Educational Trust (OLSET) Sudan Open Learning Organization (SOLO) Zimbabwe: Litraid Project(Rotary Foundation funding) + University of Zimbabwe + UK Open University
5	Donors, including non-governmental organizations, in collaboration with ministries of education	ActionAid UK and DFID UK: MITEP, project for upgrading primary teachers in western Uganda (1991–5). UNICEF: project for reorienting primary teachers to new concepts and methods in Mongolia (1996–2001) UNDP and DFID: Project for improving the quality of teachers in poor provinces in western China (2002–7)
6	Ministries of education	National Grid for Learning, UK College of Leadership for School Managers, UK
7	International agencies (sometimes in collaboration with ministries of education or with private companies)	Commonwealth of Learning (COL) STAMP 2000+ programme, to improve science, technology and mathematics teaching in eight southern African countries. <http://www.col.org/clippings/stamp2000+.htm>. European Union Telematics for Teacher Training (T3) project (1996–8) World Bank World Links for Development (WorLD), designed to link students and teachers around the world and create school partnerships <www.worldbank.org/worldlinks> Consortium International Francophone de Formation à Distance (CIFFAD) for headteachers in West Africa UK government's Department for International Development Imfundo Project (a public + private initiative to develop the use of ICT and distance education in Africa)

an existing infrastructure which new programmes for teachers can use, an accumulation of professional skills in open and distance education, a range of facilities and often university-wide agreements with media providers and others which can benefit teacher education provision and often the resources to commission leading specialists in the field to contribute to programmes. On the other hand, they can be bureaucratic and slow to respond to a changing environment (such as sudden changes in national regulations for teacher qualifications or in the national teacher education curricula) because of lengthy course production cycles or difficulties in changing internal systems designed to service courses from many other faculties. Many of the open universities have had freedom to determine their own roles in teacher education and as a result have tended to diversify provision. Although this has widened choice for teachers, it has sometimes resulted in losses of economies of scale, and the creation of an array of teacher education programmes that are difficult to manage, or to keep up to date, or to back with local student support.

Increasingly, traditional universities and colleges offer distance education programmes for teacher education, either to extend access to existing campus-based courses or to create new ones for new teacher audiences, enabled in many cases by ICT. This approach can make use of an institution's facilities, expertise and reputation and is not so constrained by the need for economies of scale as dedicated distance teaching institutions – in fact, too large a number can create problems for the systems and staffing. Traditional universities can also be quicker and more flexible in responding to environmental changes since the scale of the enterprise and investment in it is smaller. Limitations in this approach often lie within the institution: allocation of inadequate resources, resistance to the changes required in institutional systems, unmanageable workloads for the few staff involved and marginalization of the programmes in strategic planning and management.

In both the above models, students follow wholly distance education programmes even though they may have group meetings or small college-based elements such as summer schools. A less common model is an integrated one, where teachers spend part of a programme on residential courses in college and part in supported self-study while teaching in schools. This model, mostly used for initial teacher training, has the advantages of combining substantial amounts of school practice and deploying the limited capacity of college buildings, facilities and staff in different ways, increasing the numbers of student-teachers making use of them in any one year. It also has the potential to combine the best of both modes of teacher training (campus-based and distance education). However, it has been used in only a handful of cases, for example, in the Zimbabwe Integrated Teacher Education Centre (ZINTEC) programme (Chivore 1992). Despite its apparent success in this case (which was discontinued because the government could not afford to pay the larger volume of qualified teachers being produced), it has not been widely adopted, though a more recent programme, the Malawi Integrated In-service Teacher Education Programme (MIITEP) in Malawi is currently making use of it in an endeavour to meet acute teacher shortages (Kunje, forthcoming). This model offers considerable scope for reconceptualizing initial teacher training within an education system and reducing the cost per trained teacher if vested interests can be overcome.

The ZINTEC model, like many other distance education initiatives in teacher training, was introduced in the form of a project. The project model has often been used in donor-funded initiatives in distance education for teachers. Many have been successful, particularly in meeting emergency demand for trained teachers. However, relatively few have resulted in distance education becoming institutionalized as a regular part of the education service (Uganda is one case where this eventually happened after several projects). The strengths of the project approach are that it can meet urgent needs in a relatively short time-span, act as a tested pilot for larger-scale applications, demonstrate the feasibility and limitations of distance education in a particular context, and by-pass the conservatism of educational systems in order to innovate.

However, using distance education involves a steep learning curve for inexperienced providers and in one-cycle projects, the organizational learning cannot be transferred to the next cycle of presentation. At the end of projects, the personnel and their newly acquired expertise may be lost. Where several separate projects are in progress, perhaps funded by different donors, transfer or pooling of learning from the experience may be lacking through weak co-ordination. It can in any case be difficult for governments, especially in contexts where open and distance education is new, to co-ordinate efforts to establish clear policy and plans for open and distance education with different donors providing different advisors, perspectives and priorities. Because of its temporary nature, and perhaps small scale, a project's impact on the teacher education system as a whole may be marginal and its status uncertain. The odds are against its being institutionalized without strong intervention at the policy level. Many successful projects have failed to dent the armour of traditional provision.

Whatever the model used, all distance education providers are faced with challenging tasks in co-ordinating partners and agents in teacher education programmes, especially for initial training programmes where practical teaching and its assessment is involved. In programme planning, providers may need to co-ordinate their efforts with national policy-makers, teacher education departments or regulatory authorities and national examination boards or accreditation agencies. In implementing a distance education programme where practical work is involved, others who are likely to be involved are local tutors or mentors (either through a provider's own regional organization or through delegated arrangements), teachers' colleges, local in-service teacher education centres, administrators and co-ordinators, district education officers, school inspectors, headteachers and schools. This requires consultation, interaction and often participation in national and regional teacher education bodies and

> The complexity, time and cost of managing these crucial relationships with partners tends to be underestimated at the outset, especially when negotiated at a distance and involving different layers of personnel and several regional or district authorities. Furthermore, consistency of quality is not easy to achieve in large geographically dispersed programmes with decentralised field operations which at the same time need to be responsive to local conditions. Problems revolve around issues of responsibility, role definition, accountability, locus of decision-making, communication and the control and co-ordination of part-time support staff.
>
> (Robinson 1997: 126)

Articulation with mainstream teacher education and development is important for achieving legitimacy, sustainability, integration within the teacher education system and at a practical level, smoothly running operations. Too often, distance education functions as a supplementary or marginal system, disconnected from teacher education departments in ministries and decision-making bodies.

SOURCES OF FUNDING

The models described also relate to sources of funding for teacher education programmes. Generally, sources of funding are the usual sources for education: government budgets, student fees, the private and NGO sector and funding agencies. Governments usually provide funding for pre-service initial teacher training programmes of a conventional kind but not always for in-service initial training programmes by distance education (as is the case in China). Programmes which implement curriculum reform are usually sourced by government funds, central and provincial, though they may be implemented by universities or colleges or special projects. Teacher education programmes aimed at developing ICT often, at present, come from special government funds. Programmes of continuing education (such as bachelor's or master's degrees or specialist diplomas) taken by individual teachers and leading to career enhancement or salary increments are generally funded by the individuals concerned and

Table 2.3 Funding sources of ten distance education programmes for teachers

Programme	Source of funding			
	Government	Student fees	Private, local, NGO sector	Donors and funding agencies
Brazil (television-led continuing education on many topics, non-formal: 'journalism in the service of teacher education')				✓
Burkina Faso (structured programme of headteacher training)				
Chile (structured programme for ICT training)				
China (structured programmes, mostly academic subjects, leading to qualification for teaching)	✓	✓		
India (structured programme for teachers and others on child guidance)	✓	✓		
Mongolia (resource-based, non-formal provision of materials on child-centred teaching methods)	✓			✓
Nigeria (structured programme of studies leading to teaching qualification)	✓			✓
South Africa: OLSET (radio-based programme for improving English learning and teaching methods)	✓			✓
South Africa: UNISA (structured programme leading to teaching qualifications)	✓		✓	
United Kingdom (structured school-based programme of initial teacher training, leading to qualification)	✓			✓

Source: Perraton et al. 2001: 37

contribute to the fee income of institutions. Large distance teaching institutions providing distance education programmes can sometimes cross-subsidize programmes, using large profitable programmes to subsidize smaller, less popular programmes of social worth. Table 2.3 illustrates funding sources for ten programmes of teacher education and shows a fairly typical distribution of funding sources.

THE ROLES OF INTERNATIONAL AGENCIES

International agencies are providing increasing support for the use of distance education for teacher training, especially where it involves ICT, and are influencing policy in many cases. UNESCO has a long tradition of work in this area. One of the earliest ventures into distance education for teacher training was a UNESCO/UNRWA initiative to train Palestinian refugee teachers. The success of this initiative prompted many similar projects in the 1960s designed to help various African countries train the very large numbers of teachers needed for their rapidly growing primary systems (Perraton 2000: 63). UNESCO has supported the use of distance education in the world's nine most populous countries (the E-9 countries) as a means of solving some of their educational problems and has supported initiatives in ICT (see Box 2.4). More recently, UNESCO commissioned research into distance education programmes in nine countries, carried out by IRFOL (International Research Foundation for Open Learning, UK, summarized in Perraton *et al.* 2001 and used as the basis of planners' guidelines in Perraton *et al.* 2002).

International agencies like the World Bank are supporting countries' efforts in distance education through:

Box 2.4 Learning networks for African teachers

Creative Learning Networks is a UNESCO-supported project which aims to equip up to four teacher education colleges in each of twenty African countries with a computer and access to Internet as the first steps in developing local, national and regional networks. It will also fund curriculum development for teacher education in mathematics and science and help create twenty national websites. The pilot stage has taken place in Zimbabwe.

Source: Perraton and Creed 2000

- sharing knowledge and information through websites and special events <www.worldbank.org/disted/>;
- supporting international partnerships with agencies such as Commonwealth of Learning, International Council for Distance Education, Consortium Africain Francophone de Formation à Distance (CIFFAD), Réseau Africain de Formation à Distance (RESAFAD), UNESCO and regional co-operation through associations such as the Asian Association of Open Universities;
- providing technical assistance to develop and cost country plans, and sometimes providing financing.

The Commonwealth of Learning (COL, <www.col.org>) has been active in a number of ways: supporting collaborative efforts (see Table 2.2), facilitating regional partnerships and events, providing training, developing guidelines and tools for planners and practitioners and disseminating information. It is an intergovernmental organization created by Commonwealth heads of government to encourage the development and sharing of open learning and distance education knowledge, resources and technologies. The promotion and development of distance education and open learning for teachers has been a major focus of its work.

These and other agencies have been instrumental to varying degrees, depending on the knowledgeability and interest of agency staff and the agency's policy, in promoting and supporting the use of distance education and ICT for teacher education.

EFFECTIVENESS

Are distance education programmes effective in educating and training teachers? The evidence suggests that they often are (Perraton 1993; 2000). They are able to reach teachers, sometimes on a large scale and within a shorter time-scale than institution-based alternatives. They have also achieved high or acceptable pass rates in many programmes even if completion rates for distance education programmes tend to be lower than for on-campus equivalents. However, the completion rates for teacher education programmes tend to be higher than those for many other distance education courses, especially if teachers receive promotion, qualifications or salary increments as a result.

In recent research by UNESCO of nine case studies completion rates varied widely (Perraton *et al.* 2001). In one, in Burkina Faso, very few headteachers dropped out. In the case of Nigeria, drop-out rates varied from 27 to 39 per cent and the pass rates of those completing the programme varied from 55 per cent to 64 per cent. In the British Open University, completion rates appeared to be relatively high for initial training programmes and very high for master's level programmes. In a programme designed to help teachers in Chile learn about using ICT in education, about half the teachers did not complete the course, partly because of difficulty in paying their fees. The issue of whether students enrol as individuals or as part of a group nominated by their employer also appears to affect completion rates.

In terms of success rates, Perraton (1993: 393) concludes that

> while examination success cannot be equated with teaching capacity, we can legitimately assume that a reasonable examination pass rate demonstrates that a programme was effective in teaching academic subjects.

The effectiveness of distance education in helping teachers to teach well or teach differently is a larger issue which will be addressed in later chapters.

CONCLUSIONS

In reviewing the achievements of distance education for primary teacher education, Robinson (1997: 125) concluded that

> Not all courses have worked well, or provided good quality, though enough have to demonstrate the capacity of distance education for training and educating teachers, and for enabling new models of training to be explored.

This conclusion holds in general. As well as offering solutions to teacher training problems, distance education presents a number of challenges for planners and practitioners in terms of programme and materials design, media and technology use, operational logistics, partnerships for initial training and assessment, and achieving good quality, cost-effectiveness and an enabling policy framework. The chapters which follow address these aspects.

REFERENCES

Belawati, T. (2001) 'Indonesia', in O. Jegede and G. Shive (eds) *Open and Distance Education in the Asia Pacific Region*, Hong Kong: Open University of Hong Kong Press, pp. 171–88.

Burpee, P. and Wilson, B. (1995) 'Professional development: what teachers want and universities provide – a Canadian perspective', in D. Sewart (ed.) *One World Many Voices: Quality in Open and Distance Learning*, selected papers from the 17th World Conference of the International Council for Distance Education, Birmingham, United Kingdom, June, Milton Keynes: The International Council for Distance Education, pp. 236–9.

Chacón, F. (1999) 'Distance education in Latin America: Growth and maturity', in K. Harry (ed.) *Higher Education through Open and Distance Learning*, London and New York: Commonwealth of Learning/Routledge, pp. 137–49.

Chen Xiangming (2000) 'Teacher training with TV technology', *TechKnowLogia*, November/December <http://www.techknowlogia.org/TKL_active_pages2/CurrentArticles/main.asp?IssueNumber=8&FileType=HTML&ArticleID=199>

Chivore, B. (1992) 'Pre-service teacher education at a distance: the case of Zimbabwe', in P. Murphy and A. Zhiri (eds) *Distance Education in Anglophone Africa*, Washington, DC: World Bank.

Creed, C. (2001) *The Use of Distance Education for Teachers*, Cambridge: International Research Foundation for Open Learning (IRFOL) (reported to Department for International Development).

Creed, C. and Perraton, H. (2001) *Distance Education in the E-9 Countries*, Paris: UNESCO.

Deshmukh, M.N. (1995) 'Distance education in training of primary education personnel: an Indian experience', in conference proceedings of Quality Assurance in Distance and Open Learning, 11th Annual Conference of the Asian Association of Open Universities, Kuala Lumpur, 11–14 November 1997, pp. 56–68.

Ding, X. (1999) 'Distance education in China', in K. Harry (ed.) *Higher Education through Open and Distance Learning*, London and New York: Commonwealth of Learning/Routledge, pp. 176–89.

Evans, T.D. and Nation, D.E. (1993) 'Educating teachers at a distance in Australia: some trends' in H. Perraton (ed.) (1993) *Distance Education for Teacher Training*, London and New York: Routledge, pp. 261–86.

Harry, K. and Khan, A. (2000) 'The use of technologies in basic education', in C. Yates and J. Bradley (eds) *Basic Education at a Distance*, London and New York: Routledge/Commonwealth of Learning, pp. 122–37.

Islam, M.A. and Haque, H. (2001) 'Bangladesh', in O. Jegede and G. Shive (eds) *Open and Distance Education in the Asia Pacific Region*, Hong Kong: Open University of Hong Kong Press, pp. 255–72.

Jung, I. (2001) 'Korea', in O. Jegede and G. Shive (eds) *Open and Distance Education in the Asia Pacific Region*, Hong Kong: Open University of Hong Kong Press, pp. 103–30.

Kunje, D. (forthcoming) 'The Malawi Integrated In-service Teacher Education Programme: an experiment with mixed-mode training', *International Journal for Educational Development* <www.sussex.ac.uk/usie/muster/>

Ministry of Education, Egypt (2001) *Distance Training of Egyptian Teachers via Video-conferencing Technology*, paper prepared for the E-9 Ministerial Meeting in Beijing, June, Cairo: Ministry of Education, Technological Development Centre.

Mouli, C.R. (1997) 'Assuring quality of teacher training in higher education by distance mode: an Indian perspective', in conference proceedings of Quality Assurance in Distance and Open Learning, 11th Annual Conference of the Asian Association of Open Universities, Kuala Lumpur, November 11–14, pp. 319–27.

Mussaret Anwar Sheikh (2001) 'Pakistan', in O. Jegede and G. Shive (eds) *Open and Distance Education in the Asia Pacific Region*, Hong Kong: Open University of Hong Kong Press, pp. 288–317.

Perraton, H. (ed.) (1993) *Distance Education for Teacher Training*, London and New York: Routledge.

—— (2000) *Open and Distance Learning in the Developing World*, London and New York: Routledge.

Perraton, H. and Creed, C. (2000) *Applying New Technologies and Cost-effective Delivery Systems in Basic Education* (thematic study for Education for All 2000 assessment), Paris: UNESCO.

Perraton, H., Creed, C. and Robinson, B. (2002) *Teacher Education Guidelines: Using Open and Distance Learning*, Paris: UNESCO.

Perraton, H., Robinson, B. and Creed, C. (2001) *Teacher Education through Distance Learning: Technology, Curriculum, Evaluation, Cost*. Paris: UNESCO.

Prescott, W. and Robinson, B. (1993) 'Teacher education at the Open University', in H. Perraton (ed.) *Distance Education for Teacher Training*, London: Routledge, pp. 287–315.

Robinson, B. (1997) 'Distance education for primary teacher training in developing countries', in J. Lynch, C. Modgil and S. Modgil (eds) *Innovations in Delivering Primary Education*, vol. 3 of *Education and Development: Tradition and Innovation*, London: Cassell Education, pp. 122–38. <http://wbln0018.worldbank.org/hdnet/hddocs.nsf/>

—— (2001) 'Mongolia', in O. Jegede and G. Shive (eds) *Open and Distance Education in the Asia Pacific Region*, Hong Kong: Open University of Hong Kong Press, pp. 131–52.

World Bank (2001) *Distance Education and ICTs for Learning in Africa*, Washington, DC: Human Development Group, Africa Region The World Bank.

Chapter 3

Policy, planning and management of distance education for teacher education

Chai Hon-Chan and Hena Mukherjee

This chapter addresses the key questions that policy-makers and planners face when making strategic decisions about the use of distance education for teacher education. It attempts to find some answers while acknowledging that these will not be exhaustive and may themselves raise other issues for policy-makers and planners.

The key questions to be explored in this chapter are:

- What are the imperatives that drive teacher education and what factors shape these?
- Under what circumstances is distance learning a viable option?
- What do national-level policy-makers and planners need to know about distance learning for teacher education?
- What are the key factors to be considered in determining priorities in teacher education and distance education?
- What is needed for successful management of distance learning programmes for teachers?
- What organization structures and training strategies need to be adopted?
- What are the strengths and weaknesses of top-down and bottom-up approaches to national policy-making and programme planning?

POLICIES ON TEACHER EDUCATION

National education policies may be explicitly enunciated by governments or implied in the educational structures and processes. They are typically determined by some mix of national and regional political, social and economic goals, community interests and international factors such as globalization, technology or economic competition. National education systems are shaped by previous policies and provide the contexts for reshaping current policies or formulating new policies in the face of new or envisioned opportunities and challenges. Because education is an important means of transmitting political, social and economic aspirations as well as moral or religious values, the selection, training, performance and management of teachers, the primary transmitters of such beliefs as well as subject knowledge, are also a matter of political concern (Wilkin 1996). It therefore follows that the policy thrusts and changes for teacher education, or lack of them, reflect the particular goals and roles ascribed to education and that, regardless of locus of control, teacher training providers are subject to political or stakeholder influence. All of these factors need to be taken into account in considering the what, how, when and by whom of educational policy-making.

The nature and extent of policy-making for initial and continuing teacher education varies from country to country. In some countries, for example China, such policies are clearly articulated. In others, they are partial or minimal. Some countries have national policies for their teacher education systems. Others, for example those with federal structures such as the United States, have pluralistic and devolved policies. Some countries are slow to change or revise their policies for teacher education. In others, the policies are changed so rapidly and so frequently that those implementing them can be hard pressed to cope.

An important issue to be considered within this policy-making relates to how, when and where open and distance learning might be an option for initial teacher education or in providing continuing professional development. The following sections explore these policy issues.

OPEN AND DISTANCE LEARNING AS A POLICY OPTION

In many countries, and particularly in the developing world, policy-makers and planners face challenges in developing, expanding and improving school systems. Providing trained teachers is one such challenge, particularly in developing countries. The use of distance education as a solution is increasingly on the agendas of educational policy-makers and planners and appearing in policy documents on teacher education. In the past, such a strategic option has assumed a marginal role but the increasing familiarity of distance education and the growth of information and communications technology (ICT) are stimulating greater interest in finding effective and affordable alternatives to traditional forms of teacher training and professional development.

In determining the role of distance education in teacher education, policy-makers and planners need to ask some strategic questions. An example of these is presented in Box 3.1. This particular set of questions was prepared by a consultant as the basis of workshops, seminars and discussions with policy-makers and planners of teacher education

Box 3.1   Strategic questions for policy-makers and planners

1   What are the specific teacher education problems needing solution? Is teacher training or professional development of any kind the appropriate solution to the problem?

2   What role should distance learning play in solving the identified problems or in meeting the teacher education needs identified in this context? What functions should it serve? Where should the distance education options be avoided?

3   Which teacher education needs are best met by distance education and which by more traditional means? What are their relative strengths and limitations? What comparative advantages does each offer? How can distance education be used to make existing teacher training systems and provision more efficient and effective?

4   What existing distance education programmes for teachers are already in place? What is their quality, status and legitimacy? Should these be retained or improved or discontinued?

5   What kinds of distance education would be most appropriate for the selected purposes, target groups and tasks? What will the infrastructure and funding support?

6   What relationship should distance learning have to traditional provision and structures? (A supplementary role? An alternative route? A temporary substitute? A complementary role? An integrated form of provision?)

7   What status should the qualifications gained through distance education have? Equivalent to those of conventional institutions for equivalent programmes? Should they be regarded as equivalent in terms of pay scales, terms and conditions of service, academic awards and promotion prospects?

8   What separate representation, if any, should distance education have in decision-making bodies (for example, in ministries of education, curriculum boards, bodies responsible for the governance and quality of teacher education, funding and resource allocation committees, national examination agencies)?

9   Where should responsibility for distance education for teacher training be located within ministries (in the teacher training department, or the non-formal education department, or the educational technology department)? How should responsibility for it be co-ordinated at the national, provincial, local administrative and institutional levels?

10 What are the financial implications of the programmes for the system? If the output from the teacher education system is increased through large-scale distance education programmes, what are the financial implications for education budgets of larger numbers of trained (and higher-paid) teachers on the payroll? What are the implications of moving large numbers of previously unqualified teachers (who may have 'temporary' status and no claim on the benefits available to established or tenured teachers) to 'established' or permanent posts? Is it affordable?

11 What policy and policy documents exist on the use of distance education for teacher education? Is the policy up to date? When was it last reviewed? What gaps are there?

12 What mechanisms are there for policy dialogue and consultation on the use of distance education for teacher education? Do they work effectively? Do they need to be changed?

13 What regulatory roles do government departments and agencies play in the use of distance education for teacher education? Does this need reviewing?

Source: Robinson 1999

in Vietnam in preparation for a large primary teacher development project.

In finding answers to strategic questions like these, policy-makers need to be well informed about the principles, successful practices, potential pitfalls and constraints of open and distance learning in order to align its use with national and institutional policy goals. Weak understanding and knowledge about the potential and limitations of distance education has been a problem in some countries, probably the result of three things:

- the lack of an adequate research and evaluation base in distance education for teacher education, needed to support informed policy choices;
- poor access to information about distance education for teacher education;
- inexperience in using distance education for teacher education.

However, the situation is changing. The research base, though small, is growing and evaluation is receiving more attention. Dissemination of findings has improved with the use of electronic communication and the establishment of web-sites. International organizations, such as the World

Bank, have established web-sites which offer practical guidance and resources on using distance education for teacher education (such as the
Global Distance Education Network at <www1.worldbank.org.disted>).
UNESCO has sponsored research into the use of distance education
for teacher education (Perraton *et al.* 2001) and has commissioned planning guidelines from the International Research Foundation for Open
Learning (IRFOL) in England (Perraton *et al.* 2002).

Practitioners too have a role to play in informing national policy and
plans:

> Distance educators have a responsibility to assist policy makers to
> formulate sound policy and make sensible and progressive decisions.
> They need to establish good channels of communication, provide
> relevant information, raise issues, educate, debate and guide, and
> act as a pressure group. They need to find ways of building bridges
> between high-level and general policy statements and the concrete
> implementation of policy-in-action. Often there is a gap, with the
> rhetoric not matching the reality. Practitioners need to identify ways
> in which they can work more collaboratively with policy-makers
> and decision-makers to support the development of policy for open
> learning and distance education.
>
> (Robinson 1998a: 4)

POLICY ISSUES AND PLANNING IMPLICATIONS

A clear policy for open and distance education is always needed but
often lacking. Policy has been defined as an 'implicit or explicit speci-
fication of courses of purposive action being followed or to be followed
in dealing with a recognised problem . . . and directed towards the accomplishment of some intended or desired set of goals' (Hough 1984: 13). In
practical terms, a programme operation requires a public policy which
clearly expresses the goals, strategies and desired outcomes, in other
words, clear articulation between the policy and plans. However, it is
often the case that

> Reference to open and distance education may appear in very general
> statements in official policy documents on education and training
> or even in the Education Law, but is not visible in strategic plans,
> activity plans (short and long term), departmental plans, local gov-
> ernment plans, job titles or responsibilities, or in budget allocations
> for central and regional use.
>
> (Robinson 1998a: 2)

Turning policy into plans for teacher development through distance education usually involves a process of wide consultation with a number of stakeholders. It also requires the involvement of planners in the early stages of policy-making. Planners, with their knowledge of what works and what does not, provide crucial inputs to the policy-making process. However, planners of teacher education programmes may not be familiar with, or experienced in, planning for open and distance education. Hence their need for information, guides and advice, as mentioned earlier.

SETTING PRIORITIES

In turning policies into plans, several key interrelated aspects need to be considered:

- the programme's objectives and scope;
- whether a major curriculum change is involved;
- whether initial teacher education should take precedence over continuing professional development, or both need to be given equal emphasis;
- the target group(s) and their distribution;
- the budget and resources;
- the delivery options and the choice of technology.

An analysis of these will inform choices regarding the targeting of effort, the extent of coverage and the most efficacious and cost-effective means of implementation. The priorities established are also likely to be influenced by a mix of political and social equity issues – for example, consideration given to urban–rural representation and under-served areas, or the needs of women and minority groups. Priorities will inevitably be finally determined by budgetary considerations. But faced with the various choices, each with differing cost implications, policy-makers and planners need to balance the priorities with existing policies and practices and resources. For example, where existing policy guidelines conflict with new equity criteria or availability of resources, the guidelines or the criteria, or both, need to be adjusted.

Whatever the circumstances, decision-making is facilitated by establishing clear guidelines and criteria for the teacher development purposes and target groups. An example of the criteria used in selecting the target population for a teacher development programme in western China is given in Box 3.2.

In determining the criteria for teacher selection in contexts where a significant proportion of both primary and secondary teachers are

Box 3.2   Criteria for selecting target groups of teachers in western China

A project supported by UNDP (United Nations Development Programme) and (DFID) (the United Kingdom Government's Department for International Development) was planned in partnership with national and local government in China. Its aim was to improve the quality of teachers and teaching in three of the poorest provinces (Yunnan, Sichuan and Gansu) in western China through the use of distance education and ICT. Criteria were agreed with each province for the selection of counties (administrative districts within provinces) since not all could be included in the project. The criteria agreed for selection were:

- counties which had difficulty in reaching their targets in providing basic education for all;
- counties categorized as 'national poverty level' counties;
- counties with high numbers of schools with only one or two teachers (since these were likely to be the most rural or remote, often in ethnic minority areas and with the least well-qualified teachers with the least access to training opportunities);
- counties with the highest proportions of unqualified teachers;
- the existence of two-way telecommunications connectivity (access to Internet) at the county level and electricity supply at the school level to enable township schools to function as teacher resource centres;
- counties which were not already participating in other similar international projects for teacher education.

Source: Robinson et al. 2001

unqualified, several decisions have to be made in answer to the following questions.

- Which category of teachers should have priority for training? Or should both have a lesser share of the available resource?
- Which teachers within the potential target group should be selected? Should younger teachers take precedence over older in the expectation that there would be more return on the investment over time? Should there be an age limit for participation?

- Should those with more schooling be given preference on the grounds that they are more likely to succeed at distance learning than those with very low educational levels?
- Are secondary teachers likely to cope more successfully with self-study approaches than primary teachers?
- In industrialized and industrializing countries, should preference and special incentives be given to graduates in shortage subjects (maths and science, for example)?
- What kind of entry qualification should there be? What minimum educational levels should be set?
- Should the programme attempt to address the rural–urban disparities found in many developing countries? Should rural teachers have priority over urban? Will this result in the programme being seen as a lower-level one for rural, low-qualified teachers rather than a programme of value for all teachers?
- What balance within the programme should be given to 'disadvantaged' sub-groups of teachers (with regard to gender, ethnic minority groups, second-language speakers or teachers)?

Whether the programme focus is on initial teacher education or continuing professional development, policy-makers need to examine the planning implications for any one choice since change in one part of an education system inevitably has consequences in other parts of it. For example, the introduction of a new curriculum will have a direct impact on continuing professional development as well as on initial teacher education. In particular, policy-makers should be sensitive to two critical areas of concern regardless of the programme focus, as both are vital to success. The first is the need to ensure political support, the second the need to establish legitimacy.

POLITICAL SUPPORT AND LEGITIMACY

Experience shows that key factors in achieving parity in educational provision include strong political support, acceptance by employers or the market-place and good performance outcomes. Whatever the choice, programme quality is increasingly defined in terms of outcomes, i.e., the ability of the teacher to teach well (Nielsen 1997).

Political support is essential to successful distance learning programmes for teachers because it entails a commitment to providing the necessary funding for implementation, assures programme legitimacy, recognition of credentials, and thus teachers' salaries and other benefits when they are employed by the system. A lack of political support will lead to eventual programme failure, as was the case of the Malawi experiment

in the 1980s with distance (mainly correspondence) education for alternative secondary schools (Perraton 2000: 44).

Clearly, political support must be secured at the policy formulation
stage, when policy-makers must have all the relevant information for
informed decision-making. Such support will then have a firm foundation when the decision-making process involves consultation with, and
winning over, key government decision-makers, teachers' unions, teacher-
educators, parent-teacher associations and other concerned stakeholders.
Support and consultation will help ensure ownership at all levels to
provide a firm basis for programme relevance and sustainability.

Establishing legitimacy and public acceptance of distance education
for teacher education is essential for successful implementation. Despite
the generally positive experience of a number of countries, developing
and industrialized, many educational policy-makers and planners are
sceptical about the legitimacy and quality of distance education for teacher
education (Perraton 1992) on grounds that the distance mode does not,
and cannot, offer the same quality as conventional, on-campus education. Securing recognition requires getting employers, especially public
agencies, to accept distance education as equal to traditional education.
Unfortunately, some of the decisions that ministries and policy-makers
take militate against this. For example, it will be difficult to persuade
the various stakeholders of the comparable quality of distance education
when

- distance education programmes have lower entry standards;
- quality is judged on input levels rather than output levels of
  achievement;
- different lower-value qualifications or certificates are provided for
  distance education programmes even when programme content and
  credit weighting are comparable to conventional programmes;
- teachers trained by distance education are placed at a lower salary
  level;
- the qualification earned is not accepted as an entry qualification for
  further study.

The legitimacy of distance education initiatives can only be achieved
through demonstrating that the quality of content, delivery, assessment
and outcomes is equal to, or better than, in traditional forms of teacher
education. However, students achieving the same examination standards
is a necessary but not sufficient condition for claiming legitimacy, since
the providers must establish the comparative quality of the process of
distance education (Perraton 1995).

Establishing the legitimacy of distance education programmes for
teachers is crucial in a number of respects. It has legal and financial

implications for a teacher's service: salary scales, career and promotion prospects, entry to further education and training, and status with colleagues as well as its impact on teacher morale. These policy issues must be resolved at the outset by planners to ensure that the distance programmes are of at least equal standard to those of conventional programmes.

The ability of planners to deal with resistance from potential clients and funding sponsors is critical, particularly if the institution or programme is new and there are competing established, reputable providers. In order to assess support for or opposition to new programmes and policies, planners need to consult with a wide spectrum of stakeholders: programme beneficiaries; appropriate government authorities at central, state and district or local levels; potential partners such as non-governmental organizations, private sector providers, service providers, publishers, media and telecommunications providers, teacher unions and accreditation agencies.

NEW PROGRAMMES AND EXISTING POLICY

New programmes or projects for teacher education need to align with existing policy frameworks, to ensure that they are not discounted or marginalized but considered a legitimate part of teacher education provision. They may also require changes to policy. Planning distance education for teacher education can require alignment to several sets of policies, as Figure 3.1 illustrates in the context of China.

At an institutional level, when initiating new programmes within existing conventional on-campus provision, policy-makers have the choice either to parallel the content and methods of the on-campus courses or to use the introduction of distance education as an opportunity for change, developing improved approaches, new content and new pedagogies. With the growing use of ICT, a new approach is often likely to combine on- and off-campus provision. Here three key questions arise:

- Are there compliance issues in relation to existing policy and, if so, what actions need to be taken to introduce such an innovation?
- To what extent will combined provision help to integrate theory courses with practical work?
- How can the programme be designed to focus on better learning outcomes?

The experience of the Open University in the United Kingdom, when it launched its postgraduate certificate in education (PGCE) in 1994, illustrates this issue (Box 3.3).

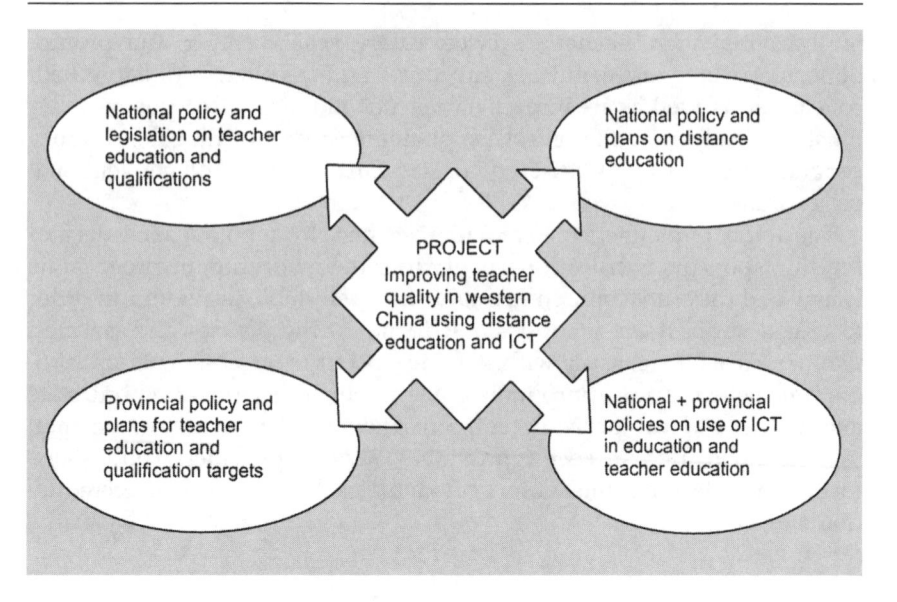

Figure 3.1 Aligning a distance education project for teacher education with relevant sets of policy in China (Robinson *et al.* 2001).

Box 3.3   Introducing an innovative programme in the United Kingdom

The launch of an Open University, UK, postgraduate certificate in education involved the development of new forms and styles of initial teacher training. While the national criteria set out in government circulars had to be met, the means of doing so would inevitably depart from conventional provision.

It was impossible, and undesirable, to try and replicate all aspects of the criteria and practice of conventional providers. Yet, inevitably, initial evaluations and judgments of a programme are heavily influenced by established conventions. The task was to define planning criteria congruent with the philosophical and logistical rationale of the programme. We needed to differentiate between regulated input factors (the minimum number of weeks to be spent in schools, for example) and discretionary input factors (how the school experience was sequenced). We had also, however, to look at this in the same way with regulated outcomes (competencies, for example) and discretionary input factors (the form of any achievement profile developed through the course).

Source: Moon and Mayes 1995

However, institutions such as the UK Open University have well-established reputations and evidence of quality assurance systems which provide a strong platform for launching and gaining acceptance for innovative approaches. In many developing countries with limited and recent experience in open and distance learning, policy-makers and planners may need to work within a long-term time-scale before new strategies gain recognition and acceptance. In Uganda, for example, a number of individual distance education projects over twenty years eventually led to the institutionalization of distance education for teacher education. Lessons drawn from a small-scale initiative, the Mubende Integrated Teacher Education Project (MITEP) in western Uganda (Robinson *et al.* 1995) shaped Uganda's Northern Integrated Teacher Education Project (NITEP), which then obtained acceptance from the national accreditation agency, the Institute of Teacher Education, Kyambogo. One of the lessons learned from MITEP was the need to engage in close dialogue with the Ministry of Education and the National Examinations Board from the outset to ensure compliance with regulations or to agree variance. In this case, lack of clear agreement on variance (the lower academic level of some entrants) put in jeopardy the recognition of their final award even if they were successful in the examinations taken by all teacher education students in Uganda. This issue for MITEP was resolved only as student-teachers were taking their final examinations (Robinson *et al.* 1995). The project which followed it, NITEP, worked closely with the Ministry of Education and the National Examinations Board and was accredited by the national accreditation agency, the Institute of Teacher Education, Kyambogo. The work of NITEP eventually became institutionalized with the establishment of the Teacher Development Management Services (Wrightson 1998).

In establishing the status of distance education programmes, a policy issue for decision-makers is whether they are viewed as a regular part of the existing teacher education provision or as separate or supplementary or impermanent. If they are to be ongoing and integral to the system, then there are likely benefits through building on and sharing existing physical, human and financial resources for teacher education. If viewed as separate, then a parallel or conflicting and fragmented structure may be the outcome and, as experience has shown in several countries, the programmes may become marginalized.

RELEVANCE, LINKAGES AND PARTNERSHIPS

The next step for the policy-makers and planners is to ensure the relevance, linkages and partnerships of the planned-for programmes or courses. They need to ask:

- How will these policies and plans translate into provision and activities that are relevant and responsive to local needs, taking into account the availability of expertise, infrastructure, logistics, and support?
- Who will the programme providers be?
- How can the programme providers effectively combine the expertise, experience and resources available at national, regional and local levels?

For programmes to be effective, organizational logistics and the conduct of training must respond directly to specific local needs. An example of policy translation into relevant action in response to a felt need is found in Bangladesh. There, a hitherto untapped resource, literate but unemployed rural adult females, were trained to become female teacher-aides, in order to augment the predominantly male teaching force and become a means of retaining adolescent girls in schools. Although this example did not involve distance learning, it illustrates the translation of policy decisions into practical programmes. Examples in distance education can be found in the training of individuals living in rural communities to become local teachers when qualified teachers cannot be recruited from elsewhere.

In advanced countries, centrally developed courses using sophisticated media and instructional materials may be delivered in a fairly standardized way, augmented by face-to-face tutorials. In less developed countries, especially those with sparsely populated or poor areas, policy-makers and planners may well need to consider a combination of print, media and face-to-face student support, according to the availability and dependability of technology and postal and electronic communications. The approaches and technology adopted will also need to take account of the curriculum, the availability or need to construct instructional materials, staff development requirements, programme delivery, learner support and assessment, quality assurance and programme evaluation. In planning programmes, one aspect for attention is the mechanisms and regulations that link teacher training, accreditation and certification at national, regional and local levels.

As has been illustrated in many programmes of teacher education, the application of teaching-learning theory is more relevant when closely articulated with local conditions relating to the learner's working (school and classroom) realities and study environment. This was a key principle on which the design of the United Kingdom's Open University PGCE was based. There is also some evidence that strengthening student motivation through support services, including face-to-face tutorials, improves learner retention, completion and graduation rates (Robinson 1995). An example of how the support system might be organized (and the complex management task involved) is found in the case of NITEP,

Uganda (the features are similar to a number of other projects). In this project the delivery system, which included a core of learner-focused modules based on the new primary teacher education curriculum, depended heavily on its student support system. This incorporated district primary teachers colleges (PTCs) which co-ordinated all district-level learning programmes. The college-appointed district student support officer implemented the district's student support system. A PTC-appointed tutor counsellor guided trainees' studies at twice-monthly weekend tutorials at the local study centre. Subject-specialist tutors provided intensive twice-yearly tutorial sessions at the residential course periods at the PTCs. Tutor markers (college subject-specialists) marked assignments and provided feedback to students while a teacher colleague in the same school as the trainee acted as personal tutor, offering professional advice (Wrightson 1998).

Partnerships

The cost, scale and complexity of distance education provision have often encouraged policy-makers to enter into working partnerships of different kinds for policy, planning and implementation. For example, partnerships have been between ministries (of education, science and technology, telecommunications, broadcasting and rural development), between ministries and donor agencies, among national, provincial and local teacher education administrations, teacher training institutions, local schools and communities. The challenges facing policy-makers and planners in developing and sustaining partnerships include achieving clear consensus and agreement, locating authority and decision-making, allocating resources and roles, ensuring technical expertise, establishing co-ordination and communication mechanisms and organizing teacher support at the grassroots level. Because government policy-makers are close to regulatory authority, they possess a built-in leadership advantage in partnerships. However, while they have an edge in decision-making, they need to consult and collaborate closely with partner agencies, institutions and individual experts to reach solutions which have technical credibility and wide acceptance.

A pilot project in China (Box 3.4) illustrates the conscious policy choices that national, provincial, county and local agencies made to harness financial, human and physical resources and expertise to support the professional development of primary and junior secondary village school teachers. The pilot project also exemplifies an effort to co-ordinate multi-level structures where rural teachers' needs provide the impetus for professional development programmes. Centrally developed distance training materials have increased relevance to trainees when set within a contextualized learning environment.

Box 3.4   Partnerships for professional development in China

The Teacher Services Network (TSN) is a pilot project in twelve counties categorized as poor, spread over six provinces. TSN was established to provide professional support services for village-level, school-based activities aimed at improving teaching and learning through peer-group professional support for isolated qualified rural schoolteachers.

Set up as hubs in town central primary schools (TCPS), the TSN serves rural school clusters. The activities are co-ordinated by a TSN organizing group comprising representatives from the prefecture Normal Teacher Training School, County Teaching and Research Group, and the TCPS principal. TSN teachers' groups comprise the TCPS principal (as head) and village schools' teacher representatives. The groups' function is to identify and respond to teacher needs and liaise with the TSN organizing group. The Normal Teacher Training School curriculum review group oversees activities.

Starting with a needs assessment study, the TSN organizing group works with all the concerned groups to plan annual activities, many of which take place in the central primary school, whose modest resource room has a television set and other simple apparatus. Videotaped programs from the Central China TV University are used for discussions and other TSN activities. Printed materials developed by the Teachers' Groups, assisted by the County Teaching and Research Group, are distributed to all teachers within the cluster.

Source: World Bank 1997

Many developing country governments have secured donor financing by either initiating distance education projects for teachers (e.g. Bangladesh through the Asian Development Bank) or planning to develop existing ones further (e.g. Sri Lanka through the World Bank). What are the policy and planning issues to be considered in donor-borrower partnerships like these? There are several that government policy-makers need to consider:

- the large initial capital outlay required to establish a distance and open learning training network;
- access to technological and professional-technical expertise which usually accompanies the financing (depending on the lending instrument selected);

- realistic programme financial projections which include identification of public resources for operational funding when donor financing ends;
- national capacity to institutionalize training programmes by the end of project implementation to ensure sustainability.

Experience of donor-borrower programmes indicates that it is important for policy-makers and planners to consider at the initial planning stages the extent to which proposed training programme features (a) mesh with existing and projected national and local level training needs and (b) can be articulated with national, regional and local structures. Box 3.1 (see above) gives the kind of strategic questions (developed as part of a World Bank operation in Vietnam) that can be used as a planning guide for policy-makers. Box 3.2 (also above) illustrates how principles established in donor-financed projects have become institutionalized as part of the Chinese national strategy, irrespective of source of financing, for expanding access and quality in basic education. Except for the fifth bullet point, which is specific to the western China project described in Box 3.2, these selection criteria for the identification of target groups are established now in four World Bank projects (first identified in China's Education Development in Poor Provinces, and subsequently refined in three ensuing World Bank projects in basic education). They have passed into the lore of policy-makers and planners and are used in all national and provincial basic education projects in poor counties in China (Ministry of Education, Ministry of Finance and the State Development Planning Commission).

MANAGING PROGRAMMES

As is apparent from preceding sections, a wide range of policy and planning decisions determine the purpose and scope of an education programme for teacher education. It is therefore crucial that a well-qualified and experienced management team is put in place at an early stage so that it can be involved in the policy-making and planning processes. A management perspective is critical to the formulation of practical, implementable policies, plans and programmes and early involvement in planning ensures management commitment, 'the central determinant of success' in distance education (Curran and Murphy 1992: 27). Unfortunately for some projects or programmes, the management team is only put in place after most of the policy decisions have been made.

Following the appointment of a management team, what are the organizational and structural prerequisites planners must ensure are in place prior to programme organization and delivery? Management commitment presupposes an efficient organization and management structure to oversee the implementation of the teacher education programmes. Various organizational models have been used for managing distance education for teachers; these are generally embedded in organization and management structures for distance education in general. In any case, national differences require selective adaptation of a model to suit a new situation. Nevertheless, there are certain basic organizational features to be taken into account when designing a management structure for distance teacher education. At a minimum, the structure needs four functional units, as illustrated by Taiwan's National Open University:

(a) administration (personnel; budget and accounting; academic, student and general affairs and public relations, etc.);
(b) teaching (teaching staff, curricula, teaching and learning materials, delivery of programme or course materials, evaluation);
(c) programme support (a printing or publishing centre, a computer centre, library and resource centre, educational media, research and development, etc); and
(d) regional or local learning centres (learner-support services).

(Chung 1999: 216)

Programme managers need to ensure that all the above are in place well ahead of time and are in line with policy objectives. It is not always easy to ensure that organizational structures are in accord with policy objectives. The management team is likely to face difficulties in, for instance, establishing distance learning programmes in institutions where conventional training programmes are the norm and the distance programmes are seen as inferior 'add-ons', or in converting programmes to distance education delivery and ensuring equal status. Experience from six African countries shows that the common factor among the various organizational structures was their dependence on an established institution as a base for organizing and implementing their programmes. Many, in fact, were funded and staffed by the parent institution (Curran and Murphy 1992). This issue relates to earlier discussions on where to locate new programmes in relation to existing provision.

Whatever the structure and organization chosen, distance education programmes for teachers are determined, to a large extent, by the provider's objectives, available funds, values and approaches to teaching and learning. Open and distance learning for teacher education clearly implies change in key areas such as curriculum, programme delivery, teaching methodology and assessment. However, any innovation, even when politically supported and adequately funded, can meet with resistance from teachers and teacher educators if they do not understand or accept the need for change. Overcoming resistance to change calls for, at the least, collaborative decision-making between management and teaching staff on all key issues through frequent, reliable and open communication (Rowntree 1992: 265–6) – a situation sometimes easier to describe than to achieve. Decision-making is also strongly affected by cultural differences in how authority and communication operate within organizations.

Monitoring and evaluation

Monitoring and evaluation are critical elements in managing distance education programmes for teachers. They provide an evidential base and establish linkages between expectations, policy, plans and implementation and between the theory, research and effective classroom practice. The functions and benefits of a monitoring and evaluation system, which should be established and financed at programme inception and as an integral part of the programme or project, are summarized in Box 3.5.

Co-ordination of administrative tasks, such as hiring and deployment of personnel, budget planning and accounting, student registration and records, and public relations, is best handled by senior managers, supported by managers and administrators at the middle and local levels.

Box 3.5   Functions and benefits of monitoring an evaluation system

A monitoring and evaluation system provides critical support to effective management of open and distance learning in teacher education by systematically recording all relevant information on how effectively policies and programmes are being implemented. This process enables management to anticipate problems and take proactive action to address them. Key activities include the following:

- systematic collection, analysis and presentation of key statistical data on students, staff, student assignments and assessment and staff feedback;
- monitoring of operation of trainee support in regional or district centres;
- periodic analysis and assessment of programme status, including staff performance and resource utilization; and
- review of policy in light of information from all the above as part of the process of policy-making and programme planning.

However, responsibility for publicity on programmes must be shared with middle and local level staff. The management team has to ensure that all the essential parts of the programme are properly articulated and ready for delivery before deadlines. This requires co-ordinating the

- adoption, adaptation, development and delivery of courses and materials;
- organization of study centres, mentors and other support systems including partnerships and any computer conferencing or online provision;
- provision of infrastructure, technology and logistics to support the learning or training;
- assurance of prompt assessment and feedback on all coursework.

Managers at all levels must ensure that critical policy decisions are effectively translated into actions for programme delivery. For example, a policy decision to adopt a learner-centred approach will need to be turned into practice by:

- designing courses, materials and a learning system which reflects this (courses and materials relevant to the learner's context, making use of learner experience and problems, taking the learner's level of knowledge and experience as the starting point, providing opportunities for interaction with the materials and with tutors and peers, providing feedback on progress and a learning system which is convenient and affordable to use);
- setting up a strong learner support system, an important element of student success (Robinson 1995; Reid 1995; Light 2001);
- ensuring personal, regular contact with trainers who directly address trainee needs, a practice which appears to have a positive effect on learner performance and completion rates;
- ensuring adequate staffing and staff training and equipment for support centres;
- establishing management roles, procedures and mechanisms to ensure effective day-to-day administration, monitoring and quality of the above.

Staff training and development

Institutions and learning programmes are as effective as the people who run them. It is therefore important to delineate carefully the roles and responsibilities of staff at national, provincial and local levels since they will be responsible for planning and managing the programmes. They must also be provided with appropriate training aimed at achieving total quality management (TQM) in which the process is as important as the outcome. Staff training needs to be part of the distance education provider's strategic planning (Robinson 1998b), an ongoing process which responds to institutional and individual needs, reinforces staff commitment to the enterprise and maintains staff morale. Training and staff development is needed for all of those involved in providing the programme: the management team; curriculum planners; materials designers and producers; writers and editors of text materials; media specialists new to distance education programmes, teachers and tutors, administrators and the support staff. A major challenge for planners is to get staff development for distance education seen as an investment, not only a cost.

TOP-DOWN AND BOTTOM-UP CHANGE

Policy-making and planning approaches to change in the curriculum, pedagogy and teachers' roles can be 'top-down' (by far-sighted ministries, donor agencies, teacher training providers or professional associations) or 'bottom-up' (by far-sighted schools, departments and groups of teachers). There are strengths and weaknesses in both these approaches when planning and managing open and distance learning-based teacher education. A top-down approach may facilitate systematic planning, ensure national commitments are made and upheld, and may help in ensuring continued funding and support. At the same time, plans may change in response to changed political imperatives and there may be gaps between national aspirations and local realities. Bottom-up approaches, in contrast, are likely to increase the involvement of local stakeholders, who can gauge local realities and preferences, while local input should help ensure the relevance of programmes to local needs and circumstances. But they face the dangers that there may be inadequate knowledge, resources or funding locally and that bottom-up and top-down drives may be in conflict.

What is needed is a judicious blend of both approaches with a shared commitment at the national and local level. Hammer and Stanton (1995) observe that without top-down leadership and any real commitment to change at the top, bottom-up initiatives may succeed for a while but will almost invariably fail in the longer term.

Experience from a project in China, aimed at improving the quality of teacher training although not by distance learning, illustrates the complementary top-down and bottom-up approaches to mobilizing and channelling the hitherto untapped creativeness of administrators, teacher trainers and trainees to design and carry out action research directed at introducing innovative classroom practice (Box 3.6).

Box 3.6   Teachers participate in innovative teaching research in China

In the World Bank-funded Effective Teaching Services (ETS) project, the *Quality Enhancement Element* included an innovation programme in which over 6,000 personnel from the provincial education commissions, normal college (NC) and normal university (NU) teachers and their students. Working in teams, they submitted proposals for school management and classroom-oriented action research projects aimed at introducing innovation in education management and classroom teaching. The first few batches of proposals were largely academic and theoretical, reflecting the traditional approach to teacher education which the ETS project was designed to change. After a few iterations, with patient coaching by the project task manager, 460 sub-projects covering eight major research areas were selected and successfully carried out. The research findings and the involvement of the NC and NU teachers in action research provided a substantive foundation for the quality improvement in teacher education. The quality and scale of the research sub-projects, unprecedented in the history of teacher education in China, helped to unleash the research potential and enhanced the quality of teaching of the teachers colleges and teachers universities and the work of the provincial education commissions.

Source: World Bank 2000

CONCLUSIONS

The exploration of policy-making, planning and management issues in this chapter leads to the following conclusions in designing and implementing teacher education programmes using open and distance learning.

- Policy thrusts in teacher education reflect the goals ascribed to education. As such, the providers of teacher education are subject to political and stakeholder influence.
- Policy-makers and planners need to be well informed about the principles, successful practices, potential pitfalls and constraints of distance learning. They should work collaboratively with planners, whose inputs in the policy-making process could avoid major pitfalls in translating policies into action, and with teacher educators, whose ground-level experience provides an important bridge between policy

and planning for teacher development on the one hand, and actual classroom practice on the other.

- Policy-makers need to secure political support for new policies on teacher education through distance education by involving key national decision-makers as well as local stakeholders in the policy-formulation process. Political support will help establish legitimacy at the outset by assuring that the quality of the programmes is at least on a par with that of conventional teacher education.
- The policy-formulating process involves setting priorities which are influenced by political and social equity issues but aligning them with existing policies, practices and resource availability.
- A fundamental policy decision is whether to focus on initial teacher education or continuing professional development, or both.
- The management team should be established early enough for it to participate in the policy-formulating and programme-planning process to ensure effective implementation and management.
- Monitoring and evaluation activities and responsibilities should be established as an integral part of the programme at inception to provide systematic evidence on programme effectiveness and a basis for policy review, programme research (including technology use) and effective classroom practice.
- The organizational structure and training strategies must be responsive to the specific environment in terms of the types of teachers needed, the technological infrastructure available, the instructional materials and media to be used, and the geographic area to be covered and regional variation to be accommodated.
- There needs to be a judicious blend of top-down and bottom-up approaches to policy-making and programme-planning to ensure relevance and shared commitment to the programme at national, regional and local levels.

REFERENCES

Chung, Hung-Ju (1999) 'Contemporary distance education in Taiwan', in K. Harry (ed.) *Higher Education through Open and Distance Learning*, London: Routledge.

Curran, C. and Murphy, P. (1992) 'Distance education at the second level and for teacher education in six African countries', in P. Murphy and A. Zhiri (eds) *Distance Education in Anglophone Africa* (EDI Development Policy Case Series, Analytical Case Studies no. 9, Washington, DC: World Bank.

Hammer, M. and Stanton, S.A. (1995) *The Reengineering Revolution: A Handbook*, New York: HarperBusiness.

Hough, J.R. (ed.) (1984) *Educational Policy: An International Survey*, London and Sydney: Croom Helm.

Light, R. (2001) *Making the Most of College: Students Speak Their Minds*, Cambridge, Mass.: Harvard University Press.

Moon, B. and Mayes, A. (1995) 'Frameworks, Competencies and Quality: Open Learning Dimensions to Initial Teacher Training', in H. Bines and J. Welton (eds) *Managing Partnership in Teacher Training and Development*, London: Routledge.

Nielsen, H. Dean, (1997) 'Quality assessment and quality assurance in distance teacher education', *Distance Education*, 18(2): 284–317.

Perraton, H. (1992) 'A review of distance education', in P. Murphy and A. Zhiri (eds) *Distance Education in Anglophone Africa* (EDI Development Policy Case Series, Analytical Case Studies no. 9, Washington, DC: World Bank.

—— (1995) 'A practical agenda for theorists in distance education', in F. Lockwood (ed.) *Open and Distance Learning Today*, London and New York: Routledge.

—— (2000) *Open and Distance Learning in the Developing World*, London: Routledge.

Perraton, H., Robinson, B. and Creed, C. (2001) *Teacher Education through Distance Learning: Technology, Curriculum, Evaluation, Cost*. Paris: UNESCO.

Perraton, H., Creed, C. and Robinson, B. (2002) *Teacher Education Guidelines: Using Open and Distance Learning*, Paris: UNESCO.

Reid, J. (1995) 'Managing learning support', in F. Lockwood (ed.) *Open and Distance Learning Today*, London and New York: Routledge.

Robinson, B. (1995) 'Research and pragmatism in learner support', in F. Lockwood (ed.) *Open and Distance Learning Today*, London and New York: Routledge.

—— (1998a) *Developing Open Learning and Distance Education: Some Questions and Issues for Policy-makers*, IIEP Workshop on the Planning and Management of Open and Distance Learning, Bangkok: UNESCO, International Institute for Educational Planning.

—— (1998b) 'Taking a strategic perspective on staff development for open and distance learning', in C. Latchem and F. Lockwood (eds), *Staff Development in Open and Distance Learning*, London: Routledge, pp. 33–44.

—— (1999) *A Guide to Planning Distance Education in the Primary Teacher Development Project, Viet Nam*, Hanoi: World Bank and the Ministry of Education and Training, Vietnam.

Robinson, B., Tuwangye, E., Serugga, S. and Pennells, J. (1995) *Evaluation of the Mubende Integrated Teacher Education Project (MITEP)*, report prepared for ActionAid Uganda and the Overseas Development Agency, UK government on behalf of IEC, Cambridge: International Extension College.

Robinson, B., Zheng Dawei, Li Jing and Huang Rongwei (2001) 'Improving the quality of teachers in the poorest areas of Western China using distance education and ICT', project planning document for United Nations Development Programme, Department for International Development and the British Council, Beijing: UNDP/DFID/British Council.

Rowntree, D. (1992) *Exploring Open and Distance Learning*, London: Kogan Page.

Wilkin, M. (1996) *Initial Teacher Training: The Dialogue of Ideology and Culture*, Washington, DC: Falmer.

World Bank (1997) *Fourth Basic Education Project. Staff Appraisal Report, No. 1637-CHA*, Washington, DC: World Bank, East Asia and Pacific Regional Office.

—— (2000) *Effective Teaching Services Project: Implementation Completion Report*, Credit *2471-CHA*, June, Washington, DC: World Bank.

Wrightson, T. (1998) *Distance Education in Action: The Northern Integrated Teacher Education Project*, Cambridge: International Extension College.

Chapter 4

Open and distance learning for initial teacher training

Bob Moon and Bernadette Robinson

A major use of open and distance learning has been for initial teacher training, especially for primary teachers and as a means of providing unqualified serving teachers with qualifications. In industrialized countries it has been used to reach new constituencies of potential teachers (such as mature entrants) who would not otherwise have become teachers, to provide university graduates with teaching licences or professional qualifications and to support school-based training. These initiatives have been prompted by teacher shortages in many countries (developing and industrialized), a new emphasis on the training of teachers for their professional roles (not just in academic subjects) and a search for more effective ways of training teachers in response to criticisms of traditional institution-based training. Most provision for initial training has, traditionally, been pre-service and residential with the emphasis on concurrent models of training (academic subjects studied alongside professional studies and pedagogy). Varying emphasis in different countries has been placed on the practical aspects of teaching in terms of time, status and assessment weighting within programmes (see Chapter 1). However, demands for large numbers of teachers within short time-scales and re-appraisal of initial teacher-training needs have caused many to question the traditional roles of teacher-training institutions and to seek alternative modes. The urgent needs for large numbers of additional teachers, especially in some African countries, have focused increased attention on the potential of distance education, especially with the advent of information and communication technologies.

In this chapter we examine the use of open and distance learning for initial teacher training and address some commonly asked questions: Can distance education be effective for initial teacher training? Can teachers develop practical teaching skills through distance training? What kind of organization and management is needed? How can practical skills be assessed on distance education courses? Do distance education programmes produce adequately trained teachers? In responding to these questions we draw on the accumulating experience of such programmes around the world.

INITIAL TEACHER TRAINING

The nature of initial teacher training is problematic. Debate revolves around the kind and amount of initial preparation required. Since some unqualified teachers begin teaching without any preparation and apparently succeed, why are large proportions of training budgets invested in initial teacher preparation? How much teacher preparation is necessary anyway? What should the balance be between pre-service and continuing education? Which should come first, the theory of pedagogy or the experience of teaching, or should they come in parallel?

What the research says

Despite the many criticisms of teacher education over the last decade, and inconclusive evidence from earlier research, the weight of substantial research evidence now indicates that teachers who have had more preparation for teaching are more confident and successful with pupils than those who have had little or none. A growing body of empirical evidence about the outcomes of different approaches to teacher preparation and recruitment suggests that the extent and quality of teacher education and preparation influences teachers' effectiveness:

> many people believe that anyone can teach, or at least, knowing a subject is enough to allow anyone to teach it well. Others believe that teaching is best learned, to the extent that it can be learned at all, by trial and error on the job. The evidence suggests otherwise. Reviews of research over the last 30 years have concluded that even with the shortcomings of current teacher education and licensing, fully prepared and certified teachers are generally better rated and more successful with students than teachers without this preparation.
>
> (Darling-Hammond 2000: 167)

Across a wide range of subjects and school levels, researchers have found that teachers who have greater knowledge of teaching and learning are more effective with students, especially at tasks requiring higher-order thinking and problem-solving (see Darling-Hammond 1999 for a review of the research). Adequate subject knowledge is essential for teaching but research in the American context indicates that 'its relationship is curvilinear; that is, it exerts a positive effect up to a threshold level and then tapers off in influence' (Darling-Hammond 2000: 167). It is safe to say that in some countries and in some subjects (particularly in mathematics and science) large numbers of teachers regularly teach to a knowledge level below this threshold. For example, in an analysis of Mexican teacher education, Tatto and Velez (1997: 180) concluded that 'the lack of preparedness on the subject matter teachers will teach seems to be an endemic weakness of teacher education programs not only in Mexico but worldwide'. Their analysis of the curricula of different teacher education programmes in Mexico revealed a lack of emphasis on subject learning, especially for the pre-service preparation of primary teachers. They argue that, though it is necessary to provide teachers with guides to the subjects in the school curricula, the capacity to teach subjects appropriately requires conceptual understanding and learning experience that goes well beyond such guides. They also suggest that distance education offers an effective in-service means of improving teachers' subject knowledge, as demonstrated through Mexico's PARE project (*Programa para abatir el rezago educativo*). There is plenty of evidence to support this suggestion from the field of distance education in general.

The relationship among these three elements of teacher training (academic subject knowledge, professional studies or pedagogy and practice) is complex. Clearly, subject-matter knowledge, pedagogical knowledge and practice interact strongly and some of the differences in conclusions about their relative influence must relate to the levels of teachers' knowledge and previous training. The relative emphasis given to them depends on the nature of the training programme and the entry levels and experience of the teacher-trainees. Two models can be distinguished. In concurrent models, academic subjects and professional studies are followed in parallel, while in consecutive models professional studies follow on a previous programme of academic studies. The point here is that 'initial teacher training' can refer to different kinds of programmes, with differing emphases on subject knowledge, professional studies and practice. Each of these places different demands on distance education programme designers and providers.

EXPERIENCE SO FAR

Distance education has been used widely for initial teacher training. Some countries have made use of it on a large scale; the China Television Teachers College, for example, and the National Teachers' Institute in Nigeria provide it as an institutionalized part of the regular teacher-training system (see Box 4.1). Many other countries have provided initial training through time-limited projects.

If we compare the content and curricula of different distance education programmes around the world, we find variations in what is included within 'initial teacher training'. In some countries, the content of programmes is almost wholly focused on academic subjects, assessed by written examinations. Teachers may gain qualifications not in the subjects that they are to teach but in those that seem the easiest route

Box 4.1 Initial teacher training in Nigeria

The National Teachers' Institute, Nigeria, is a parastatal organization, with headquarters in Kaduna and offices in thirty-six states. It has made a significant contribution to teacher supply (48,204 National Certificate in Education (NCE) graduates between 1990 and 1999) and is now an institutionalized part of the teacher education system. Though there is little government policy on distance education and no ministry section with overall responsibility for it, distance education has played an enduring role in Nigeria's teacher education and, to meet Education For All targets, is likely to do so in the future.

The NCE programme leads to the national standard qualification for primary teachers. It combines printed self-study materials, tutorials, field trips and supervised teaching practice over four years (the college-based equivalent takes three years). The curriculum covers general subjects (50 modules) and specialist academic subjects (36), education (36), communication and the use of English (4), field trips and four weeks of supervised teaching practice each year. Learner support is provided at weekends and in school vacations in 220 study centres around the country. Students attend them for tutorials, revision and examination sessions. Supervision of practical teaching in schools is carried out by educators from local higher education institutions who visit students three times during each four-week period and assess them against standardized performance-based assessment criteria. Continuous assessment, tests and practicals constitute 40 per cent of the final grade, examinations 60 per cent. Teaching practice is compulsory but to qualify for it, students have to attain a grade of 60 per cent in coursework.

The programme has steadily rising enrolment rates: 7,324 (1994–97 cohort), 7,581 (1995–98), 8,398 (1996–99) and 8,521 (1997–2000). However, these are matched by significant drop-out rates: 27 per cent (1994–97 cohort), 30 per cent (1995–98), 35 per cent (1996–99) and 39 per cent (1997–2000). Of those completing the course, only 56.5 per cent passed in the 1994–97 cohort, 66 per cent in 1995–98, 61.4 per cent in 1996–99 and 55.6 per cent in 1997–2000.

Source: Aderinoye (forthcoming)

towards qualification. In this case the qualification is important for job security or career advancement but bears little relation to the real work of teaching. By contrast, other programmes give pedagogy and the practical aspects of teaching a central role. Most programmes fall between these two extremes; the emphasis is likely to be different for trainee teachers who already hold qualifications in academic subjects, and are following a professional studies course, as contrasted with trainees who are combining academic subject study with professional studies. They are also influenced by local traditions in teacher training and the emphasis given to inputs as opposed to outcomes in planning programmes. One international trend at present is a shift to stronger definition of outcomes-based standards of competency for what a newly trained teacher should know and be able to do on completing a programme (see Box 4.2). This requires assessment of individual performance against standards – an exercise that is challenging and costly for a distance education provider alone.

The implications of all this are that

(a) claims for the effectiveness of distance education for initial teacher training may refer to quite different kinds of programmes;
(b) distance education has produced many graduates with the qualifications needed to enter teaching but the programmes may have little or no training elements in them;
(c) the professional studies and practical part of initial teacher training has varied enormously between programmes, whether through distance education or by conventional means in terms of time allotted, status and value for teachers in training.

In general, teacher-training programmes have been criticized on two main grounds: weak integration of theory and practice, and poor quality and inadequate time for school experience. How does distance education deal with these issues? The problem of inadequate time for school experience can diminish with distance education programmes, since teachers are

---

Box 4.2   Outcome-based profiles of teachers' competence: three examples

An assessment profile of teachers' competencies defines what teachers should be able to do at the end of their training.

An example from Australia

Each area has detailed 'elements' defined and each of these elements is accompanied by a statement or indicator of effective practice plus an example of the practice.

- Using and developing professional knowledge and values.
- Communicating, interacting and working with students and others.
- Planning and managing the teaching and learning process.
- Monitoring and assessing student progress and learning outcomes.
- Reflecting, evaluating and planning for continuous improvement.

An example from the United Kingdom

Standards are specified within three broad strands or areas and qualified teacher status depends on the detailed standards being met. Assessment against standards is recorded at the end of the training programme on individual profiles indicating areas of strength and where further development is required.

- Professional values and practice (attitudes and commitment and adherence to the code of the General Teaching Council for England).
- Knowledge and understanding of the subjects they teach and the curriculum for each key stage, and competence in the use of ICT.
- Teaching, skills of planning, monitoring and assessment, teaching and class management.

An example from Vietnam

Standards for primary teachers (currently in development) are being built around three broad strands, each of which has three different levels of competence listed against it with detailed standards for each. The profiles are intended to apply to the whole range of a teacher's development, from the outcomes expected of a newly trained teacher on exit from initial teacher training to the competences expected of experienced senior teachers.

- Personality, ideology and politics (a love of the country and socialism, and moral characteristics required for the teaching profession and fulfilling the functions and duties of teachers as set out in the Education Law).
- Knowledge (of the primary school curriculum so that they are able to teach all subjects except for music, arts and sports but including ICT).
- Pedagogical skills (teaching, educating, and organizational skills).

Source: World Bank *et al.* 2000

usually school-based and programmes take place over a longer time-scale, giving teachers more time to absorb ideas, try them out and reflect on practice. Integrating theory with practice presents more challenges, as the next section shows.

INTEGRATING KNOWLEDGE, THEORY AND PRACTICE

Achieving integration makes demands in three areas: curriculum and course design, learning materials, and assessment. We look at them separately but they are, of course, linked.

Integrating through curriculum and course design

An example of this comes from the PARE project (*Programa para abatir el rezago educativo*) in Mexico, which integrated different areas of teacher knowledge with curricular knowledge by selecting an important aspect of the primary school curriculum (for example, teaching fractions) and treating its pedagogical content knowledge in depth. This increased the likelihood that teachers would not only understand the pedagogy but also the subject topic. Though this treatment of curricular knowledge required an investment of time when designing the materials as well as when learning from them, it is also likely to have increased the use that teachers make of the materials and teaching content. This kind of approach, and the materials to support it, can be further extended through peer activities and mentoring and experiment in use (Tatto and Velez 1997). This approach also reduces the tendency to provide programmes as compartmentalized and disconnected areas of knowledge, leaving any integration to individual teacher effort.

A similar approach was adopted in Fort Hare University's distance education programme for teachers in the Eastern Cape, South Africa. The course design was built around a series of key areas, linked to the curriculum taught in schools and providing teachers with extensive guidance on practical activities for everyday use in classrooms. In doing this, the programme chose to give particular attention to mathematics, science and technology, subjects where teachers upgrading their qualifications (the main focus of the programme) needed particular support (Mays 2001: 16–17).

Integrating through materials design

The design of materials, which may also include on-line elements, can also be used to promote the integration of theory and practice. For example, the British Open University's initial teacher-training programmes emphasized the need for material designers to show the relevance to classroom practice of all the readings and activities set. A study guide which helped students work through the course readings and classroom activities also demonstrated this same unifying principle of practical relevance (Leach and Moon 2000).

Integrating through assessment design

Contemporary approaches to open and distance learning for teacher education in some countries make the assessment of practical activities a core part of the learner experience. For example, the programmes at Fort Hare University and the British Open University aligned their assessment design with their course and materials design, linking training and practice in classroom activities with assessment as a central feature of programme design (SAIDE 1996; Moon and Shelton Mayes 1995). In Albania, the Kualida programme made extensive use of assessment tasks as the central driving force for teacher improvement (Leach 1996b). However, control over assessment design is not always possible for a distance education provider when the distance education programme is required to use the same national examinations (often traditional and only summative) as the regular colleges. The scope for innovation may be constrained by regulatory requirements.

MANAGING SCHOOL EXPERIENCE

A distinguishing feature of initial teacher-training programmes is their inclusion of a component of practical experience in schools. Distance education courses for initial training of unqualified primary teachers usually include the supervision and assessment of teaching practice in schools, though not always – this was not possible with the Logos II programme in Brazil for reasons of 'distance, shortage of resources and lack of qualified personnel' (Oliveira and Orivel 1993: 72), so micro-teaching sessions were substituted. In many cases, teachers on initial teacher-training programmes are unqualified but experienced, serving teachers. Programme design does not always take sufficient account of this, especially where such teachers have to sit the same examinations as inexperienced students on pre-service college-based programmes.

Though the inclusion of a practical component presents challenges for a distance education provider, the problems of managing school experience do not belong to distance education programmes alone. College programmes have not always managed it well and readers may recognise some of the weakness illustrated in Box 4.3. Criticisms of the practical component of teacher-training programmes generally include inadequate

Box 4.3 Teaching practice in Malawi

Teaching practice at the college is fraught with problems. First the schools and college calendars are not synchronized, which cuts the number of weeks available. This means that a student is given a grade from one teaching session only. Sometimes these grades are given by school teachers who are not trained to do so. Tutors agree that this practice is ineffective because there is no micro-teaching or peer teaching adequately to prepare the students for the task. In addition the classes used in the schools are small and have adequate equipment while in reality the students will teach overcrowded classes with a few teaching/learning aids. The grade given during this teaching practice does not carry much weight towards the final grade of the student. It is only used in the event of a student failing teaching practice during school-based training. As a result this activity is not taken seriously and hence some tutors decide to leave the task of supervising to school teachers.

There is one consolation to the whole process. Discussions after each practice session provide opportunity for students to look critically at their own practice. In addition each student observes nine other students teach, providing opportunity to learn from others. However, the discussions that follow are said to be rather low key with very little participation from most students. Tutors need to be motivated enough to make this exercise worthwhile and get students to realize the importance of discussions after practice. Feedback from students indicate nevertheless that they value these opportunities to teach in a supportive and supervised atmosphere.

Source: Stuart and Kunje 2000: 28

length of the practice period, poor quality of supervision and support and superficial assessment of achievement and skills.

Supervising and managing school-based practical work presents distance education providers with major logistical problems of organization and management, especially in large systems. The staffing levels and costs for distance education providers to carry out this function alone are too high even if they were practicable. (Student numbers often mean it is not.) It is a labour-intensive activity with no economies of scale. To solve this problem, partnerships have been formed with other education agents – district education officers, headteachers, schools, local tutors and primary teachers' colleges. These have involved differing degrees of delegation, collaboration and formality of contract and the complexity, time and cost of managing these crucial relationships with partners is often underestimated (Robinson 1997). Consistency of quality is not easy to achieve across distance with decentralized field operations which need, at the same time, to be responsive to local conditions. However, if discernible improvements in classroom practice are to be achieved, then finding ways of providing effective local support is essential. In setting up such partnerships, distance education providers need to define partners' roles and responsibilities, areas of accountability, the locus of decision-making, communication routes and reporting requirements.

Managing the development of teachers

The literature and research on teachers' professional development indicate that teachers proceed through a series of stages in becoming competent teachers (though these mostly refer to inexperienced pre-service teachers-in-training, not experienced unqualified teachers). Is it possible for a distance education provider to support the development process when numbers are large and provision is often on a mass scale? One illustration of managing staged development is given by the British Open University's postgraduate certificate in education (Table 4.1) which specified outcomes to be reached and assessed at the end of each stage. These outcomes reflected the standards set by the national Teacher Training Agency (2002).

Table 4.1 Course structure for the Open University Postgraduate Certificate in Education (PGCE), UK

Supported self-study units			Study time (hours)	School placements (weeks)
Stage 1	Block 1	Introduction	20	
	Block 2	Subject studies and application	40	3
Stage 2	Block 3	Planning, methods, classroom management, assessment, wider professional role	80	
	Block 4	Subject studies and application	80	
	Block 5	Language and learning, equal opportunities, special needs, effective schools	90	4
Stage 3	Block 6	Subject studies and applications	120	5
	Block 7	Preparation for induction and professional development	10	6

Source: Moon and Leach 1997: 14–15

Learner support

Experience has shown that learner support is an important element of any distance education programme though what counts as learner support varies (Robinson 1995). The functions of learner support staff are:

- *tutoring*, normally in the sense of mediating the course resources in group and individual tutorials;
- *counselling or advising* individuals or groups on course requirements, but sometimes on a more personal guidance basis, depending on role definition and provider policy;
- *facilitating and supporting*, to assist students gain access to further learning activities (e.g. in school activities);
- *assessing* formally (as part of the continuous or summative course requirements) or informally (in the sense of giving feedback on progress or performance).

The way that these functions are distributed among roles and the location of these role-holders vary widely between programmes. Dedicated open universities may establish a cadre of specially trained tutors to support courses. New regional or national programmes may draw on an existing network of colleges or departments of teacher education to serve this function (as the NITEP programme did in northern Uganda or as the China Television Teachers College does throughout China).

Leach (1996a: 124–5) suggests six functions that learner support can serve in teacher education courses:

- provide model learning environments and model best practice;
- build on existing frameworks as far as possible and be consonant with the culture in which the programme is developed;
- offer developmental and exploratory support, providing experience of a wide variety of teaching and learning opportunities;
- recognize and build on the variety of professional experiences of participants, since the teachers in training are adults;
- acknowledge both the private and professional aspects of learners' experiences and their interconnectedness in the development of learning (computer communication supports this where available);
- ensure that the support has a firm base in schools and classrooms.

In carrying out these roles, the people involved may need to learn new ways of relating to the adult learners they are responsible for, so the role may also require a culture shift. In programmes like these, the role of mentor has become important if problematic. A distance education provider in most cases has to plan for multi-level training, not only for the trainee teachers but also for the agents who support them.

Interaction with others is an important part of learner support and the learning programme. Some opportunities for this are possible through existing school networks and administrative structures in an education system and new possibilities are offered by electronic communications, especially where governments are increasing the connectivity of schools. Through the use of electronic conferencing on the British Open University postgraduate certificate programme, students were encouraged to make explicit their reflective thinking, to share it with others and to exchange experiences. Electronic conferencing enabled students to support each other during their school-based periods (these constituted more than 50 per cent of course time) and between students and their university tutors, giving them access to guidance and support which would not otherwise have been available. Interactive modes of communication open up possibilities for new forms of support and for rethinking the way the tutorial role is conceptualized (Leach and Moon 2000).

ASSESSING PRACTICAL SKILLS AND TEACHING COMPETENCE

The inclusion of practical work and its assessment increases the costs of distance education courses, introducing a component which approximates more closely to the costs and cost-structure of conventional face-to-face courses. It also increases a number of labour-intensive activities for a distance education organizer. For example, it adds to the field operation tasks of management, training, liaison and monitoring local support staff in roles of mentor, tutor, supervisor or co-ordinator. Also, a second and different assessment system has to be set in place for an institution when examining practical teaching. Problems in assessing practice tend to centre on three aspects of the field operation: the performance of headteachers as tutors or mentors or assessors of practising teachers; the task of facilitating communication between all the agents involved in student support; and the major shift in role needed by headteachers and college tutors in becoming facilitators of adult learning and teachers' partners in professional dialogue and consultation rather than inspectors or supervisors. Despite these problems, the focus on practice presents opportunities for distance education programmes to inject new life and ideas into customary and sometimes outdated school supervision practice. However, to do this requires the distance education provider to allocate it sufficient importance, effort and resources within the overall programme.

Open and distance learning programmes in teacher education are increasingly recognizing the need for more comprehensive assessment policies. Traditionally the tutor-marked essay and the end-of-course examination have been the predominant forms of assessment. Examinations in particular have been used to verify that the work completed is that of the student claiming it. The shift in emphasis towards developing classroom-based activities, often backed up by reflective assignment exercises, has in many cases prompted a move towards more comprehensive portfolio approaches to recording and judging student progress. In using this, experienced teachers or inspectors can participate in assessment activities. Furthermore, the language of outcomes, with a more precise formulation of the knowledge, understanding and skills to be developed can be used to enhance the process of reflection.

Options in assessment include:

- informal self-assessed course activities;
- formal, reported, self-assessed course activities;
- externally assessed course activities;
- tutor-marked assignments;
- timed tutor/supervisor assignments;
- formal examinations.

All of these can involve varying degrees of school-based activities. The assessment of outcomes can be administered on a continuous basis with school and/or tutor supervision or through a portfolio model where a variety of assessment activities are recorded and retained towards a summative assessment. Portfolio assessment, however, deals with different and individual sets of work, a relatively costly and time-consuming form of assessment.

Whatever form of assessment is chosen, different kinds are needed to assess the different kinds of learning that take place in initial teacher training, whether the model is concurrent or consecutive. Through course assignments, teachers can display some kinds of mastery and understanding in written form but other kinds need to be demonstrated by doing. Knowledge and understanding are easier for a distance education provider to assess than practice and performance. As Table 4.2 shows, assessment becomes more complex organizationally for a distance education provider and the costs rise, as assessment moves from Level 1 (knowledge and understanding) to Level 3 (practice and performance), that is, from standard patterns of assessment of knowledge for large groups to assessment of individual performance and difference. For assessment of classroom practice, partnerships with local agents or surrogates are needed to enable distance education providers to delegate some of the functions they cannot do.

Table 4.2 Assessing teachers' knowledge and practice at a distance

Teachers' knowledge and practice	Nature of assessment	Implications for distance education
Level 1 *Knowledge and understanding* • of academic subjects to be taught • of pedagogical concepts, ideas and theory	Written work (assignments), essays, course tests or final examinations	• Can assess learning and give feedback to students on a large scale (hundreds or thousands) • Can achieve economies of scale (standard assignments) • Can provide well-designed assignments because of the resource put into course design; may also retreat into over-use of multiple-choice questions for administrative convenience • Assignments may remain too theoretical or unrelated to the realities of classroom life, or lack regional relevance
Level 2 *Knowledge applied to practice* Application of knowledge to teacher's own context; testing out and interpreting ideas about pedagogy; evaluating practical activities and experiments, and reflecting on them.	Written reports and accounts of things done (description and analysis of activities such as teaching a mathematical topic a new way; collecting evidence in a child observation study; organizing a classroom differently; or developing new language and reading activities)	• Good learning materials can structure this process for the teacher (distance not a barrier) • Can support linkage between theory and practice • Not possible for a distance education provider to tell from the student's reports how authentic an account is being given, for example, that classroom practice matches what is described • Can be more time-consuming and expensive for a distance education provider to assess (non-standard assignments, greater individual differences)
Level 3 *Practice and performance* Enactment of knowledge and ideas; demonstration of competences and skills	Direct observation and authentication of individual teacher performance	• Much more complex to organize and manage than Level 1 • More labour-intensive and expensive than Level 1; approximates more closely to costs of conventional training • Requires more support staff in a variety of roles than Level 1; needs more staff training provision, more support materials, more monitoring and management • Requires local partners. Cannot be done at a distance (without sophisticated interactive technologies) • The only way of assessing the impact or effectiveness of some of the course materials and ideas

Source: Robinson 1997: 132

QUALITY AND STANDARDS

Managing the quality and standards of initial teacher training is essential for the credibility of open and distance learning. Some countries closely specify the teacher education curriculum and outcome standards, while others do not have clearly defined national standards and leave assessment to the discretion of individual colleges within broad ministry of education guidelines. No matter how far standards are prescribed nationally, distance education programmes have to manage their own internal quality in relation to learning materials, the learner support system, delivery systems, administration and management, and assessment. Low quality in any of these can lead to student dropout (see Box 4.4).

Usually, the distance education provider has to combine compliance with external standards of quality for teacher education with internal standards for various operational aspects. An example of a quality assurance framework for a distance education programme is given in Table 4.3. This shows the procedures targeted at different aspects of the course and the kinds of evidence appropriate for demonstrating that quality assurance mechanisms are in place and working. One challenge for distance education providers is to find the right balance between the

---

Box 4.4   Quality in initial teacher training in Nigeria

The National Teachers Institute has high dropout rates. These occur for several reasons: the inability of trainees to afford course materials; the time needed for other income-generating activities; the disruption to the studies of female trainees as they follow a relocated husband; the demands of farming at examination time (especially in the northern states like Sokoto and Kano); late delivery of materials because of poor postal services; long distances to travel to study centres; failure to participate in the practical teaching element (a compulsory part of the course) and low pass rates in assignments and tests. Problems in the quality of learner support contribute to this situation. Study-centres are under-resourced and overstretched, dealing with more students than planned for when established; appropriate local tutors are difficult to recruit; and the activities provided at study centres tend to mimic the formal practices of conventional colleges or traditional ways of teaching, eroding the intention of providing opportunities for interaction between learners and tutors.

Source: Aderinoye (forthcoming)

Table 4.3 Quality assurance framework for the Postgraduate Certificate in Education (PGCE), British Open University

Aspect of course	Procedures for assuring quality
Admissions	Prescribed framework Interview monitoring Admissions review
Development of course structure	Prescribed generic framework for all courses Teacher and specialist consultative groups School of Education and university committee approval External assessors
Development of materials (print and audio-visual)	Prescribed framework Developmental testing External assessors' reports Mentor/student/tutor surveys
Tutor and mentor briefing and training	Prescribed framework and materials Evaluation and review
School experience	Prescribed framework (school experience guides, partner handbook, mentor guides) Monitoring (school visits) External examiners
School reports and tutor marked assignments	Guidance Monitoring Procedures for 'limited progress' External examiners
Final award	Prescribed portfolio – competences and qualities External examiners Assessment board
Destinations	Destinations survey
End-of-course reports	—

Source: Leach and Moon 2000: 8

costs (financial and time) and benefits of implementing a quality assurance system so that it achieves its goals of improvement and validation of the teacher education programme.

CONCLUSIONS

Experience suggests a range of policy options for the planners and demonstrates three potential benefits from the use of open and distance learning. The first relates to efficiency in the use of resources deployed for initial

Box 4.5 MIITEP in Malawi: a mixed-mode experiment

As a result of primary education expansion in 1992–4, the untrained teacher population of Malawi increased to more than 50 per cent of the teaching force. The total output capacity of the regular training college system was at most 1,500 new teachers a year.

As a solution to this problem the Malawi Integrated In-service Teacher Education Programme (MIITEP) began in 1997. It is implemented by the University of Malawi with funding from the World Bank, Deutsche Gesellschaft für Technische Zusammenarbeit (GTZ) and Ministry of Education. It provides a two-year initial training programme for secondary-school leavers who have worked as unqualified primary teachers for at least one year in schools. It operates a mixed-mode delivery system: three months of college-based courses + twenty months of distance study and course-work (with local support and visits from college tutors) + one month of college-based residential review courses and final examination.

Up to 2001, 18,000 teachers were successful in achieving training and qualifications through this approach. Colleges have been able to accommodate three cohorts of trainees a year (7,500) and over a three-year period have trained as many teachers as the traditional college-based mode could do in twelve years. The cost of producing wholly college-based training is three to four times as expensive.

Source: Kunje (forthcoming)

teacher training. The use of open and distance learning, in combination with college-based courses, enables resources (buildings, teaching staff and funds) to be used differently to accommodate more trainees and, if done well, the quality can be at least acceptable and at best very good (see Box 4.5). It can also produce a trained teacher at lower cost. The second relates to supply. Open and distance learning has shown that it can draw on new constituencies of teachers, such as mature entrants or rural members of a community and also, as emerging evidence shows, retain them for longer as teachers – an important consideration when assessing the cost-benefits of different modes of training and the overall costs of investment in a teaching force with high rates of turnover. It can also provide more trained teachers in a shorter time than more traditional institution-based approaches. The third relates to the nature of the curriculum and training. Construction of programmes around school experience, if well designed, increases the chances of programmes being relevant to the practicalities of teaching, strengthening the relationship between theory and individual practice and offering an important means of influencing classroom practice and school improvement.

REFERENCES

Aderinoye, R. (forthcoming) 'Nigeria: an alternative route to primary teacher qualification', in Perraton, H., Robinson, B. and Creed, C. *International Case Studies of Teacher Education through Distance Learning*, Paris: UNESCO.

Darling-Hammond, L. (1999) *Teaching Quality and Student Achievement: A Review of State Policy Evidence*, Seattle, Wash.: Center for the Study of Teaching and Policy, University of Washington.

—— (2000) 'How teacher education matters', *Journal of Teacher Education*, 51(3): 166–73.

Kunje, D. (forthcoming) 'The Malawi Integrated In-service Teacher Education Programme: an experiment with mixed-mode training', *International Journal for Educational Development*.

Leach, J. (1996a) 'Learning in practice: professional development through open learning', in A. Tait and R. Mills (eds) *Supporting the Learner in Open and Distance Learning*, London: Longman, pp. 101–26.

—— (1996b) 'Teacher education in change: an intellectual practice issue for Albania, *Mediterranean Journal of Educational Studies*, 4(2): 53–76.

Leach, J. and Moon, B. (2000) 'Changing paradigms in teacher education: a case study of innovation and change', in A. Scott and J. Freeman-Moir (eds) *Tomorrow's Teaching: International and Critical Perspectives on Teacher Education*, Christchurch: University of Canterbury Press.

Mays, T. (2001) 'Innovative ways to support teacher learners', *Open Learning through Distance Education* 7(1): 16–17.

Moon, B. and Leach, J. (1997) 'Towards a new generation of open learning programmes in teacher education: the Open University (UK) pre-service teacher education programme', paper presented to the Distance Education for Teacher Development Colloquium, Global Knowledge 1997 Conference, Toronto 22–25 June.

Moon, B. and Shelton Mayes, A. (1995) 'Integrating values into the assessment of teachers in initial education and training', in T. Kerry and A. Shelton Mayes (eds) *Issues in Mentoring*, London: Routledge.

Oliveira, J-B. and Orivel, F. (1993) 'Logos II in Brazil', in H. Perraton (ed.) *Distance Education for Teacher Training*, London: Routledge, pp. 69–94.

Robinson, B. (1995) 'Research and pragmatism in learner support', in F. Lockwood (ed.) *Open and Distance Learning Today*, London: Routledge, pp. 221–31.

—— (1997) 'Distance education for primary teacher training', in J. Lynch, C. Modgil and S. Modgil (eds) *Innovations in Delivering Primary Education*, London: Cassell, pp. 122–38.

SAIDE (1996) *Teacher Education Offered at a Distance in South Africa*, Johannesburg: South African Institute of Distance Education.

Stuart, J.S. and Kunje, D. (2000) *The Malawi Integrated In-service Teacher Education Project: An Analysis of the Curriculum and Its Delivery in the Colleges*, discussion paper, Centre for International Education, University of Sussex Institute of Education <www.sussex.ac.uk/usie/muster/>

Tatto, M.T. and Velez, E. (1997) 'A document-based assessment of teacher education reform initiatives: the case of Mexico', in C.A. Torres and A. Puigros (eds) *Latin American Education: Comparative Perspectives*, Boulder, Col.: Westview, pp. 165–218.

Teacher Training Agency (2002) *Qualifying to Teach: Professional Standards for Qualified Teacher Status and Requirements for Initial Teacher Training*, London: Teacher Training Agency, DFEE.

World Bank, Department for International Development and Government of the Socialist Republic of Viet Nam (2000) *Primary Teacher Development Project, Viet Nam, Draft Standards*, Hanoi: Government of Vietnam.

Chapter 5

Open and distance education for teachers' continuing professional development

Helen Craig and Hilary Perraton

It is widely agreed that initial teacher training alone is an inadequate basis for achieving good quality in teachers and teaching. Continuing professional development is receiving increasing attention for several reasons. Education is changing rapidly and teachers need to keep pace with the changes so there is pressure from governments, and from the teaching profession itself, for updating. As more teachers gain initial qualifications, so the focus of governments has tended to shift towards the improvement of quality. At the same time, lifelong learning in many professions, including teaching, is seen as a necessity for economic development in the competitive global economy.

Employers and managers of teachers do, however, face two major challenges in supporting their continuing professional development: providing access to learning opportunities for large numbers of teachers dispersed across schools in a country or region, and funding them. The budgets allocated to teachers' continuing professional development are usually small and, if traditional forms of training are used, too limited to provide for more than a small proportion of teachers.

Distance education has played a role in meeting both these challenges and is likely to play an increasing one, given the gap between the range, volume and continuity of demand and the limited availability of resources. This chapter examines the forms and role that distance education has taken and the decisions that planners need to make in using open and distance education for teachers' professional development.

FORMS OF TEACHER EDUCATION

In this and other chapters we draw a distinction between the initial education and training of teachers and their continuing professional development. While this distinction is useful, it may in practice sometimes be blurred; where both qualified and unqualified teachers are employed in schools, some programmes of continuing education are addressed to both groups. Indeed, in-service courses may be the only professional training some teachers receive. Good planning demands that we consider pre-service and in-service education together. Hawes and Stephens made the point,

> For many unqualified teachers in-service training may be the only training they receive. For others, pre-service education may well have been of a general kind, an extension of their secondary education with some study of education thrown in for good measure. In-service education (if they are fortunate to receive any) may constitute their only source of *professional* training. . . . We will also suggest that the current divisions between 'pre-service' and 'in-service' training may prove increasingly unprofitable to maintain and that we may do well to evolve a more unified and more flexible concept of 'Teacher Education and Training'.
>
> (1990: 93)

We can then distinguish between various approaches to professional development. It may be structured or unstructured. There are many programmes that have a formal structure, in which teachers are enrolled on a course, and expect to proceed through it in a structured way, sometimes to the point at which they are awarded a formal qualification. Some of these programmes can be seen as supply driven, as when a ministry of education decides to organize a training course and encourage or even require teachers to enrol on it. Others are demand driven; several open universities, for example, have developed courses that lead to formal qualifications for which there is a demand from learners. In contrast, within unstructured programmes, often made available through broadcasts but beginning to be available through the Internet, learners are not expected to enrol or follow a formal course; instead resources are simply made available to learners with the intention of strengthening their professional practice as teachers. For their part, teachers are likely to appreciate, and benefit from, a range of different approaches to continuing education. Box 5.1 shows the variety of opportunities available to teachers in Zhejiang province in China. A recurrent theme of professional development is the need to seek structured as well as unstructured approaches, to allow demand and supply to lead, even within resource constraints.

Structured in-service education

There is a wealth of experience here, of courses that are driven by both supply and demand and that use a variety of different technologies. In

Box 5.1 Channels of professional development in Zhejiang Province, China

Zhejiang is a relatively prosperous coastal province with wide disparity of development levels within it. In-service teacher training at the county level is provided by an in-service training school or centre which co-ordinates professional development activities (providing upgrading courses, seminars on curriculum changes, new teaching approaches and using new equipment). Some in-service centres also provide tutorial facilities for teachers following television-based distance learning courses or preparing for self-study examinations. At the township level, the main primary school acts as professional development centre, with better-qualified teachers from the area making an input to regular monthly or weekly activities.

What kinds of in-service activity do teachers participate in? Which do they prefer? Interviews with 127 teachers from a variety of schools (in urban, rural and ethnic minority areas) identified nine different channels of in-service professional development available to them. Self-study was the *most frequently used* channel overall for professional development, despite other more formal options being available, though it was used more often by rural than urban teachers. Urban teachers participated more often in departmental meetings than in self-study (which was their second most frequently used option). Informal channels of support and development were used most often. Overall, the *most effective* channels identified by teachers were short courses (22 per cent), self-study (21 per cent) and peer discussion (12 per cent). This pattern applied to all the rural areas but not to the urban (the capital city of Hangzhou), where cross-school observation, advisers and short courses were seen as most effective. The channels seen as effective in rural areas were school based or individual based. 'In other words, teachers and schools [in rural areas] are very much left to their own devices in terms of professional development. In the city, between-school interactions and systemic channels (e.g. advisers) are more active' (p. 170). The most highly appreciated sources of training and improvement were those closest to the teacher.

Channels of in-service development	Participation rates overall (percentage of teachers)
Self-study	57.3
Department meetings	50.4
Peer discussion	48.1

continued

Cross-township activities	35.9
Classroom observation in other schools	35.1
Supervision by principal	29.8
Supervision by inspectors or advisors	25.2
Seminars	25.2
Short courses	23.7

Source: Carron and Ta Ngoc Châu 1996: 163–70

the cluster of examples presented in Table 5.1, some programmes tend be formal longer-term programmes that assist teachers to obtain qualifications, to match needed skills for changing curricula, or are an extension of basic education. These examples tend to be more print-based with some radio and, where possible, satellite television broadcasting. Others are shorter programmes held over vacation periods or each week to raise awareness of issues, and to improve teachers' knowledge and skills on various themes. These shorter programmes are more likely to be in the form of weekly radio broadcasts, or workshops with television support.

A structured approach involving the integration of several elements is taken by the Special Orientation for Primary Teachers in India, outlined in Box 5.2. It uses a range of technologies and trained facilitators to provide interactive support for teachers. Like many programmes, it brings together actors from a number of different institutions, calling on the specialist skills of an open university and applying them to the needs of teachers. It is also significant in that the programme is embedded within a national programme to strengthen schools.

Unstructured and resource-based approaches

There is a strong argument that, as experienced or qualified teachers will have demonstrated a capacity to learn, there is no need to create a formal system of training for their continuing professional development. Rather, provided educational resources are available for them, they should be able to choose what meets their needs and learn without a formal structure.

As shown in Table 5.2, both industrialized and developing countries have used resource-based approaches in order to strengthen the teaching force, using discussion forums, general information and networking opportunities, and a variety of different media. Increasingly, and especially within the industrialized world, use is being made of the Internet. A British programme, TeacherNetUK, for example, aims to support professional development by selecting appropriate web projects, facilitating

Box 5.2   Mixing the technologies in India

As part of the Special Orientation for Primary Teachers programme, the National Council for Educational Research and Training (NCERT), the Indira Gandhi National Open University (IGNOU) and the Indian Space Research Organization have initiated several in-service teacher-training courses using interactive video technology. Studio-based educators make live one-way video presentations about different teaching areas – aided by prerecorded video clips – to groups of teachers in different sites. These teachers engage in the particular subject both before and after the broadcast through print materials and activities produced centrally by the twenty-strong course team but mediated at the local level by trained facilitators. Activity sheets are produced in the language of the participants. The teachers can ask direct questions of the educators through telephone and fax links. The approach uses satellite transmission for the one-way video and two-way audio interaction, the production of video clips, computer systems, cable television, telephone, and radio and television broadcasts.

Source: Creed and Perraton 2001: 29–30

links to national and international networks of teachers and developing on-line discussions. Examples can be found in other countries too.

But resource-based approaches are not limited to the advanced technologies. The example from Bhutan in Table 5.2 relies on radio, and the example from India upon television. Again, in both the North and the South, broadcasting agencies make programmes for teachers. Some of these go beyond national frontiers; the BBC World Service has begun to make and broadcast programmes designed for teachers internationally. These learning opportunities for teachers are less well documented than those that are structured, and little evaluation of them is available. But it seems likely that, just as many adult learners benefit more from unstructured programmes than structured, so teachers are likely to be influenced by programmes of this kind.

THE PLANNER'S DECISIONS

This analysis suggests that the planner's primary choices are about the allocation of resources between initial education and continuing professional development, closely followed by choices between structured and

Table 5.2 Unstructured programmes of general ongoing support

Country	Project	Purpose	Date	Outcomes	Other comments
Australia	Education Network Australia (EdNA)	To support and promote the benefits of the Internet for learning, and provide resources useful for teaching and learning	n/a	A directory about education and training in Australia. A database of web-based resources useful for teaching and learning. Facilitates growth of learning networks	EdNA is a network across government and nongovernment schooling systems, vocational education and training, adult communities and higher education
Bhutan	Distance education support	To extend skill support and information to teachers, especially in rural areas	n/a	Weekly radio broadcasts to all primary teachers	—
Canada	SchoolNet: virtual resource for teachers and students	To provide a set of Internet-based educational services and resources that stimulate learning and put creativity directly in the hands of the users	n/a	Provides discussion groups, teacher-designed networking projects, a virtual environment for situation-based learning, interactive curriculum resources, on-line career materials and access to special prices from hardware and software companies. 9,000 schools and 900 libraries connected by 1997 to access these resources	—
India	Hints for Teachers, national television	To raise awareness of innovations in teaching	n/a	45-minute TV broadcast once a week	—
Global	UNICEF: The Teachers' Place	To provide resources, discussion forum and networking opportunities for those involved in Education for Development	1999–	—	Provides a web-site for teachers around the world to talk and share ideas

Source: Creed 2001

unstructured approaches. Such choices are seldom made on an either/or basis. More often, and for good reason, a variety of different approaches are deployed so that a ministry of education is likely to be concerned both with initial and with continuing teacher education, and with both structured and unstructured approaches. In considering whether and how to apply open and distance learning to them, the planner is usually then faced with a similar set of decisions to be made regardless of the form of teacher education – about the functions of the programme and its curriculum, the organization and infrastructure needed to make it work, arrangements for funding, the choice between different technologies and pedagogical decisions about teaching methods. We look at each of these in turn. As with other types of teacher education, good planning also demands that we build evaluation into the programme, using a variety of approaches.

The location of these decisions is important as well as their outcome. Few decisions are made, or should be made, by a single planner or even a single agency or department. Within large states some may be located at provincial or district level; in small states, key decisions may depend on regional decisions and involve co-operation with a university or accrediting agency beyond national frontiers. Effective open and distance learning often demands co-operation between a number of different institutional actors and stakeholders. It may, for example, demand activity by an open university, under one jurisdiction, local teachers' centres that may be under a second, and a national agency with broad responsibility for teacher qualifications under a third. Thus, while considering the best way of implementing a particular strategy of teacher education, the planner is also likely to face decisions that involve a wider range of stakeholders than is the case for much conventional education. This complexity will affect the choice of organizational structure, considered below, and the development of strategies for co-operation between partners. It may also influence decisions about curriculum, where several stakeholders have interests in the content of a programme, and about funding, where finance is drawn from a number of different sources.

Functions and curriculum

Programmes of continuing professional development have been launched with a variety of different purposes and so with a variety of different curricula shaped by the functions they serve.

In a recent review of international practice for UNESCO, distinctions were drawn between three different functions in continuing education: first, to raise the skills, deepen the understanding and extend the knowledge of teachers generally; second, to help the process of curriculum reform; and third, to prepare teachers for new roles as head teachers, administrators, or the staff of teachers' colleges. In relation to the first group of programmes the report noted that

> Some programmes are broadly focused while others are targeted at specialist groups. Programmes are taken either by individuals or by groups of teachers who are encouraged to participate by their schools or their employers. For example, a non-profit television station is taking the lead on supporting school groups in Brazil. In other cases, programmes are available for individual teachers who want to improve their skills and their status, often enrolling on an individual basis, and at their own expense. Indira Gandhi National Open University in India has a number of programmes of this kind. The University of South Africa also offers programmes on this basis. Their BEd programmes are for experienced under-qualified teachers and also new entrants to teaching, which serve to meet individual goals as well as contributing to the policy goal of a graduate teaching force. Some programmes are aimed at the upgrading of teachers' qualifications required by official policy as new national standards, as in China for example.
>
> (Perraton *et al.* 2001: 15)

These purposes may overlap with those of curriculum reform. Here, some programmes have been designed to reorient teachers generally. In Mongolia, for example, as part of the national process of a transition away from a command economy, radio and print have been used to reach scattered audiences of teachers who need to respond to national changes in curriculum and teaching methods. Often, however, programmes have been designed to raise capacity in a single area. In South Africa, the Open Learning Systems Educational Trust (OLSET) has used radio to raise capacity in the teaching of English. And in many countries distance education approaches are being used to support teachers who need to understand and apply the new information technologies in education.

Organization and infrastructure

There are many different organizational models from which the planner may be able to choose in designing a programme of professional education at a distance. The actual choice will be shaped by the curriculum, by national culture, by the scale of need and by the existing educational infrastructure. The curriculum may impose its own organizational demands: specialist courses may require the participation of specialist agencies, while courses accredited by a particular university or agency are likely to require their involvement. Cultural expectations will make it appropriate in some cases and inappropriate in others to involve non-governmental organizations or private-sector organizations. If, within the infrastructure, there is already an open university or specialist distance-teaching institution with the capacity to develop and deliver materials, it may not be necessary to develop capacity in these areas from scratch.

A variety of organizational models have been adopted (see also Chapter 2), with responsibility most often resting with ministry of education institutions or with universities, but also, in some cases, involving non-governmental organizations and, occasionally, international co-operation.

Many countries have made perhaps the most obvious organizational choice in giving responsibility for distance education to a single college of education, alongside its other work. In Belize, for example, with the narrow range of options that were possible in a small state, this was the ministry of education choice. Identifying a college of education in this way may help eliminate conflict between different approaches to teacher education but demands that conventional teachers develop new skills in distance education alongside their specialist skills. Programmes of this kind are generally supply driven, with a college responding to a definition of educational needs made by the college's parent ministry. In other cases a ministry of education has itself run programmes, as in Uganda in the 1990s or, in a much less structured programme, through the National Grid for Learning set up on behalf of the Department of Education and Skills in Britain. A much more unusual approach was adopted by Nigeria in establishing a specialist, distance-teaching, institution for teachers – the monotechnic National Teachers' Institute.

More often, distance education for teachers has become the responsibility of universities. Where there are open universities these have often included faculties of education and attracted many teachers on to their courses. In Britain, the initial cohort of Open University students was dominated by qualified teachers, who held a teaching certificate but not a degree, and wanted to raise their status. More recently the university's education faculty has run a variety of general and specialist courses for teachers ranging from specialist certificates to doctoral programmes designed mainly for teachers looking for administrative or teacher-training posts. It has also sought to meet the continuing demand for higher qualifications by moving into master's degree programmes as the qualification levels of many teachers increased. Many conventional universities that have introduced distance education have seen teachers as important audiences or been called upon by governments to play a part in teacher education. The University of the South Pacific began its, now extensive, programme of distance education by making distance education a responsibility of its education faculty.

A variety of non-government and international programmes contrast with these national, public-sector, approaches. In some jurisdictions non-governmental organizations have developed programmes for teachers in response to perceived need. In South Africa the programme (mentioned above) to raise the quality of the teaching of English offers one example: the Open Learning Systems Educational Trust (OLSET) runs radio programmes, with some support for teachers, and has subsequently moved into teacher education in order to strengthen its programmes for schools. In doing so it has, however, had to build up its own structure for distributing materials and monitoring its work in schools and was not able to rely on existing structures for this purpose. So far it has not been successful in becoming institutionalized into the education system, despite positive evaluations. In the differing culture of Brazil, where there is a tradition of co-operation between profit and non-profit sectors, programmes for teachers are offered by a consortium of agencies that makes television programmes for teachers and supports them on the ground. Consortia are also a feature of the small number of international programmes being launched for teachers. The francophone Réseau Africain de Formation à Distance (Resafad) has worked with educators in West Africa to develop international programmes of professional development. In Europe, there have been the beginnings of co-operative telematic programmes in teacher education, with funding from the European Commission, that demanded co-operation between different member states.

This analysis has concentrated on identifying the lead agency for the programmes mentioned. In practice, as noted above, much teacher education demands co-operation between a number of different agencies: few institutions have the capacity to carry out all the necessary functions. Even where teacher education is the responsibility of a body with considerable autonomy, like the National Teachers' Institute in Nigeria or the Open University in Britain, able to award its own qualifications, co-operation with other agencies is usually necessary. The Institute is a federal agency and needs to work with those operating under state governments if it is to use their resources. The University has to rely on the BBC for broadcasts and, as in most countries, ultimately needs government recognition of qualifications for teachers. Often the organizational structure is more complex with separate agencies responsible for, say, the development of teaching material, the supervision of classroom practice, and the award of credit.

There are therefore two sets of critical issues for the planner when looking at organizational choices. One is about the location of the various specialist services needed for teachers' continuing education, and the possibility of using existing institutions or structures rather than creating new ones. The second, and probably more important and difficult, is about structures for co-operation between them.

Experience suggests that this kind of articulation between partners is likely to be particularly difficult and important in relation to learner support, teaching practice (most often part of initial teacher training) and accreditation. Distance education, of its nature, tends to centralize decision-making, and academic staff. Programmes are developed at the centre and delivered at the periphery. And yet the students and schools are also at the periphery and arrangements for the management and supervision of any face-to-face support, or of meetings between teachers, or classroom practice, need to be local, not central. Responsibility for recognition and accreditation often rests outside the teaching organization, and is seldom the responsibility of those drawing up a teacher education curriculum or developing teaching materials. But if teachers' motivation is to be maintained, recognition of their study and qualifications is likely to be all important.

Generally we can conclude that any organizational structure needs to ensure that there is adequate support for students, including communications, transportation, and library resources. One of the continuing frustrations is that teachers in remote areas often have the greater professional development needs. Meeting these involves facing obstacles of irregular or non-existent telephone lines and electricity, limited postal services, poor roads, and limited transport. Technology may help here, provided that its infrastructure is in place.

Funding

While open and distance learning has often been promoted on the grounds that it will save costs, it will not necessarily do so and inevitably requires resources for which there will be competing demands from other parts of the education service. Distance education programmes may not require halls of residence but they do need an infrastructure, upfront investment in the development of teaching materials and setting up arrangements for student support. Some of the resources needed may be found by redeploying them from elsewhere in the educational system. As suggested in Chapter 11, the planner needs to consider both the fixed costs, for capital, equipment and course development, and the running costs of a programme. There has sometimes been a tendency to neglect running costs and the expenditure needed to keep programmes and materials up to date.

Distance education may have an economic advantage over conventional through one or more of three mechanisms. First, if the duration of face-to-face and residential education can be reduced, then the costs of running conventional colleges or in-service training institutions can be reduced or spread over a larger number of students. Second, materials developed and distributed on a large scale can bring down the unit cost per learner. Third, distance education can save travel costs. Many conventional programmes have to devote a significant proportion of their budget to the costs of bringing teachers to one location, and paying them a daily allowance while away from home. In both Burkina Faso and Mongolia, for example, decisions to move towards distance education were based in part on this opportunity to cut travel costs for teachers (Perraton *et al.* 2001).

Programmes of continuing education have been funded from a variety of sources, according to the nature of the project. Often, the costs of unstructured and resource-based programmes have fallen on those who are producing them: a broadcasting station, or a ministry of education, or in some cases a consortium of agencies that are making resources available free of charge to teachers or schools. In Brazil, for example, a consortium of for-profit and non-profit agencies runs a television-based programme for teachers with the costs being met mainly by the consortium. For structured courses, there are two main patterns. The costs of supply-driven courses tend to be met from public funds, often from a ministry of education. In contrast, at least a significant proportion of demand-driven courses require learners to pay a fee so that some or even all of the costs fall upon the teachers who are seeking a qualification.

The planner's challenge is to look at the variety of expenditure that may be required and to see where this may be found. Some of the options are set out in Table 5.3, drawn from a UNESCO study that concentrates mainly on the needs of ministries of education. This distinguishes between capital and recurrent costs and also distinguishes areas, like the production of materials, where economies of scale are possible, from those, notably arrangements for student support and supervision of practical work, where costs vary with student numbers. It is also intended to encourage the planner to ask where the costs will fall. Even programmes that do not charge a fee to learners may, in practice, ask them to incur costs: for materials, for radios, perhaps for travel to a learning centre.

Decisions about the proportion of cost that can be passed on to the learner are important and often difficult. In a climate where cost-sharing is increasingly favoured, it follows that the planner is likely to ask, or be required to ask, whether the learner should pay some or all of the cost of a course, since it benefits individuals as well as the teaching force. This argument is reflected in the widespread practice of making no charge where teachers are nominated to non-award-bearing updating courses, or required to take part in them. There are also risks that need to be faced in developing a fee policy. There is some evidence that higher fees may act as a disincentive to students to enrol (Nielsen and Tatto 1993). Where, as in Asia, open universities have been under pressure to shift their costs from public subsidy to student fees, planners have inevitably been attracted by the notion that fixed costs can be met from public subsidy while variable costs should be met from student fees. This makes it easier to expand student numbers within budgetary constraints but means there is a tendency to hold down expenditure on student support. There is also

Table 5.3 Activities and resources

Activity to be funded	Type of funding required	Comments on possible sources
Planning and initiation	One-off	May be from ministry of education funds but often also from funding and international agencies
Materials development	Funding mainly for staff time but can be treated as capital where materials are used over several years	Upfront funding usually from ministry of education, NGO or funding agency grants. Funds for revision and updating also required
Materials reproduction and distribution	Recurrent	Regular expenditure that may be recovered from operating grant or from student fees. Where distribution is through public broadcasting, government mail, or by Internet, costs may be borne on other budgets
Reception costs	May be some capital (e.g. supply of radios, development of videoconference facilities) but recurrent costs then arise	Initial funding may be from one-off grant (e.g. funding agency). Individual recurrent costs (e.g. maintenance of radios, computers) likely to fall on individual learner/centre
Student support and classroom practice	Recurrent	Regular expenditure that may be recovered from operating grant or from student fees. It may be possible for some costs (e.g. for deployment of school or college staff to support students) to be met from other institutional budgets
Training and capacity building	Recurrent	Heavy initial expenditure needed, especially where project is unfamiliar to those working in it, but continuing expenditure then required
Maintenance	Recurrent	Continuing expenditure that is often neglected (especially for materials updating) and needs to be built into budgets for previous areas

Source: Perraton, Creed and Robinson (2002)

always a temptation to disregard the opportunity cost for a teacher in enrolling on a course: study takes time which could otherwise be used productively or profitably or both. Students of a BEd programme in Kenya reported that the time they spent studying cut down their income from offering private tuition (Makau 1993). Upgrading and updating programmes are pointless if teachers cannot afford them.

The level of funding required is likely to be a function of the scale of the programme, the amount of student support especially at a field level, and the sophistication of the media used. Comprehensive networked learning courses, complete with multimedia and customized computer-assisted instruction components can only be developed and delivered economically if there is a large number of participants. These large numbers provide sufficient revenue to spend more time and money on extensive course development, especially by teams of specialists with highly developed technical, artistic and instructional skills (Haughey and Anderson 1998). Generally speaking, the higher the interactivity of the technology used in the programme, the higher the cost. However, professional development courses that depend less on lots of pre-packaged materials and more on the simple interaction between learners and instructors, such as discussion forums, can be developed with less initial expenditure, with smaller teams and often by a single instructor. If they require heavy support at local level, their recurrent costs are, how-ever, likely to be high. If it is possible to develop teacher learner groups and build on the advanced skills of other teachers, friends, peers, and colleagues, then the costs falling on the manager's budget are likely to be reduced (Haughey and Anderson 1998).

Choices of technology

Open and distance learning depends on communication technologies and, in using them to reach learners, does so for two different purposes: to distribute materials to students and to encourage interaction with them. There is a distinction, for example, between using a computer network to distribute materials to learners and its use to facilitate dialogue among students, or between them and a tutor, or between them and an interactive computer program. The second use – to promote interaction and activity – is different in educational function, and different in its economics from the first. Thus the planner needs to decide both how to get learning materials to the student and how they can be used to encourage learning. Two other chapters in this book (Chapters 8 on media and 9 on ICT) examine these issues in some detail. But from a planner's perspective, Perraton (2000) suggested that five questions need to be answered in devel-oping a national or institutional policy for the use of communication technologies in education.

First, we need to ask what technology is available for a particular audience and acceptable to that audience. . . .

Second, and the point is closely related, we need to look at international variations in the ways in which technologies can be used. Issues here may be geographical, regulatory, or economic. . . .

Third, once we have considered the availability of a particular technology, and related it to our national situation, it is possible to move on and consider what makes sense educationally. . . .

Costs come next. In order to make sound decisions about technology choice, we need to know how much they cost . . . [and] to distinguish between the use of technology to provide an alternative type of education, thus reducing the cost of teaching staff, and its use to raise quality without affecting staff numbers.

Finally, new communication technologies are a double-edged sword. On the one hand, they may allow a small island developing state, for example, to have wider access to sources of information than was ever previously possible. On the other hand, there is an ever greater danger of cultural hegemony by the large countries and large international companies who control the production of hardware and software.

(Perraton 2000: 32–7)

When we turn to recent experience of using the technologies, both to distribute materials and to help teach, we find a wide range of technologies being used but also a continued heavy reliance on print. Broadcasts and video-conference links have been used with some evidence of success in overcoming teachers' sense of isolation. There are also the beginnings of the use of Internet-based approaches, though there is a shortage of good evaluations or cost data on which to base guidance for decision-making. At present, the Internet has been used more for unstructured programmes than for structured ones. Here, for example, teachers have benefited from compilations of resources on a web-site and delivered via the Internet. UNICEF and UNESCO have begun to develop materials that are available both on the Internet and in CD-ROM format. In Central Africa attempts have been made to provide computer links between teachers' colleges. In the case of structured courses, industrialized countries have begun to use Internet-based methods for course delivery and dialogue with students. (See also Chapter 9.)

Pedagogy

Decisions about pedagogy are a function of the curriculum and of the choice of technologies, and they demand attention to questions about materials development, participation and student support. They also make demands on many different stakeholders, well beyond the distance-teaching institution offering a programme. Stakeholders are at all levels, and often in schools, colleges and teachers' centres as well as in central agencies.

The development of effective materials makes similar demands. Materials need to be targeted to teachers' needs and to match the relevant curriculum. Adequate time is needed for their preparation and pre-testing and they are likely to benefit from inputs by skilled instructional designers. This in turn poses training demands.

While materials design can encourage participation and dialogue, this is often the central purpose of some of the other components of open and distance learning, and in particular of face-to-face sessions and on-line tuition. Dialogue is important to help exchange meaning about various topics and concepts, to internalize this meaning and to share ideas. When undertaken effectively, it should also lead to greater learner autonomy and independence. The often isolated learning environments of many teachers create the need to provide interaction with others.

Even with good materials design and arrangements to encourage participation and dialogue, teachers will continue to need support in their role as learners. If continuing professional development is to motivate them, teachers need to be able to see its relevance to their jobs and their future. Support is needed in the form of follow-up to training programmes to provide teachers with opportunities to relate what they have been learning to their own classrooms, preferably with the assistance of peers, or a mentor or tutor.

The motivation of teachers to participate in continuing education is likely to be a function of support, relevance and credibility, and reward. Programmes need to be credible and respected, and to overcome the perception that open- and distance learning in-service programmes are inferior to more traditional face-to-face courses. Appropriate incentives or rewards to teachers for successful completion of the programmes need to be established. These may take the form of accreditation for work completed, making available tangible resources and ideas that help teachers with their direct classroom needs, and possibly some extra release time to take part in a professional development programme. Any formal accreditation for distance courses needs to have parity of esteem with that given to traditional face-to-face programmes.

Motivation is a critical factor in ensuring that opportunities for continuing professional development are in fact used. Simply providing courses or distributing resources does not ensure that they are useful or usable. In China, for example, it was anticipated that there would be little take-up of opportunities for professional development without measures to ensure this. The mixture of regulation and national policy set out in Box 5.3 was adopted with this in mind.

Box 5.3 Motivating teachers and the 'iron rice bowl' in China

Not all teachers are motivated to undertake professional development to become better teachers. So providing learning opportunities and resources for teachers, whether by conventional means or distance education, may still not motivate them sufficiently to use them. In China, motivating teachers to participate in professional development is a problem. The main reason is that qualified teachers have an 'iron rice bowl', that is, secure government employment for life with little chance of dismissal in a country where, overall, there is a shortage of qualified teachers. Also there are few sanctions or rewards for performance or improvement as a teacher.

The main solution for the problem has been policy formulation and legislation. This requires teachers to undertake continuing professional development and provinces to provide it. National policy issued by the State Council says that continuing education is the right and duty of all teachers and regulations from the Ministry of Education (national and provincial) state that all kindergarten and primary teachers should accept 72 hours of continuing education every year. In addition, the State Council's 'Gardener Project' for improving teacher quality has a sub-project for Teachers Continuing Education (1999–2002), with requirements issued by the Ministry of Education though with no central government funding for it. This requires every kindergarten and primary school teacher to take 40–190 hours of continuing professional development training (in the period 1999–2002), the content to include, as a minimum, teachers' ethics, 'backbone teacher' training, training for trainers, and training in the use and creation of learning aids. Some of the poorer provinces have had difficulty in achieving these targets for lack of funding. In some, the targets have been reached through allocating part of the time for self-study by teachers.

Source: Robinson and Li Jing (forthcoming)

All these pedagogical demands in turn place demands on the management and administration. Those who are delivering the instruction themselves need to be adequately prepared and supported, especially where, with changing technology, roles and skills may be changed or expanded (Moore and Kearsley 1996). Efficient management and information systems are critical, and more complex, when students are not present on campuses. Managers also need to consider how the services usually available to on-campus students can be made available to those who are at a distance. This includes availability of information, access to library and resource material, and support at a distance from instructors. Where appropriate, technical support is also needed to help learners actively use computers and access programmes, as well as to be there to make sure equipment from the delivery side is in place.

CONCLUSIONS

The shortage of resources for conventional approaches to continuing education, and the capacity of distance approaches to reach scattered or large audiences, have led to its extensive use for teachers' continuing education (Craig *et al.* 1998; Creed and Perraton 2001).

This has demonstrated the strengths and weaknesses of open and distance education. For the continuing professional development of teachers, as for other applications, its most significant advantage may be its reach and ability to provide teachers with learning resources. By the nature of their work, teachers are often isolated. In-service programmes based on communications media are sometimes the only way of reaching them without bringing them away from home, and probably work, and diverting funding from education to transport and accommodation. Provided media are chosen that are appropriate to the scale of the problem, distance-teaching approaches have the capacity to operate at lower unit costs than those of more conventional methods. Beyond these practical benefits, a programme that reaches teachers in their schools should make it possible for the learners to integrate what they learn with their day-to-day practice in school. Where teachers are strengthening their own general education, or taking a higher degree, the effects are likely to be long-term, or may be felt when they move on to a new job, rather than be immediately applicable.

Against these practical advantages have to be set problems of practice and of perception. There are in-built practical difficulties in managing programmes of distance education, which often demand co-operation between national and local agencies and between agencies with differing primary objectives (educational, media, telecommunications). Where programmes depend on advanced communication systems, they may favour the urban teacher at the expense of the rural, widening rather than narrowing a gap in terms of access to resources. Alongside these problems of practice, we also need to recognize the negative effect of the perception of open and distance learning as a low-status way of study, offering qualifications that lack public esteem, and sometimes even formal recognition.

At the same time, distance education programmes are likely to be one among many approaches to continuing professional education which, to maximize its effectiveness, needs to be multi-level and varied. Effective programmes demand attention to all the elements examined in this chapter – from curriculum to organization to the choice of technology and development of pedagogy. Over and above them, the motivation of individual learners is likely to be all-important; formal qualifications, that lead to more pay or better promotion prospects will motivate many teachers while intrinsic rewards are not to be dismissed: many teachers want to do a better job and welcome opportunities that help them do so.

REFERENCES

Carnell, R. (1999) 'Distance education and the need for dialogue', *Open Learning*, 14(1): 50–55.

Carron, G. and Ta Ngoc Châu (1996) *The Quality of Primary Schools in Different Development Contexts*, Paris: International Institute for Educational Planning (IIEP).

Craig, H., Kraft, R. and du Plessis, M. (1998) *Teacher Development: Making an Impact*, Washington, DC: USAID/World Bank.

Creed, C. (2001) *The Use of Distance Education for Teachers*, Cambridge: International Research Foundation for Open Learning (IRFOL) (reported to Department for International Development).

Creed, C. and Perraton, H. (2001) *Distance Education in the E-9 Countries*, Paris: UNESCO.

Haughey, M. and Anderson, T. (1998) *Networked Learning: The Pedagogy of the Internet*, Toronto: Cheneliere/McGraw-Hill.

Hawes, H. and Stephens, D. (1990) *Questions of Quality: Primary Education and Development*, Harlow: Longman.

Maier, P. and Warren, A. (2000) *Integrating Technology in Learning and Teaching: A Practical Guide for Educators*, London: Kogan Page.

Makau, B. (1993) 'The external degree programme at the University of Nairobi', in H. Perraton, (ed.) *Distance Education for Teacher Training*, London: Routledge.

Moore, M.G. and Kearsley, G. (1996) *Distance Education: A Systems View*, Belmont, Cal.: Wadsworth.

Nielsen, H.D. and Tatto, M.T. (1993) 'Teacher upgrading in Sri Lanka and Indonesia', in H. Perraton (ed.) *Distance Education for Teacher Training*, London: Routledge.

Perraton, H. (2000) 'Choosing technologies for education', *Journal of Educational Media* 25(1): 31–8.

Perraton, H. and Creed, C. (2000) *Applying New Technologies and Cost-Effective Delivery Systems in Basic Education*, Paris: UNESCO.

Perraton, H., Creed, C. and Robinson, B. (2002) *Teacher Education Guidelines: Using Open and Distance Learning*, Paris: UNESCO.

Perraton, H., Robinson, B. and Creed, C. (2001) *Teacher Education through Distance Learning: Technology, Curriculum, Evaluation, Cost*, Paris: UNESCO.

Robinson, B. and Li Jing (forthcoming) 'Improving the quality of teachers in China'.

Chapter 6

Training non-formal, community and adult educators

Charles Potter and Mohammad Aslam

Many attempts have been made over the last forty years to improve the standard of education and literacy through non-formal, community and adult education programmes as well as through the formal education system. The literature of the 1970s and early 1980s, in particular, reflected an expectation that non-formal, community and adult education would be able to provide alternative forms of education and curricula in areas where the formal education system could not (Hall and Kidd 1978; Millar 1991a; Thompson 1981). It also reflected an expectation that distance education would be able to play a significant role in non-formal educational settings (Young *et al.* 1980).

While many non-formal education programmes have produced promising results, overall, the results of non-formal alternatives to the formal curriculum over the past twenty years have been mixed (Coombs 1985; Jamison and Lau 1982; King 1991). The evidence concerning the success and cost-effectiveness of non-formal education involving open and distance learning has also been generally equivocal, and in certain cases disappointing (Dodds 1996; Perraton 2000; Romain and Armstrong 1987). Nevertheless, the scale of the problems faced by developing countries and the sheer number of people who need to be provided with basic education suggest the need for finding ways of reaching and teaching large numbers of people using distance education via the mass media.

The use of mass media in education offers significant cost advantages compared to traditional face-to-face teaching (Adkins 1999; Cobbe 1994 and 1995; Dock and Helwig 1999). However, it has also become clear that distance education often works best in combination with interpersonal interaction and face-to-face contact, especially for learners with low educational levels, younger learners, rural and remote learners unused to formal education, and for some kinds of skill development where feedback on performance is needed. While mass media and distance education can provide information and learning resources for large populations of learners, they cannot easily mobilize local groups or assist individuals without the support of local agents such as tutors, facilitators, group leaders or co-ordinators. The use of such local agents has been an essential element of all kinds of non-formal, community and adult education programmes. But what kind of training do such agents need? What forms does training take? What role does open and distance learning play?

This chapter examines these questions in relation to six examples of training for non-formal, community and adult educators or tutors.

NON-FORMAL, COMMUNITY AND ADULT EDUCATORS

Non-formal education has been defined as 'any organized, systematic, educational activity carried on outside the framework of the formal system to provide selected types of learning to particular subgroups of the population, adults as well as children' (Coombs and Ahmed 1974: 8). As Robinson (1999) concludes, non-formal education has been variously described as an educational movement, a setting, a process and a system. Whatever the definition, the reality is that there are huge numbers of workers engaged in the implementation of various non-formal and adult education programmes. While these programmes typically emphasize the acquisition of basic literacy and numeric skills, in recent years their scope has widened to include a variety of development objectives enabling learners to build skills for lifelong learning.

In defining the roles and goals of adult education the 5th International Conference on Adult Education in Hamburg stated that

> the objectives of youth and adult education . . . are to develop autonomy and the sense of responsibility of people and communities, to reinforce the capacity, to deal with transformations taking place in the economy in culture and in society . . . in short to enable people and communities to take control of their destiny and society.
>
> (UIE 1997)

This definition helps in understanding the wide variety of roles (tutor, teacher, facilitator, counsellor, advisor, group leader, co-ordinator, coach) that non-formal, community and adult educators play in working in a variety of settings. They involve activities directed towards general or basic education, open schooling, literacy and numeracy, family education, community improvement, occupational training, agricultural extension work, income generation, human rights, health care, HIV-AIDS education and many more areas of focus, for adults and young people alike.

The training needs of these local agents are diverse and also overlapping. They are usually met within the operation of a particular project or programme. Only a small percentage of those working in non-formal, adult and community settings are formally trained. Often the training is very programme- and context-specific, and designed around particular roles and the people available to do the work. While some training is excellent, and a model of good practice that more formal teacher training systems could learn from, in other cases it is too limited, or reduced by time constraints to knowledge transmission alone. Considerable dilution of the quality of training also occurs because of the *ad hoc* nature of some training programmes or the lack of sufficient backward and forward linkages in the system to ensure quality (Aslam 1987). The problem is further compounded when new development initiatives, like local self-government (Panchayats) in India or a similar decentralized administration initiative in Bangladesh, are put in place, since in these cases the number of people requiring training runs into millions. This has led to a search for alternative mechanisms of training involving open learning and distance education, which can supplement or complement conventional training interventions. While very many project-specific training programmes have been developed and documented, little has been written about the training of non-formal education tutors or local agents in similar open and distance programmes.

TRAINING APPROACHES

In this next section, we provide six cases which illustrate the training provided for local tutors, leaders or counsellors in open and distance learning projects for adults (the first four cases) and for teachers in non-formal schools (the last two).

The panchayat project in India (Aslam 2000)

Across Asia, open and distance education is increasingly being accepted as a legitimate mode of education and training relevant to the emerging demands of society. According to the International Centre for Distance Learning (ICDL) database <http//www.icdl.open.ac.uk/database/asia> fourteen countries in Asia have distance education institutions which offer non-formal education. These programmes cover a variety of topics, including village administration; land and property laws; and vocational programmes in plant protection, soil problems, poultry farming, garment making, radio servicing, textile technology, functional literacy and many others. In India, there are one national open university, nine state open universities and one national open school. Each of these has identified specific areas of intervention involving open learning and distance education.

As part of this non-formal education, one specific project provided training for the large-scale panchayat (local self-government) programme. This initiative began in 1993 when, in an attempt to widen participation in democratic government, particularly for disadvantaged groups, a historic amendment was made to the Indian constitution. As a result, more than 3 million people (more than a third of them female) were elected to different tiers of local self-government.

The lack of preparedness of these key personnel for the roles they were expected to play was perceived as a major constraint in the process of social transformation. The scale of the problem was enormous. If all the conventional educational institutions responsible for training in rural development in India had been asked to do nothing else but to conduct training for elected members of the panchayats, it would have taken them more than twelve years to complete one round of training to cover the 3.4 million elected functionaries.

To meet this need more rapidly, a large-scale programme of education and training for these elected members was implemented by the Indira Gandhi National Open University (IGNOU) with support from the government of India. The main objective of the programme was empowerment of the rural masses through the elected members of panchayats, so that they could participate successfully in the process of self-governance.

The goal was to equip the elected panchayat members with knowledge about the concepts and practices of self-government and the skills necessary to formulate and implement development programmes and to work with the local community. To meet these needs a self-study package was prepared (printed materials, audio and video cassettes) and contact programmes for counselling were planned. The self-study printed material was expected to cover a wide range of subjects, ranging from 'Basic features of the Indian constitution' to 'Development with social justice'.

In the Indian rural situation, it was not possible to rely totally on state-run television as a delivery mechanism for audio-video programmes. Further constraints were created by the infrastructure in terms of the supply of electricity and the availability of equipment. Special arrangements were therefore made to enable learners to view programmes through a mobile reception system. This was made available at the weekly markets (*haat bazaars*) which are held for marketing local products in many rural areas, and these viewing sessions proved popular. But however good the materials were, they were not enough without access for the target audience (the elected panchayat members) to local advisors or counsellors, so a counselling or advisory service was provided.

The purpose of the counselling provision was to clarify any problems and uncertainties arising from the materials. A two-tier system of counsellors was planned: the first one of master counsellors, who were in turn responsible for the second one of local 'grass-roots level' counsellors.

For both levels, the counsellors were selected by the state government according to the criterion that they should be development functionaries who could become active partners in the implementation of this programme. The master counsellors' training programme was attended by twenty-two people from across different sectors (development officers, panchayat inspectors, child development project officers, district adult education officers, medical officers and assistant project officers). It was a multi-sectoral group. The IGNOU project team conducted a needs analysis and based the training on it. The training was provided by specialists from different institutions of rural development together with IGNOU staff.

Four components were the focus of the master-counsellors' programme: *knowledge* about the local self-government (panchayat) system; *understanding* of distance education and the programme system; *skills* in counselling and in training the local counsellors; and *attitude* formation among elected local government members.

The process of training was participatory and also involved demonstration and practice of the skills required of an effective counsellor. The training programme was converted into a manual and translated into local languages. This was made available to the master counsellors to help them recall various elements of their training programme and it proved a very useful tool when they themselves became involved in training the local counsellors. The cadre of 325 local counsellors produced as a result of this strategy then conducted village-level counselling, providing one- or two-day sessions in over 3,466 village panchayats and covering many thousands of elected local government members. The cost of training local counsellors and sending them to village sessions was borne by the state government.

Together, the self-study materials and counselling sessions were successful in developing knowledge and raising awareness and debate about local self-government, and in assisting the elected panchayat members to perform their roles.

Training tutors in the Learning for Life project in Mongolia (Robinson 2001)

The Learning for Life (*Surch Amidarya*) project (1997–2001) provided non-formal education for over 40,000 rural and nomadic learners across the large and sparsely populated country of Mongolia. This was achieved through radio, print materials and support from local tutors for local learning groups and individuals from a population with high levels of literacy.

Selecting, training and supervising local tutors were important activities for the programme in a context where non-formal education was new to most of the provinces. The project team began by drawing up a job description for the role of tutor, and then reviewed the human resources available in provincial and district centres around the country. One decision was whether or not trained schoolteachers should be used as tutors. It was decided that they should not be excluded, for three reasons: they had some useful skills, good community knowledge and a respected but not too high a status in the community. As a result, those who were open to learning new approaches were included. However, the learner-support provision needed to include a broad range of knowledge and skills, so tutor-teams were formed to include a range of expertise, for example, the local veterinarian, doctor, lawyer, radio journalist, agriculturalist, and schoolteacher as well as members of the community with craft skills (the schoolteachers often had good craft skills too). As well as organizing learner-group meetings in village settlements, the tutors' role was to travel round the countryside to visit herding families and help individual learners or family groups. Sometimes the distances were great, for example, a trip of 200 kilometres taken over two to three days and often in very cold weather, and learners' families acted as hosts to tutors in these circumstances. Tutors also visited learners in the course of their regular work in the countryside.

Training focused on the tutors' roles, tasks and relationships with learners. It took the form of workshops, printed guides and regular meetings in tutor-teams with a supervising tutor at the district or provincial centre level. The first training workshop, for selected national and provincial level trainers, was provided by the central project team and used a content and process plan worked out with the project's consultant. The process was modelled in the workshop by the consultant, learner-support officer and project director working together as a team and demonstrating a variety of group approaches. Opportunities were provided at intervals for participants to reflect and comment on the processes being used, and their application to their home contexts. Paying attention to the process was new for participants and at first, difficult, since the traditional education system concentrates on content. The workshop activities were gradually handed over to other tutor-trainers in the workshop. After the workshop, amendments were made to the workshop content and approach and guidelines were produced for the following round of regional and provincial workshops, covering all twenty-one provinces and involving nearly 700 tutors. All the workshops modelled the kind of active learning approaches and relationships that tutors needed for working with adult learners. These contrasted with the didactic and whole-class approach style of teaching common in the formal schools.

Over the period of the project, provincial tutor-trainers travelled to other provinces and villages to observe tutor-groups at work and share experience. The provincial co-ordinators and tutor trainers thought this was a very valuable form of staff development for them. It cost little, since they travelled in the vehicles of project staff doing field trips within the project, and it gave them a point of comparison with their own practice. The consensus within the project team was that

> several elements combined to make the training successful: modelling in workshops the kinds of interaction and activities that tutors would do with learners; a clear but not rigid job description; opportunities for tutor-trainers to practice with a supportive group and to review the experience; interaction between trainers in different provinces to share experience and to improve practices; the provision of clear guidelines for tutors and trainers; opportunities for tutors and tutor-trainers to contribute to training materials and the project news-paper; and the close and ongoing interaction between project staff and provincial trainers and tutors.
>
> (Robinson 2001: 14)

Training village group leaders in a rural development programme in Pakistan (Warr 1992)

The basic functional education programme for rural development, pro-vided by the Allama Iqbal Open University in Pakistan, aimed to provide learning opportunities for rural adults with low levels of education on aspects of rural development (for example, on childcare, poultry keeping, electricity in the village, civics education). The means of doing this was through village learning groups using audio-cassette tapes, flipcharts, illustrated handouts and facilitation by a village group leader. Members of village communities were selected and trained for this key role.

Group leaders at the village level were proposed by the village com-munity and two of the proposed candidates were selected by the project fieldworkers. The criteria for selection were that they should be respected members of the community, have no other heavy time commitments and should not be teachers (the last criterion was chosen to avoid problems with the traditionally authoritarian, didactic roles of teachers common in the formal system of education). Qualities of self-confidence and enthusi-asm were looked for as well as their social position in the village, taking into account that affiliation with a particular faction would influence group membership and cohesion. Finally, those who were literate were preferred, mainly because they were able to complete the feedback forms after each meeting. However, literacy was not an essential condition of becoming a group leader and as the project developed, it became clear that many competent group leaders were not able to read or write.

The selected candidates attended a six-day course at a temporary rural training centre within easy reach and each group leader's course had about twenty participants – about the same size as the adult learning group itself. There were several reasons for training two people from each village group. It allowed the fieldworkers to select the best to become group leader, with the second becoming a 'stand-by' leader and provided a safety-net if the group leader dropped out for unavoidable reasons. Training in pairs gave greater confidence and, in the case of females, helped to overcome the cultural problems of women travelling outside their own villages.

Training was provided by the fieldworkers who were members of the project team. Trainers worked in pairs (either two men or two women), each pair responsible for running one course a week. Two pairs of trainers ran eleven courses for over 180 trainees in six weeks.

The aims of the training course were to introduce the village group leaders to the programme, its aims and methodology: to explain their roles (presenting materials, leading discussions and practical exercises, reporting on each meeting); to help them to acquire and practise skills needed, especially in leading discussions; to take them through the materials, unit by unit; and to explain the administrative aspects of their role. The methods used in training the group leaders were the same as those to be used in the village learning groups. The learning materials (audio-cassettes, flipcharts and handouts) provided strong support for the village group leaders, who had no special teaching qualifications. A hand-book was developed for trainers, giving detailed guidance on how to set up and run a village group leaders' training course and for village group leaders, together with additional support materials. Practical learning was stressed in the training programme and village group leaders practised presenting sessions to each other. They were paid a small honorarium for their work and paid a registration fee at the start of their training course, though they received a training allowance after com-pletion. Experience from the programme showed that close supervision and support of village group leaders was essential and this was done by local assistant supervisors of several village groups and the project team. The careful selection of group leaders, the structured training, the model-ling and practising of their roles by trainers, and ongoing support and supervision were important elements in making them effective.

The Adult Basic Education and Training (ABET) project, South Africa (Bown et al. 1999)

During the 1970s and early 1980s in South Africa, a number of universities established departments of adult and continuing education, to which were linked the training of adult educators, community development initiat-ives and non-formal education projects. One of these, the Adult Basic Education and Training (ABET) project was established at the University of South Africa (UNISA) in 1994. The project's aim was to make a contribution to poverty alleviation through adult basic education and training, to improve the range of opportunity to the poorest South Africans and to increase their potential to contribute to South Africa's future.

During the first phase of the project, a core methodology was developed aimed at training practitioners through distance education (largely print based, supported by tutoring in small groups). Self-study materials were developed to meet the needs of the learners and their tutors. The project drew on a wide range of writers from local government and the water, education and health sectors. The materials were student-friendly, designed to promote active learning and supported wherever possible by discussion and activities undertaken in tutorial groups. In the context of UNISA at the time, this type of self-learning print material was unfamiliar. The courses were modular, arranged to form a continuum of qualifications in adult basic education, from certificate to diploma, and from diploma through to more formal degree courses and postgraduate qualifications. This structure reflected thinking among South African academics at the time about the potential role of non-formal, adult and continuing education in national development in post-apartheid South Africa (Hofmeyr and Swart 1991; Millar 1991a; 1991b; Prinsloo 1991). It aimed to professionalize the work of adult educators.

Training and support were provided through a three-level cascade model for tutors, practitioners and learner groups. The first level trained tutors in adult education methodology. These then trained the second level of adult education practitioners, who then in turn trained adults in community settings. Numbers grew rapidly (see Table 6.1). By 1997, the project had trained over 200 tutors, who in turn had trained 12,322 practitioners in adult basic education; by 1999, the number of adult education practitioners trained reached 21,433.

Table 6.1 Student enrolment in courses at the University of South Africa's Adult Basic Education and Training (ABET) Institute, 1995–2001

Year	ABET certificate	ABET diploma	Local government	Total annual enrolments
1995	2,240	—	—	2,240
1996	4,541	—	—	4,541
1997	5,541	—	—	5,541
1998	2,956	2,445	536	5,937
1999	1,982	2,372	262	4,616
2000	2,857	1,575	170	4,602
2001	3,911	1,922	231	6,064
Total	24,028	8,314	1,199	33,541

Source: Personal Communication, Adult Basic Education and Training Institute, University of South Africa 2001

In setting up this structure, and developing plans to put in place bachelor's and master's degrees that would be linked to it, the ABET Institute has been assisted by grants from the British Department for International Development (DFID) and has had high-level support from UNISA's management at deputy vice-chancellor level (Bown *et al.* 1999). The institute has also been assisted on the administrative level by its location as part of the efficient UNISA editing, printing and postal services, as well as the university's local infrastructure of regional centres and examination centres. The unit's staff has used considerable ingenuity to work within and build out from the existing infrastructure, and change it to suit the programme's goals (*ibid.* 30). What has resulted has been a transformation of the way in which tutoring and student support has been implemented in UNISA's regional centres, as well as in the local contexts managed by the ABET unit's 200 tutors. Whereas previously UNISA's regional centres served a mainly administrative purpose, and were used for occasional content-based lectures in support of UNISA's printed course materials, the centres are now used by the ABET Institute's tutors for tutorial support of learners, which is conducted in small groups in rooms if these are available, or in the foyer, passages or grounds if other teaching space is not available. In several respects, the work of ABET has influenced UNISA practice.

The ABET Institute's staff estimates that it costs roughly R1,000 (US$110) to train a tutor, and that once the DFID funding comes to an end, continuity will be possible from student enrolments and fees, and to a lesser extent from sale of services and materials. In terms of its cost-effectiveness, the unit is highly efficient, operating with a small core staff of three academic staff (one professor and two senior lecturers) and three additional administrative support staff and three part-time advisors.

Overall the programme organization emphasizes a close link between theory of adult education and practice of it, demonstrating this in the tutorial support provided and materials design (materials are written with participatory, experiential and co-operative learning in mind) and in coherence between the approaches to learning in the materials and learner support.

Para-professional teachers in the tribal areas of Sambalpur District, Orissa, India (Barpanda 1999)

Despite measures to increase the enrolment and participation rates of rural and tribal populations in India, success so far has been limited. To address this problem within the District Primary Education Programme (DPEP), an initiative was taken which focused on the crucial role of the teacher. This experiment aimed to empower teachers. 'Empowerment' was defined as developing capacity for dialogue and interaction with learners and the community, learning to be an educational leader and guide in the community, and becoming a decision-maker about key aspects of the programme. Individuals were chosen to be teachers by the community in which they lived and were approved by the project team. The teachers were not highly educated and were untrained, but received ongoing training interventions and support by project staff. Because the teachers came from the community, they shared the same language. The pay was very low and was supplemented from a teachers' welfare fund in times of need.

Training and support for the teachers were provided through:

- a series of regular accessible workshops using participatory methods;
- ongoing support and advice from project workers;
- study visits to other education centres and communities;
- a curriculum planning workshop which assisted the teacher to plan a locally relevant, context-specific curriculum instead of the centrally planned standardized curriculum;
- a manual, mainly developed by the teacher, which guided her day-to-day work in a flexible way and recorded changes and adaptations to the plans;
- peer support through the project's teachers' association;
- training in writing simple texts for learners and in developing low-cost learning aids;
- self-study of materials provided by the project and from other sources.

The following outcomes were reported in a study of fifteen non-formal education centres:

- higher levels of accountability by teachers to the community;
- greater community participation and teacher-led formation of village education committees;
- changes in teachers' role and style of teaching (wider repertoire of skills; more active learning methods; better diagnosis of individual learning difficulties; greater attention to individual differences; an increase in the use of locally made learning materials, better curriculum planning and record keeping of teacher activities; greater use of assessment for formative purposes);
- rates of enrolment at the centres increased from 36 per cent in 1991 to 100 per cent in 1996. Rates of retention rose from 14 per cent in 1991 to 93 per cent in 1996. Nearly all girls participated (97 per cent).

The conclusion was that the experiment led to primary education being a successful 'people's programme' in these tribal areas and that the training provided for teachers was a good model.

Training and support for teachers in the Bangladesh Rural Advancement Committee (BRAC) programme (Ahmed *et al.* 1993; Rugh and Bossert 1998)

Children participating in the non-formal primary-education programme of the Bangladesh Rural Advancement Committee (BRAC) achieve as much as or more than children in formal schools and have higher attendance, lower repetition and higher continuation rates into class four. More than 90 per cent of the children who start BRAC schools complete the three-year programme. Yet the BRAC teachers are unqualified and come from the local communities. Teachers are selected from educated members of the community by BRAC field staff and parents. They must have nine years or more of education and be articulate, committed and preferably married (single women are likely to move away on marriage). Teachers are hired on a temporary part-time basis and pay is low (about US$12 a month, twice that of an agricultural worker). About 8 per cent of teachers drop out each year. In 1995, 32,131 teachers continued in the BRAC programme, 2,002 dropped out and 9,187 new teachers were recruited.

Teacher training is provided through field officers. Teachers attend an initial fifteen days of training at a residential BRAC training centre, which are repeated at the start of each year. Further training sessions take place for a day each month at a more local venue near the teacher's school. The aim is to give teachers practical training in active child-centred learning and methods focusing on learning for understanding rather than memorization. BRAC field workers visit schools twice a month to review lesson plans, observe teaching and monitor attendance. They also meet weekly with school committees. A manual is provided for teachers on child development, lesson planning and child-centred learning approaches for a simplified curriculum.

Whereas the formal school system allocates most of its resources to teachers' pay and school facilities, the BRAC programme allocates only 29 per cent of budget to teachers' pay. About 27 per cent of the non-formal primary education budget is allocated to the management and supervision of teachers. Though this has worked well (the field officers have played a critical role), the area of pedagogy needed more attention in the support given. The lesson from BRAC is that part-time para-professionals can be effective lower-primary teachers, if adequately trained, supervised, supported, and provided with a clearly defined, achievable curriculum and learning materials. BRAC teachers also have smaller classes (a pupil/teacher ratio of 30:1) than the formal system. The conditions in this context which support the BRAC model are high rural population density and educated rural people without employment. A BRAC teacher provides 500 hours more teaching time per year to his or her class than teachers in the formal primary schools.

CONCLUSIONS

Though these examples of training tutors and teachers in non-formal education vary, they share some common features. First and foremost, they show a different starting point in approaches to training from conventional formal education, with its commonly found lengthy pre-service preparation. In these non-formal education cases, the model generally seems to include elements of short preparation, carefully designed roles with training directed towards those roles, good-quality learning or training materials, ongoing support and development while 'on the job', and selection of trainees (tutors or group leaders) not only for their educational levels but for other qualities too (even to the extent that in the case of Pakistan's functional education project, many competent group leaders were not able to read or write). The six examples combine these elements to differing degrees.

Whether the training programmes are part of a distance education project or not, the predominant means of training tutors, facilitators and group leaders is through face-to-face workshops and events. The use of distance education in these examples is primarily to provide materials (printed content and training guides; broadcasts and audio- and video-materials) and to organize an operating structure, in at least one case (ABET in South Africa) building on the structures of the project's parent institution and even transforming them in turn. Distance education is also used to support cascade training models through the provision of good-quality training materials, as the examples of the panchayat, ABET and Mongolian programmes show. The basic functional education programme from Pakistan illustrated a different model of multiplying its learning groups and training group leaders, but the heavy reliance on project field-workers to provide the training, while ensuring good quality and consistency in the training, limited the numbers who could be involved. One question is whether open and distance learning could play a stronger role in training non-formal tutors and group leaders, especially if ICT facilities are available. Linked is the question of whether some of the particular skills needed for local tutors, group leaders and facilitators can only be developed though inter-personal interaction with trainers or peers – a labour-intensive activity for a distance education provider.

Arising from some of the approaches to training are issues about its conceptual basis. While clearly defined roles, matched to the capabilities of the local agents within an overall system or programme, are part of the formula for success, they may also be seen as being based on narrow behaviourist models. Perhaps this is a necessary starting point in some contexts, in order to build confidence and enable tutors or group leaders to gain experience before venturing further. The ABET programme offers some solutions to this problem, in aiming to go beyond a particular job-role, by addressing the theoretical underpinnings and by providing a ladder of progression for tutors, group leaders and adult educators. The ABET programme is unusual in its focus on professionalizing the work of non-formal, community and adult educators. In this case, adult education is conceptualized as a continuum in which formal and non-formal education are clearly linked, and in which universities can play a role in developing the continuum. The ABET Institute's successful navigation of these tricky waters is a demonstration not only of how universities can bring their considerable resources to bear in the service of national development, but of how distance education can contribute to this area. The form and structure of the ABET Institute's courses and materials, and the way in which student tutoring and support is conceptualized and implemented, also demonstrate good practice in adult, community and non-formal education, as well as distance education more generally.

The value of formally trained teachers to non-formal education is an issue which emerges, though the focus of attention is more usually on the reverse situation. In the case of the Pakistan project, formally trained teachers were excluded from training as group leaders on the grounds that what they did as teachers in the formal system would not be good for the non-formal education project. In Mongolia, although this issue was considered, it was decided that, on balance, trained teachers' knowledge levels, skills and community status were assets if they could be retrained for a different role, one more appropriate to adults and for non-formal education, one less didactic, less teacher-centred and authoritarian. Both of these cases illuminate perceptions of teachers in the formal system of education and of what they are trained to be.

By contrast, the roles and training provided for para-professional teachers in the BRAC and Orissa non-formal school programmes appeared to be successful for their purposes: the model of training worked. However, there is often no ladder of progression to enable teachers who begin in this way to move on to further qualifications and training, and move into the formal system, if they wish. Distance education can and does play a role in enabling this, but frequently it does not if the policy framework does not allow it. Planners frequently aim to replace under-qualified rural teachers rather than develop them. Features of the training for BRAC and Orissa teachers which would be desirable for teachers in the formal system are: ongoing support in schools from field officers or local advisors, regular observation and feedback on teaching, exchanges with other teachers and study visits to other schools, and training in developing locally relevant curricula and in producing low-cost teaching aids. One of the strengths of the training approaches in the examples given is their practicality. It appears that non-formal and formal training approaches place different values on this.

REFERENCES

Adkins, D.L. (1999) 'Cost and finance', in A. Dock and J. Helwig (eds) *Interactive Radio Instruction: Impact, Sustainability and Future Directions*, Washington, DC: World Bank. Education and Technology Technical Notes Series, 4(1): 37–50.

Ahmed, M., Chabbott, A., Joshhi, A. and Pande, R. (1993) *Primary Education for All: Learning from the BRAC Experience*, Washington, DC: Academy for Educational Development.

Aslam M. (1987) *Manual for Training of IRD Functionaries: Planning, Management and Methodology*, Dhaka: Centre on Integrated Rural Development in Asia and the Pacific (CIRDAP).

—— (2000) 'Education and training for millions: pedagogical challenges for distance education', *Open Learning*, 15(3): 309–15.

Barpanda, N. (1999) 'Teacher empowerment strategies to ensure continuing involvement in the universalisation of elementary education', *DPEP Calling*, March: 19–23.

Bown, L., Kotze, H. and Myeza, L. (1999) *Trusting the Future: an evaluation of the UNISA ABET Institute Programme*, Pretoria: University of South Africa Adult Basic Education and Training Institute.

Cobbe, J. (1994) 'Economic report on "English in Action"', in C.S. Potter and S. Leigh (eds) *'English in Action' in South Africa 1992–1994*, Washington, DC: Learntech, and Johannesburg: Open Learning Systems Education Trust.

—— (1995) *Economics of Interactive Radio: The Case of South Africa*, Washington, DC: Education Development Center.

Coombs, P.H. (1985) *The World Crisis in Education: The View from the Eighties*, New York: Oxford University Press.

Coombs, P.H. and Ahmed, H. (1974) *Attacking Rural Poverty: How Nonformal Education Can Help*, Baltimore, Md: Johns Hopkins University Press.

Dock, A. and Helnig, J. (eds) (1999) *Interactive Radio Instruction: Impact, Sustainability and Future Directions*, Washington, DC: World Bank. Education and Technology Technical Notes Series, 4(1).

Dodds, T. (1996) *The Use of Distance Learning in Non-formal Education*, Vancouver and Cambridge: The Commonwealth of Learning and International Extension College.

Hall, B.L and Kidd, R.L. (eds) (1978) *Adult Learning: A Design for Action*, Oxford: Pergamon Press.

Hofmeyr, J.M. and Swart, L.T. (1991) 'Non-formal education', in C. Millar, S. Raynham and A. Schaffer (eds) *Breaking the Formal Frame: Readings in South African Education in the Eighties*, Cape Town: Oxford University Press.

Jamison, D.T and Lau, L.J. (1982) *Farmer Education and Farmer Efficiency*, Baltimore, Md: Johns Hopkins University Press.

King, K. (1991) *Aid and Education in the Developing World: The Role of Donor Agencies in Educational Analysis*, Harlow: Longman.

Millar, C. (1991a) 'Non-formal continuing education in South Africa: an overview', in C. Millar, S. Raynham and A. Schaffer (eds) *Breaking the Formal Frame: Readings in South African Education in the Eighties*, Cape Town: Oxford University Press.

—— (1991b) 'Response to Mastin Prinsloo: professionalising non-formal education or can we see your Skunking License?' in C. Millar, S. Raynham and A. Schaffer (eds) *Breaking the Formal Frame: Readings in South African Education in the Eighties*, Cape Town: Oxford University Press.

Millar, C., Raynham, S. and Schaffer, A. (eds) (1991) *Breaking the Formal Frame: Readings in South African Education in the Eighties*, Cape Town: Oxford University Press.

Perraton, H. (2000) *Open and Distance Learning in the Developing World*, London: Routledge.

Prinsloo, M. (1991) 'Adult basic education *et al.*: What Skunks behind the Rose?, in C. Millar, S. Raynham and A. Schaffer (eds) *Breaking the Formal Frame: Readings in South African Education in the Eighties*, Cape Town: Oxford University Press.

Robinson, B. (1999) 'Open and distance learning in the Gobi Desert: non-formal education for nomadic women', *Distance Education: An International Journal*, University of Queensland, Australia, November.

—— (2001) *Learner Support in the Learning for Life (Surch Amidarya) Project*, internal project document, Ulaanbaatar: UNESCO.

Romain, R.L. and Armstrong, L. (1987) *Review of World Bank Operations in Nonformal Education and Training*, Washington, DC: World Bank, Education and Training Department.

Rugh, A. and Bossert, H. (1998) *Involving Communities: Participation in the Delivery of Education Programs*, Washington, DC: Creative Associates International.

Thompson, A.R. (1981) *Education and Development in Africa*, London: Macmillan.

UNESCO Institute of Education (UIE) (1997) *CONFINTEA-V Final report*. Fifth International Conference on Adult Education, Hamburg, 14–18 July.

Warr, D. (1992) *Distance Teaching in the Village*, Cambridge: International Extension College.

Young, M., Perraton, H., Jenkins, J. and Dodds, T. (1980) *Distance Teaching for the Third World: The Lion and the Clockwork Mouse*, London: Routledge.

Chapter 7

Open and distance learning for school managers

Tony Bush and Richard Charron

The quality of leadership and management is one of the most significant variables in delineating effective and ineffective schools, yet in many countries the provision of training and professional development is minimal or absent. Hallinger and Heck (1999) show that the influence of school managers is most powerful in clarifying and articulating the purposes of the school:

> The literature exhorts leaders in all sectors to articulate their vision, set clear goals for their organisations, and create a sense of shared mission. Our review supports the belief that formulating the school's purposes represents an important leadership function. In fact, the research shows that mission-building is the strongest and most consistent avenue of influence school leaders use to influence student achievement.
>
> (Hallinger and Heck 1999: 179)

UNESCO's Delors report (Delors 1996) observes that the most important factor in school efficiency and quality improvement is the openness, competence and efficiency of the head teacher or principal. The Commonwealth Secretariat (1996a) also emphasizes the link between management and school effectiveness, focusing specifically on the role of the head-teacher in Africa. It warns that 'effectiveness' may mean operating with smaller budgets:

> The head . . . plays the most crucial role in ensuring school effectiveness. This role is, however, complex and demanding. It involves management of financial, human and material resources in a dynamic situation affected by many internal and external forces. This situation is frequently made more difficult by decreasing levels of government funding, in real terms, at a time of increasing demands for education. The school head in Africa is, therefore, in a difficult position, being

expected to deliver 'better quality' education in a period of diminish-
ing resources.

(Commonwealth Secretariat 1996b: 5)

The managerial effectiveness of principals and other school leaders may
be tested by the need to implement educational 'reforms' introduced by
national or provincial governments. This exacerbates the demands on
school managers by requiring them to introduce new initiatives successfully while still maintaining high standards for current pupils and students. The need to manage externally imposed change provides a further
challenge for principals and other school managers, leading to the now
widespread view that school managers require specialist preparation, as
well as in-service training, if they are to be effective in meeting external
requirements while also providing a satisfying and successful educational
experience for children and students (Pelletier and Charron 1998; Pelletier
2001).

A World Bank evaluation of projects successful in improving the quality
of education in developing countries recognizes the important contribution
of management training in developing school effectiveness:

> A review of Bank experience found that the most successful pro-
> grammes have a different profile than the less successful programmes.
> The former aimed at comprehensive change, encompassing a wide
> range of objectives that include administrative and management
> training and the provision of educational materials as well as the
> usual curriculum and teacher training components . . . successful
> programmes paid significant attention to strengthening institutions
> and organisational structure, including developing a capacity for
> innovative management.

(Verspoor 1989)

All this evidence points to a clear need for training and professional
development for school managers. Open and distance learning has an
important part to play in meeting this need, as we shall see later in this
chapter, but first we need to identify who these 'school managers' are.

WHO ARE THE 'SCHOOL MANAGERS'?

School managers are all of those people who exercise management
responsibilities in schools. The structures vary in different educational systems but there are always some leaders who have designated responsibility
for school management. However, a distinction can be made between

external managers who may have authority over schools, such as national, regional and local officials, and those who work inside the schools. The internal managers include principals, vice-principals, heads of department and subject leaders. The focus of this chapter is the latter group: internal managers who have direct responsibility for school activities while remaining accountable to the external agencies.

The roles and responsibilities of senior and middle managers in schools depend on both national and institutional variables. Where schools operate within a bureaucratic framework, as in China (Bush et al. 1998), Cyprus (Pashiardis 2000), South Africa (Sebakwane 1997), Zambia (Commonwealth Secretariat 1996b), African francophone countries, or much of South America (Newland 1995), many of the most important decisions are taken within the external hierarchy and passed down to principals for implementation. In such situations, management may be limited to a small number of senior staff reporting to the principal. Similarly, internal managers who prefer a 'top down' approach are unlikely to empower their colleagues by asking them to fulfil management activities.

In contrast, self-managing schools are responsible for many of the functions undertaken outside the institution in more centralized systems. In England and Wales, Australia, New Zealand, Israel, Portugal, Quebec and Switzerland, for example, schools have a significant measure of autonomy, including responsibility for some or all of governance, determination of aims, financial management, staffing, pupil admissions and management of the site and buildings. These tasks are beyond the scope of the principal so management responsibilities need to distributed among a wider group of staff, including vice-principals, senior teachers, heads of department, subject co-ordinators and senior support staff. Furthermore, training needs are likely to be more extensive for principals of self-managing schools.

Some writers broaden the definition of managers to include all classroom teachers because they have to manage their classrooms, the work of their children or students, and the implementation of the curriculum. The definition used by the UK Open University (1996) includes elements of both these positions:

> There are aspects of management in the work of all teachers and lecturers, not just those in the work of those in positions of authority ... management is ... working with and through others in order to achieve particular purposes. The purpose of educational organisations is to promote desired learning for pupils and students. The management of education, therefore, means harnessing the energies of other adults, in particular staff, parents and members of the community, in order to promote the educational purposes of the organisation.
>
> (Open University 1996: 5)

O'Donoghue and Dimmock (1998: 15) portray an all-encompassing role of principals in a contemporary setting, including:

- educational or instructional leadership; supporting, supervising and monitoring the curriculum, and teaching and learning;
- management of other aspects of the school (including personnel and human relations management) and resource management (particularly budgetary and financial management);
- management of the school community and its relations with the external environment;
- management and leadership of change.

In many developed and developing countries, with responsibility increasingly shifting from central offices to individual schools, principals are becoming accountable for the academic tone, performance goals and standards of their schools, are having to cope with teacher shortages and inadequacies, and are often required to manage with limited resources. In this work, they are accountable to their local communities, as well as to their external managers, and they need to draw upon the support of parents and other community members.

The extent of participation in managing this agenda depends upon the attitudes of principals as well as the policy context of the school. As the Open University (1995: 17) observes, 'responsibility for these tasks can be concentrated in the hands of a small number of people or widely dispersed among the staff'. Peters (1993) suggests that dispersed management is appropriate for the service sector, including education, because of the large numbers of highly qualified specialist staff who expect to participate in decisions affecting their working lives. The more people here are involved in school management, the greater the requirement for effective professional development to prepare and support these managers.

THE IMPORTANCE OF PROFESSIONAL DEVELOPMENT FOR SCHOOL MANAGERS

Headships and other senior and middle management positions in schools usually go to outstanding teachers, but good teachers do not necessarily make good leaders and managers. There is increasing recognition of the need for principals and other school leaders to be prepared for their managerial responsibilities, but training is rarely a requirement for appointment and there is still an assumption that good teachers can become effective managers without specific preparation. The Commonwealth Secretariat (1996a) shows that this is certainly a problem in much of Africa:

> The school principal carries prime responsibility for creating an effect-
> ive educational environment. Without the necessary skills, many
> heads are overwhelmed by the task. In Africa, the situation is par-
> ticularly acute. In rapidly expanding systems, experienced and skilled
> teachers are customarily appointed to run complex schools without
> adequate preparation and back-up support . . . strategies for training
> and supporting school heads [are] generally inadequate throughout
> Africa.
>
> (Commonwealth Secretariat 1996a: iii)

Within Africa, too, there are accounts of widespread mismanagement
leading to indiscipline in schools and of a respect for paper qualifications
with little regard for qualities of leadership. Some school managers are
dealing with their personal business to an extent that interferes with
their school work. The situation in anglophone and francophone countries is similar (Confemen 1995). There are typically no national training
policies or institutions and there is no distinct professional status for
school managers. The principals are teachers who occupy a managerial
position as long as the authorities renew their mandate; they can be
returned to the classroom at any time.

The Commonwealth Secretariat (1996b) identifies three overlapping
problems of school management in Africa:

- inadequate managerial capacity among principals and other school
  leaders to cope with the ever-changing demands of their jobs;
- inadequate training and support opportunities for principals and
  other school leaders to reinforce existing managerial skills or acquire
  new ones;
- an inadequate supply of training materials and resources in educational institutions that has reduced the impact of programmes directed
  towards enhancing school management effectiveness.

These problems are evident in several African countries, including Botswana, Ghana, Kenya, Malawi and Namibia (Commonwealth Secretariat
1996b). They could apply equally to many developing countries.

As writers such as Saint-Germain (1999) and international agencies such
as CIDA (2001: para. 3.6) observe, major changes are needed to enhance
the scope and nature of the training for principals and school managers.
Programmes and systems are needed to enhance their status, professionalism and morale, and there is also need for national and international
networks through which these educational managers can share their knowledge and experiences. This training is required at three distinct levels:
for those aspiring to become managers; for recent appointees; and for those
experienced principals and managers whose knowledge and skills need

to be brought up to date. A number of strategies have been identified to address these problems, including the use of open and distance learning.

OPEN AND DISTANCE EDUCATION FOR TRAINING AND DEVELOPING SCHOOL MANAGERS

Distance education is now well established as a major alternative to traditional forms of teaching and learning and is one area where new learning strategies are most progressive. There are five main reasons why this mode of education may be appropriate for providing professional development for school managers.

As noted in earlier chapters, it can reach large numbers, contain costs, reach scattered audiences, widen understanding of good practice, and meet the needs of adult learners – all factors that apply to school managers.

Models of distance education used for training school managers

Distance education is not a monolithic concept, but embraces a range of approaches which have in common the separation of teacher and learner during much or all of the learning process. The 'lone wolf' student (Peters 1993: 50) now represents only one approach to distance learning as participants increasingly join groups to enhance mutual learning. These groups are often linked to the workplace or a professional association and they provide a powerful vehicle for linking theory and practice. The Commonwealth Secretariat (1996a), in explaining how its 'Better Schools' modules may be used, shows that they may be suitable for individuals or groups and for addressing real issues in participants' schools.

> One of the most effective ways in which these materials may be used is through self-directed study or open learning. As heads your backgrounds differ. You have varying experiences and your schools are different. Your learning needs, therefore, vary considerably ... The modules may be studied by individuals working on their own or in formal or informal study groups ... Your study of the modules will not be complete without active steps being taken to address issues in your own school or in your neighbourhood. There should be no mere reading of the materials.
>
> (Commonwealth Secretariat 1996a: 25–6)

In the AFIDES programme (see Box 7.1), participants are invited to share their learning with other managers in their school, and to involve the whole community in the development of an educational project.

> **Box 7.1   The AFIDES distance education training programme in Africa**
>
> - Authors: Association francophone internationale des directeurs d'établisse-ments scolaires (AFIDES), on behalf of the Agence intergouvernementale de la Francophonie.
> - Main objective: to give African elementary and secondary principals training in basic management skills, to enable them to implement improvement in their schools and their local system.
> - Main focus: on professional abilities rather than on academic knowledge. In many countries, school managers, especially at the elementary level, do not have sufficient learning skills to follow a university programme.
> - The content progresses from simple to complex issues. Each module is divided into three parts: information, skills and implementation of an improvement in the school. The principal is expected to evaluate, compare and improve structures and processes.
> - Written by an international team of principals (from Africa, Europe and Canada), the programme was tested in Benin, Burkina Faso and Senegal. National AFIDES associations are using the programme to train 200 elementary and secondary principals.
> - Relies heavily on learning from peers, whether they be the authors of the materials or the participants in their work groups.
> - Duration: one year, with three general meetings and many voluntary teamwork meetings. National tutors are trained to provide support for individuals and teams.
> - The programme is often adapted to local realities before being used.
>
> Source: <www.afides.qc.ca>

What makes an effective programme

Successful distance education programmes for school managers usually include some or all of the following features:

High quality materials

They have good print materials which are often of publishable quality. Those produced by, for example, the UK Open University (1995, 1996), the University of Leicester (1998/99), AFIDES (see Box 7.1) and Resafad

---

Box 7.2 The Resafad programme in Africa

- The Réseau Africain de Formation à Distance (Resafad) trains national managers in the use of distance education technologies, using multimedia resource centres connected through the Internet, and situated in the capitals of partner states: Burkina Faso, Guinee, Mali, Togo, Benin, Madagascar and Senegal.
- Sponsored by the Foreign Affairs Ministry of France.
- Main objective: to help develop in each country a national expertise concerning communication technologies and distance education.
- Supported by a consortium of French and African universities, national institutions and intergovernmental agencies.
- The favoured approach is learner centred, directed 'self training' and virtual group work.
- In basic education, priority was given to the training of principals, recognized as a priority by regional specialists. Training modules were developed collaboratively by specialists from each participating state.
- At the secondary level, demand for management training is increasing. To respond to this need, a regional action plan was developed concerning the self-training of high school principals.

Source: <www.edusud.org.resafad/presentation.html>

(see Box 7.2) are often used by other providers and the University of Leicester's publications were praised by the English Quality Assurance Agency during its 2001 quality assessment.

Texts may be supplemented by video and audio materials to heighten interest and illustrate real-life situations (Open University 1995, 1996). Computer-based learning is also becoming significant, notably in the Leadership Programme for School Headteachers (LPSH), first offered by the Department for Education and Employment (DFEE) in association with the UK Open University.

The English National College for School Leadership (NCSL) is managing the 'Talking Heads' programme (Box 7.3). This is available for all headteachers in England and facilitates discussion and networking. Discussion groups may relate to the school sector (early years, primary, secondary), or to particular themes (performance management, learning and teaching, finance). The programme is successful in reducing isolation and improving ICT skills as well as in exchanging good practice.

Box 7.3   The NCSL 'Talking Heads' programme, England

- 'Talking Heads' is presented by the National College for School Leadership (NCSL) in England.
- 'Talking Heads' is a private, interactive community area of NCSL Online.
- It facilitates discussion and networking and provides opportunities to share common problems with other school leaders.
- Community members can have conversations in open forums or in private communities where the membership and audience is restricted.
- The aim is to generate a virtual community of school leaders.
- Each community member is allocated to a facilitator who provides guidance about using and making contributions to 'Talking Heads'.

Source: <www.ncsl.gov.uk>

A similar programme, albeit on a much smaller scale, is being piloted in Israel. Ten principals from all over the country, who may not know each other beforehand, are linked for the purposes of professional development. They learn and share mostly through virtual channels. The virtual sessions may be either synchronized or unsynchronized. Synchronized sessions take place once a month in a virtual chat room while unsynchronized sessions are forums that enable principals to choose the frequency, intensity, nature and timing of their participation.

Despite these interesting web-based developments, good print materials are likely to remain the key feature of programmes, particularly in the developing countries, although it is notable that the University of Leicester's programme in Dominica (Box 7.4) includes a special email facility. Print and other materials are most likely to promote professional learning and prompt school improvement if they are focused on the specific national and organizational contexts of the participants rather than based on generic concepts or practices in other settings.

School-focused assessment

Many programmes require or encourage school-based assessment to enable theory to be linked to issues and problems in the participants' schools. This often means that issues requiring attention in the school are tackled as part of the assessment process. Teachers and school managers become 'practitioner researchers' (Middlewood et al. 1999), investigating

Box 7.4 Master's degree programme for secondary school principals in Dominica

Dominica is the largest and most mountainous of the Windward Islands in the eastern Caribbean. It has a population of 71,000, of whom 22,000 live in the capital Roseau. This programme for fifteen secondary school principals is part of the Commonwealth of Dominica's Secondary Education Support Project (SESP) designed to raise standards in the secondary education sector. The University of Leicester has worked with Dominica in offering the programme.

The main features of this special programme are as follows:

- The candidates were nominated by Ministry of Education officers but subject to the university's usual admission processes.
- There is a local 'country facilitator' who acts as the focal point for the network of participants but the tutor is appointed by the University and is located in England.
- Contact between tutor and participants is maintained through a special email link. All SESP participants have access to computers for use on the programme.
- The course is text-based and involves the same course materials and assessment requirements as the courses offered in other countries.
- There was a formal 'opening ceremony' for the programme attended by the prime minister and other ministers.
- The programme is supported by funding from the UK Department for International Development.
- The programme is designed to be completed in two years.
- Successful completion of the programme leads to the University of Leicester's MBA in Educational Management.
- The programme was launched in 2001 and had not been evaluated at the time of writing.

Source: University of Leicester 2001

their own practice in order to promote school improvement. School-based assessment is evident in the course for primary school principals in Belize (Box 7.5), in the middle managers' programme in Wiltshire, England (Box 7.6) and in the AFIDES material (Box 7.1).

Box 7.5   Management training for primary school principals in Belize

Belize is on the Central American mainland and gained independence from Britain in 1981. It is sparsely populated with only 222,000 people. There are 53,000 pupils aged 5–14 in 280 primary schools, 195 of which are in rural areas.

The Belize Teachers' Training College (BTTC), in association with the Ministry of Education, introduced a one-year in-service programme for primary school principals. The programme is delivered by supported open learning with the following features:

- Principals follow the 'Better Schools' materials developed by the Commonwealth Secretariat, aiming to study one module a month.
- Workshops are held for one day each month at district education centres and cover a range of topics relevant to the basic concerns of principals.
- Each principal is assigned to a BTTC supervisor who visits monthly for a full day. The purpose of the visit is to provide guidance in the implementation of the programme and to observe progress over time.
- Assessment is based on the principal's portfolio of activities, tasks and assignments linked to the development needs of their schools plus supervisor's reports and an exit interview.
- Successful candidates receive a certificate in leadership and management and an increase in salary.
- The programme was valued partly because it was accessible to principals in all six districts.

Source: Crossley and Thompson 2000

Support by a supervisor or facilitator

In many programmes, the potential isolation of the distance learner is acknowledged in the provision of extra support. Most university or other distance education providers appoint tutors with responsibility for the academic progress of a group of distance learners. The Dominican (Box 7.4) and Wiltshire (Box 7.6) programmes both provide facilitators to support participants, while each principal in the Belize course (Box 7.5) has a supervisor who visits the school once a month. According to Kemp (1991: 7), the facilitators in Wiltshire 'have done a marvellous job in forming and building their teams and getting them to work effectively'.

Box 7.6   Management development for middle managers in Wiltshire, UK

Wiltshire is a predominantly rural county in south-west England. The local education authority introduced management development programmes for middle managers in secondary schools. The main features of these programmes are as follows:

- Programmes are based in individual schools to facilitate group work.
- School groups address issues of current concern to the school.
- The programme uses materials developed by the National Development Centre, which is based at the University of Bristol.
- There is a facilitator in each school to provide guidance and encouragement. Facilitators are chosen for their interpersonal skills and status in the school.
- The programmes involve ninety-five teachers in ten schools.

Source: Kemp 1991

Accreditation

Many of the best distance education courses include provision for accreditation. This is certainly the case of some university-provided courses, such as the Dominican programme (Box 7.4), but is also true in some other courses, including that in Belize (Box 7.5). Accreditation helps to motivate those participants who welcome the prospect of career development arising from certificates, diplomas and higher degrees. It also facilitates the identification of a recognized group of management professionals in the educational system, and the creation of a distinct status for principals, something that is noticeably lacking in many countries.

However, some distance education courses, for example the 'Talking Heads' programme provided by the English NCSL, do not lead to accreditation. The focus here is on mutual learning rather than formal teaching and such provision is likely to be more suitable for qualified and experienced principals than for those without any previous training who need some assurance that they have reached an appropriate level of competence in school leadership.

Aims, content and tuition

Good distance education courses are clear in setting out their general *aims*, as Boxes 7.7 and 7.8 demonstrate, but the specific aims may vary.

Box 7.7   UK Open University 'Effective Leadership and Management in Education' (E838)

E838 aims to improve professional capability in educational management by:

- developing knowledge and understanding of educational management theory and practice;
- promoting the self-development of effective educational managers through critical reflection on practice;
- developing an understanding of how context and values influence educational management.

Source: Open University 1996

Box 7.8   University of Leicester MBA in educational management

The aims of the course are:

- to equip students with a body of knowledge that will improve their understanding of educational management and leadership;
- to enable students to reflect on concepts, theories and models of educational management and leadership;
- to provide analytical frameworks that can be applied by students to their own working environment;
- to provide a review and experience of various research methods and processes of analysis that can be applied to educational institutions;
- to provide opportunities for the improvement of research based management skills;
- to enable students to contribute to school and college improvement.

Source: University of Leicester 1998/99: 6–7

For example, while both the UK Open University and the University of Leicester focus on developing knowledge and understanding, and on the notion of personal improvement, the former emphasizes the concept of reflective practice and the latter's aims relate to the development of research-based management skills.

The *content* of educational management courses has become standardized to the point that one might refer to an international curriculum for the subject. The main topics covered are:

- leadership and strategic management;
- teaching and learning;
- human resource management;
- finance and resources;
- links with parents and the community.

The four programmes featured in Table 7.1 below (the UK Open University course is only one part of an MA programme) include most or all of these topics. All four programmes cover the standard functions of

Table 7.1 Comparison of content of distance education courses for school managers

Open University E838	University of Leicester MBA	Commonwealth Secretariat 'Better Schools' modules	AFIDES
Professional self-development		Self-development	Study guide
Leadership	Leadership		
Understanding educational organizations		Principles of management	Fundamentals of educational management in the national context
Strategic management	Strategic management		
	Managing people	Personnel management	Human resources management
Managing professional development			
	Managing the curriculum	Curriculum and resources	Managing learning
Financial and resource management	Managing finance and resources	Financial management	Administrative, financial and resource management
Organizational effectiveness		School effectiveness	
	Managing external relations	Governance	
Teams			Leading the school-based educational project
Managing for quality			
	Research methods		
Reflective practice			

financial, staff and curriculum management but there are variations in the other topics.

Most distance learning courses supplement their teaching materials with personal tuition which is often, but not always, provided by telephone, post, fax and email rather than face-to-face contact. Devlin (1993: 265–6) sets out the purposes of tutor support in distance education:

- enrichment of the learning experience through the provision of additional information and contextualization;
- diagnosis of learning difficulties through a process of monitoring, testing and interpersonal contact;
- dealing with difficulties reported by participants;
- practical help in administrative matters;
- human support to counter the isolating effects of distance education.

Most successful distance education courses have tutors whose role includes the features identified by Devlin. University courses typically expect that tutors will meet these requirements as well as provide specific support for the course assignments. In developing countries, trainers need to be of a sufficient status to gain the respect of the course members. However, there may also be difficulties if the course leaders or tutors are also the line managers of the participants, for example, as district education officers. There can also be role ambiguity if the trainers are also responsible for appraising or supervising participants.

In addition to tutor support, the AFIDES programme emphasizes the importance of learning from peers. Most school managers learn their trade by working alongside senior principals, and it seems wise to emulate such practice in distance learning provision. Wherever possible, the process should incorporate peer learning, whether through case studies, sharing experience through written materials or electronic means, or group activities.

EVALUATING DISTANCE EDUCATION TRAINING FOR SCHOOL MANAGERS

Evaluation is a key aspect of any educational experience. It is valuable for course leaders and tutors to establish the attitudes of participants and to assess the quality of provision. Thorpe's (1993: 5) succinct definition incorporates the main features of evaluation:

> Evaluation is the collection, analysis and interpretation of information about any aspect of a programme of education and training, as part of a recognized process of judging its effectiveness, its efficiency and any other outcomes it may have.

Thorpe explains why evaluation may be particularly desirable for distance education:

- While it is always desirable to establish the quality of the learning process, this tends to be problematic in distance and open learning because much of the learning occurs as private study. 'Evaluation as a formal activity becomes more important, therefore, because it is one of the few ways of finding out learners' reactions in order to tailor provision for a closer fit with their needs' (Thorpe 1993: 2–4).
- Distance education providers require comparative evidence of the relative effectiveness of different models of open learning, and evaluation can provide this evidence.
- Evaluation is also essential for the improvement of the provision.
- Evaluation also provides evidence of how and where the competence of practitioners can be developed, leading to staff development for providers.

In relation to distance education-based training for school managers, there is also the important point that ineffective or poor-quality courses are unlikely to produce school improvement, which is the ultimate objective of such programmes. Evaluation helps to achieve quality assurance by providing direct feedback on the perceived value and relevance of distance education programmes. There also needs to be follow-up to assess the subsequent impact and ramifications of the training. Ensuring that there is appropriate evaluation, and involving the participants in the process, also helps to reaffirm and demonstrate the importance of heads employing formative and summative evaluation in managing their own schools.

The University of Leicester's MBA in Educational Management by distance learning has an evaluation policy which involves issuing questionnaires to the students on completing each of the five course modules and on completion of the MBA. In addition, the participants are sampled for their views whenever parts of the course are replaced or updated. Individual comments receive personal replies by the course team and issues of wider interest are the subject of feedback in the University of Leicester's *Professional Development News*. Improvements in response to feedback have included changes in the sequencing of the delivery of course material, the addition of more international examples in the course texts, and the provision of additional text books (University of Leicester 1998/99: 10).

The University of Leicester has also addressed the impact of its MBA on school outcomes, notably by publishing a book showing how school-based assessments are 'making a difference' in various educational settings (Middlewood *et al.* 1999). There is a similar book highlighting the positive outcomes of teacher research arising from the UK Open University school management courses (Preedy 1989).

English distance learning programmes are also subject to external evaluation through the Quality Assurance Agency (QAA). Documentation provided by departments is scrutinized by teams of inspectors who grade provision according to six criteria. The University of Leicester's MBA by distance learning was the largest course included in the 2001 QAA inspection of its School of Education and it was awarded the maximum score of 24.

Trainers and participants involved in the AFIDES distance education programme in francophone Africa identified a number of positive results which went beyond individual outcomes. These included:

- the strengthening of the participants' professional identity;
- pressure on the school systems to give the managers a distinct status and to establish professional training as an important factor in the nomination and promotion of managers;
- pressures to establish a national training policy and training institution for school managers;
- because of the decentralization of the expertise involved in the training process, an increase in the capacity of school systems to train their own managers.

These positive systemic outcomes suggest that these training activities can truly contribute to school management and school improvement.

CONCLUSION: THE FUTURE OF DISTANCE EDUCATION FOR SCHOOL MANAGERS

Perraton (2000: 82) states that: 'distance education has gone some way to establishing itself as a significant and legitimate way of training teachers' and open and distance education is now also shown to be a well-established means of developing school managers in several parts of the world, including Australia, the United States and the United Kingdom. The Commonwealth Secretariat's programme is also widely used in Africa and the Caribbean, while the AFIDES courses are widely used in francophone Africa.

The advantages of distance education for training and supporting educational managers are now well documented. They include their capacity to provide for large numbers of participants regardless of location, achieve economies of scale (which make them attractive to governments), and offer the means of combining study, reflection and practice (which provides benefits for the managers and the educational systems). Such programmes are particularly valuable when existing provision is limited and there is a need quickly to develop the knowledge and skills of large numbers of principals and senior managers. In such circumstances, there may be few trainers qualified in educational management and it makes good sense to concentrate the available talent into central teams capable of designing and developing curricula appropriate to the specific needs of client groups in the countries or regions concerned.

The strengths of distance education in such applications are considerable. There are, however, several limitations which need to be understood and addressed if distance education is to maximize its potential for developing managerial competence in schools. A major issue for many heads and managers is that they find it difficult to share their problems or ideas with others in the school or wider community and, in the distance learning process, they are isolated from other participants and their tutors or mentors. While learning styles differ, most people respond better to group activities than to monastic engagement with teaching materials, even where these are attractive and challenging. Many providers address this issue by developing opportunities for interaction with other participants and course staff. We noted earlier that the Primary School Principals programme in Belize (Box 7.5) provides for participants to meet once a month. The UK Open University has summer schools for some of its courses and the University of Leicester's MBA team holds day schools for their students. In Senegal, the participants in the AFIDES programme (Box 7.1) are invited to take part in monthly discussions with their tutors; these events have become a major source of shared learning and convinced the agency to increase the attention given to peer training within the programme.

Linked to the problem of isolation is the lack of opportunity for people to work collaboratively to address school issues and problems. Heads and teachers involved in distance education training programmes often experience difficulty in conducting in-school enquiries because the other staff may become suspicious of their motives. Encouraging groups of learners within participating schools, as in Wiltshire's scheme (Box 7.6), the AFIDES programme (Box 7.1), and the University of Leicester's school-based MBA course, can produce positive outcomes in terms of learner motivation and school improvement (Middlewood *et al.* 1999). This indicates an open learning approach which includes distance education as part of a wider approach to management development. The AFIDES programme suggests that the learning experience of the managers should be shared with the whole school team. It follows that, since a major objective of the programme is to promote a collaborative management approach, there should be a collective learning experience.

A third issue relates to the differential potential for distance education to bring about improvements in learning. Sparkes (1993: 137) distinguishes between knowledge, skills and understanding. Good distance learning materials can be effective in promoting knowledge and understanding but are likely to be relatively weak in developing skills, particularly for a practical activity such as school management. For example, chairing a meeting of staff or parents requires specific skills which are unlikely to be acquired from engagement with distance education texts. This may require role play and may be a suitable group activity when participants meet. Using case studies is another useful means of relating the learners' experiences to the underlying knowledge base. School management development programmes should utilize the principles of adult learning and aim to extract knowledge from experience.

Finally, there is a potential problem about the context of learners and the suitability of distance education courses for all the participants. Given the notion of 'organizational culture' (Bush 1995, 1998), each school has some unique features which may cast doubt on the applicability of the 'general principles' presented in course texts. There is a particular problem in the use of distance learning courses from Western countries in the developing world, unless these have been customized for the intended market. As the Commonwealth Secretariat (1996a: iii) indicates, 'management techniques appropriate elsewhere cannot be imported unmodified into African systems'. The Commonwealth Secretariat's (1996a) own 'Better Schools' modules are targeted specifically at African schools, and largely prepared by people in seven African countries. However, while acknowledging the particular problems facing school managers in Africa, even these materials inevitably underestimate differences between systems. It is advisable to adapt materials to the national context before using them in a different country.

Despite these reservations, open and distance education continues to have a huge potential for developing the capabilities of school managers. As advanced information and communications technology becomes more widespread, it is likely to have even greater impact.

REFERENCES

Bush, T. (1995) *Theories of Educational Management*, 2nd edn, London: Paul Chapman.

—— (1998) 'Organisational culture and strategic management' in D. Middlewood and J. Lumby (eds) *Strategic Management in Schools and Colleges*, London: Paul Chapman.

Bush, T., Qiang, H. and Fang, J. (1998) 'Educational management in China: an overview', *Compare*, 28(2): 133–41.

Canadian International Development Agency (CIDA) (2001) *Draft Action Plan on Education*, moderator's summary report of the online public consultation, <http://www.acdi-cida.gc.ca/cida_ind.nsf/>.

Commonwealth Secretariat (1996a) *Better Schools: Resource Materials for Heads: Introductory Module*, London: Commonwealth Secretariat.

—— (1996b) *Managing and Motivating Teachers under Resource Constraints: Training Headteachers to Face the Challenges*, London: Commonwealth Secretariat.

Confemen (1995) *L'Education de base: vers une nouvelle école*, Dakar: Secrétariat Technique de la Conférence des Ministères de l'Education Nationale des Pays ayant le Français en Partage.

Crossley, M. and Thompson, M. (2000) 'Distance education for primary teachers and principals in Belize', *Education Across the Commonwealth*, 1: 59–65, July.

Delors, J. (1996) *Delors Report to UNESCO of the International Commission on Education for the 21st Century*, Paris: UNESCO.

Devlin, T. (1993) 'Distance training', in D. Keegan (ed.) *Theoretical Principles of Distance Education*, London: Routledge.

Hallinger, P. and Heck, R. (1999) 'Can leadership enhance school effectiveness?', in T. Bush, L. Bell, R. Bolam, R. Glatter and P. Ribbins (eds) *Educational Management: Redefining Theory, Policy and Practice*, London: Paul Chapman.

Kemp, J. (1991) 'Individual, team and school management development: how distance learning has been used successfully in Wiltshire', *Management in Education*, 5(6): 6–7.

Middlewood, D., Coleman, M. and Lumby, J. (1999) *Practitioner Research in Education: Making a Difference*, London: Paul Chapman.

Newland, C. (1995) 'Spanish American elementary education 1950–1992: bureaucracy, growth and decentralisation', *International Journal of Educational Development*, 15(2): 103–14.

O'Donoghue, T. and Dimmock, C. (1998) *School Restructuring: International Perspectives*, London: Kogan Page.

Open University (1995) *E828 Educational Management in Action: Study Guide*, Milton Keynes: Open University.

—— (1996) *E838 Effective Leadership and Management in Education: Study Guide*, Milton Keynes: Open University.

Pashiardis, P. (2000) 'Cyprus at the crossroads of change', *Education Across the Commonwealth*, 1: 76–83, July.

Pelletier, G. (2001) 'Diriger un établissement scolaire: jeu de pistes pour un temps Actuel', *La Revue des Echanges*, Editions de l'Association francophore des directeurs d'établissements scolaires (AFIDES), Septembre.

Pelletier, G. and Charron, R. (1998) *Diriger en période de transformation*, Montreal: Editions de l'AFIDES.

Perraton, H. (2000) *Open and Distance Learning in the Developing World*, London: Routledge.

Peters, O. (1993) 'Distance education in a post-industrial society', in D. Keegan (ed.) *Theoretical Principles of Distance Education*, London: Routledge.

Preedy, M. (1989) *Teachers' Case Studies in Educational Management*, London: Paul Chapman.

Saint-Germain, M. (1999) 'La formation des gestionnaires de l'éducation: nécessité d'un renouveau des contenus et des méthodologies', in G. Pelletier (ed.) *Former les dirigeants de l'éducation: Apprentissage dans l'action*, Bruxelles: De Boek Université.

Sebakwane, S. (1997) 'The contradictions of scientific management as a mode of controlling teachers' work in black secondary schools: South Africa', *International Journal of Educational Development*, 17(4): 391–404.

Sparkes, J, (1993) 'Matching teaching methods to educational aims in distance education', in D. Keegan (ed.) *Theoretical Principles of Distance Education*, London: Routledge.

Thorpe, M. (1993) *Evaluating Open and Distance Learning*, Harlow: Longman.

University of Leicester (1998/99) *Professional Development News*, 12: 10.

—— (2001) *Report to the MBA in Educational Management Programme Board*, Northampton: Educational Management Development Unit.

Verspoor, J. (1989) *Pathways to Change: Improving the Quality of Education in Developing Countries*, <http://www.worldbank.org/html/extdr/educ/edu_eram/pathways.htm>.

Chapter 8

Selecting and using media in teacher education

Adrian Kirkwood and Charles Joyner

Although the situation varies from country to country and from region to region, media are undoubtedly having an increasing impact on people's lives throughout the world. Technological developments, particularly digitization, are also enabling more people to become media 'producers' and not just media 'consumers'. Media are similarly having an impact on education, including teacher education. Like many of the teachers they train, teacher educators tend to be more familiar and comfortable with the media they experienced as young learners and are wary of the newer technologies. However, it is important that teacher educators understand the potential of the various technologies and media for extending or enhancing teacher education and training and the principles, if not the detailed technicalities, of applying these in specific contexts. Depending on circumstances, teacher trainers will either produce the courseware themselves, or select and adapt existing materials. They will work with internal or external colleagues in multi-disciplinary teams or engage professional producers in developing the media products. Whatever their role and given the rate of technology change, it is important that they not only develop but maintain their knowledge and skills in using media for teacher education. The following chapter discusses these issues and offers some guidance in using media for teacher education.

USING MEDIA FOR TEACHING AND LEARNING

A wide variety of media are used in teaching and learning, and techno-logical developments are both increasing the range of media available and bringing about innovative combinations and new 'hybrid' media. Although the rate at which new media are developed and launched sometimes seems overwhelming, the fundamental point demonstrated by research and experience is that there is no single 'super medium' for education. Teaching and learning are complex processes and although some media can be used to support certain facets of those processes, each and every medium has its limitations and constraints – and very often media used in combination are more effective (Kirkwood 1998). Availability is the most important constraint on choice but the practice of selecting and using media involves addressing a combination of economic, educational and practical considerations.

Obviously, the level of decision making influences perspectives on media choice and decisions about it. Planners in ministries or donor agencies or non-governmental organizations will view things differently from those in teacher-training institutions or schools. Nonetheless, planners need to focus on three inter-related sets of practical considerations at the outset:

1   the context within which the teaching or learning will take place;
2   the pedagogical needs and purposes;
3   the characteristics of media and their potential contribution to the teaching-learning process.

If planners start with 1 and 2 above and then weigh up the potential advantages and limitations in 3, the outcomes will help inform decision-making about which media are feasible for particular purposes and groups of teachers.

THE CONTEXT

Without access, everything else is of little consequence. It may be highly desirable to use a particular medium, for example, radio, television or the web for particular teacher education programmes, but it is first essential to find the answers to the following questions.

- What media are available to the teacher training institutions and providers?
- What media do teachers have access to and where? In institutions, teachers'centres,inschoolsor at home? How do they access these media?
- What familiarity or competence do the teacher educators and trainees have in using the media?
- How large a role are media components expected to fulfil within the teacher education programme? Are they to provide resources, or enrich or complement 'traditional' methods? Do they play a leading or supporting role?
- What is the existing infrastructure (electricity, postal and telephone services, radio and television reception, technical support) and what will it support?
- What enhancements to the existing facilities (if any) seem feasible (e.g. audio- or video-conferencing facilities, Internet connection) or affordable?

Box 8.1   Some typical problems in access and logistics

A national in-service teacher development strategy in a developing country was based upon a series of radio programmes designed to be listened to in schools. These were supported by printed materials for teachers, providing additional readings, practical activities and suggestions for adapting the teaching and learning ideas presented to local needs and circumstances. Successful delivery required participating teachers to have access to a working radio, to be free of other responsibilities and tasks at the time of programme transmission, and to have received the printed materials in advance. A sample of schools was visited some time after broadcasting of the series had commenced to assess what impact the programmes were making. The evaluators found that some schools had not received the booklets for the series, and that others did not have sufficient batteries to keep their radios working.

- What impact will the costs of using media have on access or sustainability of the programme?

These questions need to be considered in relation to all the settings in which teacher training takes place and the schools where teachers work.

Although there is the potential for using a wide range of media, there will always be constraints and problems to be overcome if the full educational benefits are to be gained. Problems of access can also be compounded by operational ones (see Box 8.1), where the logistics of delivery or organization fail to run smoothly. Regardless of the educational quality of the programmes and materials, their value is greatly reduced if there is a failure in any one of the delivery operations or lack of access. Clearly, using media for teacher education involves much more than design issues in developing programmes or software.

THE PEDAGOGICAL NEEDS AND PURPOSES

Media can be used in teacher education in a variety of ways to help achieve particular educational goals, for example, in

- knowledge building
  - in educational theory, child development, classroom management, teaching methods, gender-sensitive education and various aspects of professional studies;

- in academic subjects or the subject content to be taught (history, numeracy, languages, health education, mathematics) and the school curriculum for these; and in
- skills development
  - in classroom management, teaching methods, lesson planning, multi-grade teaching;
  - in practical work in language and science teaching, and in the creation and use of basic learning aids;
  - in interpersonal and communication skills, facilitating interaction and using computers across the curriculum.

Media can also contribute resources for teacher-trainers and teachers to use in face-to-face teaching and in combination with distance education, as the examples below show. They are able to enrich the teaching learning experience.

Presenting source material

Audiovisual media can provide, for example, still or moving pictures of otherwise inaccessible people, artefacts, places and processes. They may take the form of entire instructional sessions, with their own didactic structures, or may be used in discrete segments to illustrate teacher-trainers' presentations. In training science teachers, much can be learned by observing certain phenomena in slow motion, through time-lapse photography, or by means of explanatory animations or by seeing teaching principles and procedures 'come to life' through videos that provide 'a feel' for what is involved in putting theory into practice. In training teachers in mathematics, science and technology, visual media can provide trainees with 'concrete' examples of abstract ideas or principles, and help relate theoretical concepts to everyday situations with which they can identify. Sound can also be important to understanding certain scientific or technological concepts and is often essential in teaching music and languages. As well as focusing on subject content, videos are used widely to illustrate lessons and classroom interaction, providing data and examples for teachers to observe and analyse.

Supporting the active use of learning resources

Media can help learners make active and effective use of educational resources. Although computers are generally considered synonymous with interactive learning, it is possible for other media to support active study. For example, audio commentaries can 'talk' learners through processes such as interpreting graphs, diagrams, maps or photographs or guide them through practical tasks in the classroom or laboratory or in using computers.

Video sequences can demonstrate procedures that learners will subsequently undertake, such as setting up or operating equipment or organizing a classroom or running a parents' meeting. In such cases, it is often the integration of different media that promotes the most effective learning, enabling the learners to use various senses (aural, visual, tactile) concurrently.

Responding to individual needs

Whenever media can be used by individuals (e.g. printed texts or audiocassettes) learners can proceed at their own pace rather than being tied to the 'average' speed dictated by group or class working. Another way of using media to meet individual learners' needs is adapting the style and content of the teaching to maximize understanding. Teacher educators can respond to learners' requests for clarification by modifying their presentation and providing additional media examples to overcome misconceptions or explain things differently. They can also alter the pace of their presentation, going faster or slower or repeating items according to the responses and progress of the learners, or provide media resources for learners to use in their own time.

Such adaptation of teaching to learners' needs and progress can be greatly enhanced by the use of media that enable dialogue to take place. Interactive computer-based materials can be designed to monitor the progress of learners and to adapt the presentation of teaching and tasks to suit individual development. Media that enable two-way communication to take place, for example, audio-conferencing and video-conferencing, can similarly support adaptive ways of teaching, even when the teachers and trainers are remote from one another.

Promoting professional practice and reflection

The presentational and interactive functions of media can be combined when, for example, real-life 'documentary' or 'case study' material is offered for trainees to analyse, evaluate or test or apply principles, procedures or theoretical approaches. This approach can be particularly useful in helping teachers reflect upon and prepare for classroom practice: for example, video sequences demonstrating classroom management issues or teacher-pupil interactions can be viewed by individual trainees or used as the basis of discussion between teacher educators and teachers or teachers and their peers. Short video 'triggers' or 'vignettes' in which statements or scenarios are presented directly and personally to the viewer or listener can help student teachers reflect on how they would react and respond to similar situations in the school environment and show them different strategies. Box 8.2 gives an example of how broadcast television has been used for such purposes.

Box 8.2   Television for teacher development: the *A-Plus* series in Brazil

A-Plus is a daily television series designed to stimulate interest in education, teaching and learning among teachers and the broader community in Brazil. Taking a journalistic approach, it reaches an audience of 13 million across the country with a regular daily audience of 7 million. Television ownership is high in Brazil and some urban schools record the programmes.

The series is offered by TV-Futura ('The Learning Channel'), a non-profit educational channel sponsored by a consortium of private and public organizations. The purpose of the series is to deal with education matters critically and at a practical level. The fifteen-minute programmes have a magazine format, combining general educational news with an in-depth documentary. Each programme shows two examples of real-life applications of the programme topic (e.g. a method of teaching or how to conduct parent-teacher association meetings). An education expert comments on this in a challenging way or presents arguments designed to provoke debate. Suggestions for further activities and references to other sources of information are given at the end of the programme. Twice a week, the programme is supplemented by two sets of commentaries, one on relevant research, the other on literature helping viewers to apply the topic to real-life situations. The series has no set curriculum, but aims to be responsive to teachers' needs, drawing on several sources of guidance including a phone-in service. TV-Futura states that its mission starts when the broadcast ends, so one of its goals is to mobilize teachers through its Community Mobilization Network. Follow-up activities and monthly meetings are organized around the programmes for teachers' groups who opt in to this service. *A-Plus* provides sixty community officers who facilitate the Community Mobilization Network in support of these activities. Print is used for a bi-monthly newsletter and quarterly magazine, giving programme schedules and background reading.

The series is highly popular because it communicates well with teachers, meets teachers' needs, prompts action and suggests new approaches. It allows teachers to observe, discuss, probe and interact with what other teachers are doing or trying to do. It addresses educational issues determined by teacher interest rather than by the educational authorities. Most teachers view the programmes at home but 12 per cent view them in schools. Reasons given for viewing include personal development (65 per cent), to get lesson plans (39 per cent), to stimulate classroom discussion (30 per cent), and for content information (14 per cent).

The cost per viewer per programme (based on a 7 million audience per day) is less than ten cents (US). However, the initiative is a vulnerable one since it relies totally on private funding and, as an educational television channel, TV-Futura cannot sell advertising to raise funds.

Source: Perraton *et al.* 2001

Promoting dialogue and discussion

A crucial element of active learning is person-to-person communication, particularly where differing perspectives and interpretations are important to developing understanding. Dialogue is essential for the acquisition and development of language and other interpersonal skills. Proficient communication is essential for teachers and must be developed and practised in a variety of contexts (e.g. with small groups of learners, in whole class presentations, with parents, with school managers and colleagues). While it is fairly straightforward to arrange for dialogue and discussion to take place when the teacher and learners are at the same location, difficulties arise when the teacher educators are separated from their learners.

Instructional programmes broadcast via radio or television cannot enable questions to be asked by learners and answered by remote teacher trainers. Nor can recorded audio enable learners of languages to engage in meaningful conversation. However, such one-way media can be used to inform or stimulate dialogue and discussion when combined with other means of communication. For example, teachers learning at a distance can be organized into viewing or listening groups and facilitated by local mentors or tutors to discuss the topics and issues in relation to their particular circumstances and local practices. Feedback to and from the remote locations can be provided by telephone or email. Another kind of model here is interactive radio instruction, where programmes are designed to generate activities and interaction in the participating classrooms, so that the interactivity takes place among those at the point of reception rather than over distance with the programme providers (e.g. Bosch 2001). Box 8.3 provides an example of this.

As well as using media to support discussion across and within groups, communications media can be used to extend learning groups by bringing remote teachers or 'experts' into the educational process, creating larger communities and learning networks. For many years, two-way radio has been used in sparsely populated regions to link teachers, dispersed learners and their parents, for example in the 'Schools of the Air'

Box 8.3   Interactive radio instruction to support teachers of English as a second language in South Africa

The Open Learning Systems Education Trust (OLSET), a non-governmental organization, has been working in South Africa since 1992. Its aim has been to develop a model for teaching English as a second language in South African primary schools, through the medium of interactive radio. Interactive radio is a one-way delivery system which requires learners to be active and responsive to carefully structured radio lessons in real time as they are broadcast. The daily half-hour radio lessons introduce pupils (Grades 1–3) to English through activities such as stories and songs and also make use of posters and classroom materials, workbooks, and comic readers.

However, the majority of teachers also speak English as their second, third or fourth language. Some have low levels of teaching qualifications and are inexperienced in using active learning approaches. So the radio programmes provide support for teachers too. They offer teachers structured, well-designed and carefully graded language lessons which model active learning. The lessons involve teachers as partners in the teaching process by asking them to lead language development activities, such as games or pair-work, and to mediate content, if necessary, in the mother tongue. A teacher's manual is provided together with visits from programme co-ordinators who organize training workshops and teachers' groups, with discussions on how to teach the radio lessons, and how to link the programme with other areas of the primary school curriculum. OLSET's 'English in Action' programme has grown from 14,000 primary school pupils in 1994 to over 500,000 pupils and 11,000 teachers in 2001. The cost per pupil is about US$1 a year, and per teacher, a little over US$1.

Despite its success, the programme struggles to cope with the lack of a consistent policy on educational broadcasting at national and local level and difficulties in negotiating access to airtime. Programmes are produced and recorded by OLSET but delivered through the South African Broadcasting Corporation, which provides free transmission. Problems with transmission in some locations have required the substitution of audio-cassettes, adding additional tasks and costs for the organizers.

Source: Perraton *et al.* 2001

in Australia. Such two-way communication has also been used to increase teachers' motivation, knowledge and skills, making it possible for schools to extend the breadth of their curriculum or improve the quality of their teaching and learning or supplement gaps in their knowledge. Computer-mediated communication is being used for the development of virtual classrooms, with remote teachers and learners contributing on-line via the keyboard, audiographics or desktop audio- or video-conferencing. Applications of these ICT tools are also discussed in Chapter 9.

Extending the curriculum

Various media are used to extend the curriculum in countries or school districts or village schools where there are insufficient numbers of qualified teachers to cover all levels and/or subjects. In Mexico, for example, television and associated workbooks have enabled secondary education to be offered in rural communities (Castro *et al.* 1999) and to support the underqualified teachers there at the same time.

Providing motivation

When media are used in any of the above ways, they can provide invaluable motivation and reinforcement for the learners, though much depends on the quality of the design and how they are used in particular contexts. Although it is often difficult to quantify increased motivation, there is evidence from learners that they appreciate and benefit from variety (although novelty for its own sake may be counter-productive). Where programmes are relevant and worth watching, teachers may be motivated by those that show them how to tackle classroom problems and be reassured by finding that other teachers share their experience and concerns.

The characteristics of the media

Some media are essentially for one-way communication – presenting information from a knowledgeable source to the learners. Classic examples are the lecture and the book. Various new media can extend the possibilities of presenting learning materials on a one-to-many basis and the ways in which the learners can engage with a body of information or data. While some media (e.g. lectures, live broadcast radio and television programmes) take place in real time and are transitory, others (e.g. books, video-cassettes, CD-ROMs) store information for later retrieval whenever required.

The terms synchronous and asynchronous are used to differentiate between media that require concurrent or real-time participation, and those that do not (see Table 8.1). In all cases, the content is finite and determined by the producers of the material.

Table 8.1 Synchronous and asynchronous one-way media

Examples of synchronous one-way media	Examples of asynchronous one-way media
Lectures	Books and printed texts
Radio and television broadcasts	Audio-cassettes and audio CDs Video-cassettes, CD-ROMs and DVDs. Certain applications of the Internet and the web where information or data can be acquired from a 'remote' source without the facility for users to contribute to or make amendments (as in a library)

Table 8.2 Synchronous and asynchronous two-way media

Examples of synchronous two-way media	Examples of asynchronous two-way media
Telephone	Fax
Two-way radio	Email
Audio- and video-conferencing	Computer conferencing
Computer-based messaging or 'chat' facilities	

Some other media allow two-way communication and may be seen as extensions of correspondence (written words) and conversations (spoken words). In educational contexts, these media can be used to develop and support interaction between people on a one-to-one, a one-to-many or a many-to-many basis. Again their use may be synchronous or asynchronous, as illustrated in Table 8.2.

Although similar material can be conveyed in different ways (e.g. by radio, audio-cassette or audio CD), each means of delivery enables the learners to control and use the materials in different ways. For example, a radio programme must be listened to when broadcast and offers no opportunities for learners to control or interact with its content or structure. On the other hand, learners can hear the same programme on audio-cassette or audio CD whenever it is most appropriate or convenient, and use it actively – stopping, replaying or missing out sections as required. The index facility of an audio CD gives the user precise control over the location, playing, stopping or replaying of segments as required.

SELECTING MEDIA FOR PARTICULAR NEEDS AND CIRCUMSTANCES

The emergence of digital information and communication technology has had a tremendous impact on all forms of media – both the hardware (the generic term for any capital equipment, including communication and electric power infrastructure) and the software (the computer programs, tape cassettes, compact disks, DVDs, films, printed texts and graphic materials). The convergence of digital audio, video and data transmission into manageable formats enables increased access and applications of media for distance teacher education. The availability of increasingly user-friendly media for teacher education is emerging more quickly than most educators realize. This leaves gaps in the understanding and skills of many of those designing programmes, especially in contexts where these technologies are new.

A great deal of the technological and media innovation does not occur in the educational but in the private sector, driven by the need to increase media access and gain greater market share of viewers, listeners, readers and 'web surfers'. Private-sector media researchers strive to develop products, services and techniques that will capture the imagination of young and old. These early adopters of innovation are frequently the forerunners of change in applications of educational technology (Rogers 1995). Educators need to remain current by keeping pace with the latest media and ICT developments through ongoing research and experimentation with new products, services and methods. The challenge for teacher educators is the same: to select media that match the means, methods and motivations of the users.

Decision-making levels

Selecting media hardware and software for teacher training and the providing institutions requires careful consideration of numerous factors. Apart from considerations of cost, which we return to later, decision-making begins with a scrutiny of the context and magnitude of any initiative for change. Planners first need to conduct a thorough analysis of the conditions in the environment in which the change will take place. One way of organizing this is in relation to the three broad levels of magnitude that typically influence media-based change: the mega system level, the macro and the micro. Analysis of the levels assists selection of media and, in fact, the choice is shaped by identifying the appropriate level involved as indicated below.

Mega system

When the change is to be on a global, regional, national, or provincial level, government endorsement and policy, legislation and financial support are needed to implement it. The use of mass media, including audio, video and data transmission via satellite, might be included at the mega system level. However, the change process is generally slow and complex, requiring the co-operation of various ministries, departments, private companies and other agencies.

Macro system

When the change is planned for districts, municipalities, multi-site institutions or very large educational institutions, planning and implementing change at this level is still complex but generally easier to manage than mega system changes. This is because of the proximity of locations and the relatively smaller numbers of agencies and people involved. At this level, the choice of media generally focuses more on programming through local area infrastructure and networks. Distribution of multiple copies of audio, video and print media is more achievable.

Micro system

When the change is limited to medium-sized and small institutions (colleges, teachers' centres and schools), or within selected faculties or departments or even limited to an individual, then decision-making is localized and generally requires less time than at the mega and macro levels. Small groups or individuals are generally the champions of introducing changes at the micro system level.

Cost considerations

A predominant concern is financial – finding the financial means to procure the capital equipment or hardware and to guarantee the long-term commitment needed to fund the recurring costs of purchasing, renting or developing operating software. The capital cost of the technology is only a portion of the long-term cost to the institution (or the schools or the learners). There is also the cost of providing, updating and ultimately replacing the necessary software, copyright agreements, equipment, maintenance and capital depreciation, and insurance. Decision-makers need to balance the cost of using various media with a rational explanation of the return on investment.

Another factor is teacher mastery of the skills essential for effective use of the technology and the amount and cost of time required to produce good-quality materials and learning systems. Ensuring adequate skills also requires investment in training. The proper selection and use of various media formats certainly enhances the teaching and learning experience. Conversely, improper use of media has a negative effect on the teacher, the learners and the institution. Overuse of the same techniques and media becomes mundane and boring, especially for the learners. Decisions on what, when and how to use media are crucial to the effective application of the available technology, but this requires informed choices. The kind of information required is given in Table 8.3. This provides a matrix of available media, key indicators for selection, and outlines some

Table 8.3 A comparison of the advantages and disadvantages of different media used by teachers

MEDIUM	Good for	Advantages	Disadvantages
Printed text	*Imparting information*; telling a story; presenting an argument; describing events, activities and processes; posing questions and giving details of exercises; providing accounts of human interactions; etc.	Very familiar and flexible to use (individually or shared with others); portable; a 'permanent' resource that can be referred to many times. Learner does not require a power source or special equipment. Can include diagrams, tables, illustrations, images, etc.	One-way communication – readers cannot 'talk back' to the author (but can use ideas in text as basis of discussion). However, readers sometimes consider printed text to contain 'the truth' – not to be questioned or interrogated. Usually has linear structure (telling a story or presenting an argument).
Audio (radio, audio-cassettes and CDs, audio on the Internet, etc.)	*Sound resources*, e.g. music and performance, non-native languages, natural and mechanical sounds, etc. *Presentations, talks*, etc. *Tutoring and guidance linked to other media*, e.g. interactive exercises, overviews and summaries of main points, revision, updating, etc. Native language introductions to resources in other languages.	*Radio* – can deliver quite cheaply over a very wide area. Offers immediacy through 'live' or 'almost live' transmission. *Audio-cassettes and CDs* – a 'permanent' resource that can be referred to many times. Learners have some *flexibility and control* over when (and possibly where) they listen – use is not tied to transmission schedules and study can be undertaken when most appropriate.	*Radio* transmissions not always scheduled at appropriate times; impossible to pause for reflection, discussion, application, etc.; must have equipment in working order. A 'transitory' resource, unless users make a recording. *Audio-cassettes and CDs* require access to equipment and distribution of materials.
Two-way audio (audio teleconferencing, two-way radio, etc.)	*Dialogue* between two or more people, immediate feedback to questions, discussion, group activities and problem-solving, etc.	Enables teachers and learners to ask and answer questions in real time – for clarification, active learning, discussion, etc.	Synchronous – all participants must be available at same time and in a location with suitable equipment.
Video (broadcast television, satellite and/or cable TV, video-cassette, CD-ROM or DVD)	*Visualization* – where this is important for learning – demonstrations, animation, performance, 'vicarious' visits or experiences, real-life cases or examples, etc.	*Television transmissions* can reach a widely dispersed audience and be very topical or up to date. Programmes can motivate and hold attention through use of narrative structure, by providing 'concrete' (real life) examples to which learners can relate, by making learning less impersonal, etc.	*Broadcast TV* – a 'transitory' resource, unless users make a recording. Transmissions require all participants to be available at same time and in a location with suitable equipment. Programmes usually have a linear structure, a fixed length and a regular schedule.

Table 8.3 (continued)

MEDIUM	Good for	Advantages	Disadvantages
	Can work at an *affective* level – conveying feelings and emotions, challenging attitudes and preconceptions, etc. Humanizes 'remote' teaching.	*Video-cassette, CD-ROM or DVD* – a 'permanent' resource that can be referred to many times. Can contain many sequences in a non-linear structure – users can access any of these as and when appropriate for their learning needs.	For most effective use, programmes or sequences must be closely related to or integrated with other study materials or learning activities.
Two-way video (video-conferencing, interactive video)	Dialogue between two or more people, discussion, group activities and problem-solving, etc.	Enables teachers and learners to ask and answer questions in real time – for clarification, active learning, discussion, etc.	Synchronous – all participants must be available at same time and in a location with suitable equipment. A 'transitory' resource, unless users make a recording.
Computer-based learning materials (not requiring connection to a network)	Combining features of text, sound and pictures (still and moving) – and the educational benefits of each. Engaging learners with interactive tasks; adapting sequence to users' needs and progress; enabling learners to manipulate or explore information and data; providing a bank of resources, etc.	*CD-ROM or DVD* – a 'permanent' resource that can be referred to many times. More likely to have a non-linear structure. Learners can search a large collection of information – text, pictures (still or moving), sounds for resource-based learning. Interactive exercises enable the presentation of information to be combined with opportunities for learners to interrogate and experiment with resources and for feedback and progress to be directly related to individual users' needs and development (adaptive).	Access to suitable equipment of required specification. Navigation and outcomes: learners must have a clear understanding of the tasks they are expected to undertake or goals to be achieved – otherwise they might 'get lost' or be overwhelmed by the volume of information and/or complexity of the structure. Reading large amounts of text from a screen is often difficult for learners – printing extensive amounts can be very expensive for users.
Internet materials and resources	Combining features of text, sound and pictures (still and moving) – and the educational benefits of each.	Can give learners access to documents and other sources of information, collections of pictures, sounds, moving images, etc.	Access to suitable equipment of required specification and connection to an appropriate network.

Engaging learners with interactive tasks; giving them greater control over what is studied, when it is studied and in what order resources are accessed.	Educational sites can be created to serve the needs of particular groups of learners, providing study advice and guidance, activities and exercises as well as links to a 'library' of resources (N.B. Copyright laws must be observed when linking directly to external sites). Easier to modify and update than printed texts, videos, etc. Does not incur the costs of making, storing and distributing multiple copies of teaching/learning materials (N.B. Does require technical as well as educational development costs).	Reading large amounts of text from a screen is often difficult for learners – printing extensive amounts can be very expensive for users. Navigation and outcomes: Learners must have a clear understanding of the tasks they are expected to undertake or goals to be achieved – otherwise they might 'get lost' or be overwhelmed by the volume of information and/or complexity of the structure. Learners' searching and evaluation skills need to be developed for effective use of on-line resources. Sources on the World Wide Web are currently dominated by North American and/or English language sites.
Internet communications (computer conferencing can be text-only or may involve audio or video elements) *Dialogue between two or more people, feedback to questions, discussion, group activities and problem-solving, etc.*	Communication can be in real time (synchronous) or over an extended period (asynchronous). Synchronous activities have the advantage of immediacy, but do require all participants to be available at same time and in a location with suitable equipment. Asynchronous communication gives participants more flexibility and time to reflect on questions and answers. Text messages can be stored as a 'permanent' resource that can be referred to many times.	Access to suitable equipment of required specification and connection to an appropriate network. Teachers and learners need to develop on-line communication skills in order to make effective use of participation.

Source: Perraton *et al.* 2001

of the advantages and disadvantages for use in teacher education. It does not include estimated costs for the development, procurement and use of media. The broad range in cost for equipment procurement, operation and software development makes it difficult to quantify the real cost of media usage. It is equally difficult to determine the return on investment. In addition to direct costs, two other factors must be considered: the number of learners viewing or using the media and the value-added effectiveness of the selected medium or media mix compared with the alternatives.

Scale and selection

The selection of a medium is greatly influenced by the size of the audience or number of learners. As a general rule, the greater the number of people, the more cost-effective the medium and the easier it is to justify the investment of time, money, human resources and facilities. Using a mass medium such as television for teacher training has high production costs but may be justified in situations such as in the People's Republic of China where approximately 10 million teachers work in primary and secondary schools. As an example of mega system change, since 1986 state-operated television in China has provided educational programming to help teachers upgrade their qualifications and improve their knowledge. However, it must also be said that the overriding characteristic of curriculum development and teacher education in China has been the central control of a nationally unified curriculum. Dividing the total production and presentation cost by the very high number of learners (teachers) involved results in low cost per learner and a potentially high return on investment for media development.

Canada and China provide contrasting examples of cost. The two countries, the first and second largest in the world, are similar in size but vastly different in population. China's population of 1.3 billion people is approximately forty times that of Canada's 33 million. Unlike China's centrally controlled education system, jurisdiction of education in Canada is a provincial responsibility. Consequently, there are thirteen ministries of education (one ministry per province). The Canadian model of educational governance frequently results in costly duplication of efforts, significantly lowering the return on investment particularly in media development and distribution. Devolution and pluralism come at a cost.

The final consideration when choosing the most appropriate media is to assess how the selected medium or combination of media will enhance learning compared with other media formats. Planners and developers of programmes need to determine the instructional advantage of using one format over another before deciding on the most appropriate. One way of doing this is to prepare a clear written description of the desired outcome and result of each teaching or learning activity. An excellent reality check when selecting a medium is to consider alternative instructional methods to achieve the same learning outcome. Then, it is possible to question the reasons for selecting one medium over another. For example, is it to:

- describe a situation or condition better, to stimulate learner reflection and reaction?
- help a greater number of students to understand concepts or issues more easily?
- illustrate ideas and teaching practices more graphically?
- demonstrate classroom processes?
- demonstrate examples of skills in various teaching situations?
- save time and energy in achieving the same learning outcomes?
- show different teaching styles at work and structure reflection on models of good teaching?
- develop attitudes and values which are thought desirable in teachers?
- use the media because the hardware is readily available and the programming (software) matches learner needs and desired learning outcomes?
- demonstrate a variety of innovative methods and techniques suitable for different teaching and learning environments and resource levels?
- promote critical thinking on key topics of current interest and concern to teachers?
- compensate for weaknesses in teachers' subject knowledge and lesson planning?
- improve the quality of learning materials and programmes?

If the answer is 'yes' to seven or more of the above questions, it is likely that the selection of media is appropriate to the learners' needs and the institutional providers of teacher education.

DESIGNING AND DEVELOPING MEDIA

In some teacher-training contexts, the teacher educators and trainers will have little or no influence on how media materials are designed and developed. This may be due to limitations in the infrastructure or media equipment available, or because the materials are designed and developed as part of a national or regional initiative. However, there is still much to be gained from developing the skills of the teacher-trainers and tutors in the effective and flexible use of media resources available (for example, integrating class-based discussion with individual study of media resources or developing supplementary materials to localize standardized packages). In other situations, there will be possibilities for teacher educators to become involved to some degree with instructional design and teamwork in materials development.

Instructional design

Whether teacher educators produce, adopt or adapt the materials for their courses and programmes, it is important that they apply the principles of instructional design. Regardless of the media selected, attention to quality is essential. Visual and audio media not only amplify the messages conveyed to the learners, but magnify any errors in the instructional design, development or delivery of the material. Print material that is badly constructed and presented without adequate illustrations, audio material that is inappropriate, improperly sequenced or barely audible, and video images that are not clearly visible or relevant can have an extremely negative impact on the learning and learners' attitudes to learning from the media.

There is not space here to detail all of the techniques of instructional design but there are numerous excellent books available on this topic. They are consistent in their advice and in urging designers to begin with learners' needs and circumstances, to sequence material and to provide appropriate ways for learners to check their own progress. In summary, when designing and developing instructional materials, the emphasis must be on quality, relevance, and ease of access and use by teacher educators and learners alike. The more complex and sophisticated the media, the greater the possibility of inaccessibility at the time and place needed.

Teamwork in developing media

There may be times when an individual and multi-talented educator can design, develop, produce and deliver instructional media with little or no assistance from other skilled professionals, but the vast majority of quality media production requires a team approach. The size and diversity of each team will differ depending on:

- the level of the project (whether it is 'mega', 'macro' or 'micro');
- selection of the most appropriate media;
- the time available for media design and development;
- the nature of the instructional content;
- the funding available for the media design, development and delivery.

Instructional materials produced for the mega and macro systems levels generally have the resources and time to employ teams of specialists for preparing materials. Such teams typically include the teacher educators (the content or subject specialists), instructional designers, graphic designers (and possibly photographers), content editors and substantive editors, copyright clearance specialist, desktop publishers, video and audio specialists and web designers. As the size of the team increases, so does the complexity and the need for someone to act as project director.

Teacher-trainers with little or no experience of designing and developing instructional materials using different media might consider such a team approach unnecessary or extravagant, but experienced materials producers are well aware of and respect the expertise available through such an approach. Regardless of the media selected, the quality and clarity of the final product is greatly enhanced by the team effort.

Whenever a media development team is formed for a specific project, there is a need to ensure that all of the members understand and respect one another's areas of expertise and experience and develop a shared understanding of the project's purpose and goals. It is not unusual to find that people who usually work in separate fields have rather different concepts, attitudes, approaches and concerns. For example, content specialists' concern will be the content and clarity of understanding, but a graphic designer's main concern may be that all materials produced are visually attractive (though they might not communicate effectively with the learners), and a video producer's notions of what makes 'good television' may be in conflict with some specific teaching or learning goals. It is always advisable to make explicit, at an early stage of the team's work, what educational outcomes are expected from the development project, how these are to be realized, and how the expertise of the individual team members is expected to contribute to these outcomes.

An example of a team approach on a macro level change initiative for teacher education may be seen in a project funded by Canadian International Development Agency (CIDA) in Malawi. The country was faced with a shortage of about 8,000 qualified secondary school teachers but existing teachers' colleges had too limited capacity to train them through conventional on-campus residential programmes. The solution for increasing the quality and quantity of secondary school teachers was to design, develop and implement an in-service teacher education programme using a combination of intensive on-campus residential sessions and distance education. The curriculum and instruction on-campus provided the main source of content for the distance education modules. Constraints such as poor communication and electric power infrastructure, low income and limited budgets influenced the decision to select print media for the distance education instructional modules.

In Malawi, course authors worked with a team of specialists to write the content for each of the modules. Once completed, each module was sent as an email attachment to Simon Fraser University in British Columbia, Canada where another team of editors, instructional designers and other specialists further developed the modules. The final stage of module production was to send the completed files back to Malawi for printing, production and use. This international team approach to producing good-quality instructional materials for teacher education is an example of how ICT can be used to combine the strengths and resources of institutions halfway around the world from each other.

Formative and summative evaluation of media

Whether media-based education materials are developed by multi-talented individuals or interdisciplinary teams, evaluation should always be planned into the development process. Evaluation is essential to determine how well materials serve the educational purpose for which they were designed. It should address issues of access and usability, and learning effectiveness. It should not simply focus on the technology and software design but also be concerned with the context of use and pedagogical structure and design. There are two main types of evaluation: formative and summative.

Formative evaluation

This takes place during the materials development stage. Media and materials are piloted with sample learning groups with a view to resolving any problems or difficulties before an improved version is prepared for wider use. The evaluation findings are primarily intended to inform the materials developers in making change and improvements.

Summative evaluation

This gauges the overall suitability and effectiveness of 'completed' educational materials and resources. The purpose of the summative evaluation is to assess the outcomes in terms of overall success and effectiveness. The findings are more likely to be directed towards policy-makers, funding bodies or sponsors and local or national government agencies. Such bodies often require evidence of the effectiveness of the programme or project (to meet demands for accountability) or to persuade others that such approaches can be used in similar situations (to disseminate best practice). Evaluation findings may also be required by a variety of stakeholders – managers, providers, teachers, teachers' unions and employers – to verify that learning with educational media is effective and worth undertaking.

The precise nature of the questions asked in any particular study will depend upon a number of contextual factors. However, in all situations there are likely to be issues for investigation in relation to:

- technical and operational factors, e.g. access to equipment and infrastructure; delivery; ease of operation or navigation, legibility and design;
- pedagogical design factors, e.g. appropriateness of teaching strategies and approach; range of activities and tasks; supporting worthwhile learning outcomes;
- contextual factors, e.g. the integration of media within the course or curriculum and the assessment and examination requirements and whether the materials increase or decrease flexibility for learners in terms of when, where and how they study.

CONCLUSIONS

This chapter has shown that educational media can be used to enhance teacher education in a variety of ways. The appropriate selection and use of media can be complex and subject to potentially conflicting interests, constraints, expectations and demands. Whatever the level of decision-making involved, planners may find the following principles a useful guide:

- Educational concerns should always have higher priority than technologies; consider what are the teaching/learning challenges in a particular context.
- No single medium can support all aspects of teacher education and training; consider how media in combination could be used to satisfy the full range of needs and contexts.
- Access and availability are vital preconditions for training teachers via media; without access, no media materials will achieve their goals.
- One important goal should be to exploit the particular strengths and characteristics of any available medium or media.
- When media are used in combination, it will be difficult to attribute 'learning gains' to any one component. In judging the effectiveness of media and materials, the qualitative as well as quantitative outcomes should be evaluated.

The only certainty about the future of educational media is that there will be continuous change in the hardware and software, in the availability of systems and facilities, and in the media expectations and experiences of users. We predict, however, that the inevitable technological and infrastructural changes will be of much greater magnitude than the changes in the fundamental educational concerns and problems in designing effective materials for teacher education and training.

REFERENCES

Bosch, A. (2001) 'Interactive radio instruction for mathematics: applications and adaptations from around the world', *TechKnowLogia*, March/April. Available on-line at <http://www.techknowlogia.org/welcome.asp?IssueNumber=10>

Castro, C. de M., Wolff, L. and Garcia, N. (1999) 'Mexico's Telesecundaria: bringing education by television to rural areas', *TechKnowLogia*, September/October. Available on-line at <http://www.techknowlogia.org/TKL_active_pages2/CurrentArticles/main.asp?IssueNumber=1&FileType=HTML&ArticleID=6>

Kirkwood, A. (1998) 'New media mania: can information and communication technologies enhance the quality of open and distance learning?' *Distance Education*, 19: 228–41.

Perraton, H., Robinson, B. and Creed, C. (2001) *Teacher Education through Distance Learning: Technology, Curriculum, Evaluation, Cost*. Paris: UNESCO.

Rogers, E.M. (1995) *Diffusion of Innovations* (4th edn), New York: Free Press.

Chapter 9

Uses of information and communication technologies in teacher education

Betty Collis and Insung Jung

The following chapter discusses the use of information and communication technologies (ICT) for teacher training. It starts by providing an overview of ICT applications and their functions for learning purposes and drawing a distinction between ICT applications as core or complementary to the learning process. Via a variety of examples, we show that ICT use is not only a matter of new possibilities but brings with it new implications and new challenges. We extract key factors that can stimulate or frustrate the use of ICT for teacher education and teachers' initial and ongoing development. The chapter concludes with a discussion of key future developments in teacher training made possible by developments in ICT.

THE EVOLVING USE OF ICT IN TEACHER EDUCATION

'ICT' stands for 'information and communication technologies'. Information technologies involve computers. Communication technologies can include telephone and video-conferencing, but in the combination, 'ICT' is generally taken to mean technologies that support communication via computers. Currently, this implies the Internet or local networks, email, and World Wide Web technologies. We begin with a brief historical perspective on the evolution of ICT in teacher training.

In the late 1970s a new wave of teacher training emerged, whose major focus was introducing teachers to microcomputers and programming. Students and teachers alike learned languages such as LOGO and BASIC. The LOGO language, and to a lesser extent, BASIC, were vehicles not only to create useful (small) programs, but also to learn how to program, to control the computer, to be 'ready for the information age'. Also, LOGO led the way in terms of intertwining information technology and a curriculum area, as LOGO programming was primarily used in the context of exploring mathematical ideas.

The focus on teaching teachers how to program faded during the 1980s as a number of regional and national initiatives in Britain, Sweden, the Netherlands, Australia, France, Mexico, the United States, Canada, Israel and other countries led the way to the professional development of educational software. Schools needed support staff to select, license, and install the software packages and to train their teachers how to use such packages. Teacher training began to switch towards introductions to the use of these professionally made software packages, training which was sometimes provided by teacher training colleges or faculties of education, sometimes by support groups financed by ministries of education, and sometimes by representatives of computer companies. Also, the educational value of using computer software that was not necessarily developed for learning, particularly word processing and spreadsheet applications, became known, and teacher training began to routinely include courses on how to use and apply such generic applications in the classroom. A persistent concern was the growing divide between teachers in wealthier and less-wealthy countries due to differences in access to computers, appropriate teacher training, and (costly) educational software.

A major breakthrough in computer use in education came with the emergence of the Internet and the web as technologies commonly available to individuals during the mid-1990s. A new phase of computer use began and is still continuing for teachers and teacher-educators. In this phase, teachers are still making use of stand-alone computers, but are increasingly having online contact with other teachers, teacher-trainers, and networked resources via the Internet or intranets. This has powerful implications for ICT in teacher training. Teacher education frequently focuses on how to make use of the Internet and the web and teachers themselves are learning via the Internet and the web.

TEACHER TRAINING IN HOW TO USE ICT

For *teacher training in how to use ICT*, the major types of ICT products currently being studied by teachers include: tutorial software and simulations for knowledge transfer and conceptual development, email and conferencing software for communication support, groupware and other tools for collaborative learning, concept mapping and other tools for conceptual manipulation, software for access to educational databases, specialized computer-based tools for subject areas such as mathematics and technical drawing, software for testing and assessment, and different forms of web-based resources (Collis 2001). Video segments are increasingly a part of Web and CD-ROM resources. For all of these, the focus of teacher training is how to use such products in the classroom or off-campus. Teachers face new roles with respect to using ICT, being called upon to:

(a) Select and use appropriate ICT tools and support students in the use of these tools.
(b) Think of new forms of student activity and determine how ICT can help support these.
(c) Learn how to set up and monitor ICT-related learning activities.
(d) Determine and communicate how learners will be evaluated in the new forms of ICT-related activities, particularly for group projects and peer evaluations.
(e) Monitor and intervene when there are problems with group work or using the technology.
(f) Manage contact with students, web submissions, e-mail, discussions, and comments on each other's work.
(g) Develop new methods of grading student performance.
(h) Monitor the quality of what students find via the Web and share with others.
(j) Keep records of student participation and process for monitoring and grading.
(k) Manage incoming and outgoing e-mail and contacts with individual students.

(Collis and Moonen 2001: 106)

Teacher education must help the teacher to use ICT in all of these activities.

TEACHER TRAINING WITH ICT

For *teacher training with ICT*, the major ICT products are web-based course management systems and other forms of database-driven web systems, simpler web environments, and email and computer conferencing software (increasingly integrated within web environments). Web environments or systems offering an integrated range of tools to support learning and communication are becoming a major medium for learning in every discipline, and thus also for teacher training. Table 9.1 provides an overview of how current web environments can support teacher training with ICT, even if the teachers or trainee teachers are not in the same place at the same time.

ICT AS CORE OR COMPLEMENTARY IN THE TEACHER-TRAINING PROCESS

ICT may be the major or core technology in a learning setting, or a complement (Collis and Moonen 2001). A core technology refers to the major way of organizing the learning experience, the component around

Table 9.1 Web-based technologies to support teacher training courses

Course component	Increasing flexibility in participation	Supporting new ways of teaching and learning
General course organization	– Post all announcements about course procedures on a course web-site – Make a calendar of relevant dates and times available on the web-site	– Have teachers add links to web-based resources and to the work and homepages of experts related to their courses and the subjects they will teach
Lectures and contact sessions	Extend the lectures and contact sessions for persons who cannot always be present so that: – the most relevant points are expressed in notes (PowerPoint, document files, images) available via the web-site – discussions and presentations during the class session can be captured as digital audio and/or video and linked to the course web-site for later reference	– Extend the interactivity of the contact sessions by having teachers work in small groups and post the results of their discussions on the course web-site – Extend the impact of the contact sessions by having all teachers reflect on some aspect of the sessions and communicate with each other about the aspect with some form of structured comment via the web page
Self-study and exercises; practical sessions	Assemble a set of resources (text as well as images and video) which the teachers can refer to in terms of lesson planning or course materials. Teachers can compare their own experiences as teachers with resources in the collection (available via the course web-site or a CD-ROM) and also add information (text and images, and in special cases, video segments) about their own experiences	– Stimulate communication and interaction among the teachers via the web-site or email. Teachers can build up a portfolio of instructional ideas or experiences, saving the files in a shared workplace environment that can be electronically accessed by other teachers

	– When student teachers are engaged in teaching practice or practical work in schools, invite regular reflective reports and stimulate email contact among supervising teachers in the schools, staff in the teacher-training institutions and the teachers themselves. Web-based discussion boards are a good tool
Multi-session projects or activities	– Make available shared workspace tools along with other communication and reporting tools in the web-site to allow group members to work collaboratively on projects at one site or at different locations – Use real-time communication tools via the Internet for teachers in different locations who wish to meet electronically and discuss their teaching experiences, to support action-research projects by teachers, and to make contact with subject specialists as individuals or via professional associations
Evaluation and assessment	– Use the web environment to submit assignments electronically without having to come to a physical location. – Provide self-evaluation tools and guides for reflective practice – Integrate new forms of assessment, such as teachers maintaining their own portfolios, within the course web environment. Lead the teachers to comment on each other's portfolios
General communication	– Add a communication centre to a course web-site so that groups of teachers as well as individuals can be easily contacted via email – Use real-time collaborative tools so that teachers can see and/or hear their instructor or each other during a fixed-time appointment, but without being face-to-face – Add a web board for discussion about course topics as a major activity in the course; have the teachers take responsibility for moderating the discussions, adding links to external resources to justify their comments when appropriate – Involve experts from outside the course to join in or lead the discussions

Source: Collis and Moonen 2001: 83–5

which all other components are planned. In traditional teacher train-ing, for example, the core technology is the face-to-face classroom session, led by the teacher trainer. Without the core technology more or less as planned, the learning experience is likely to be unable to continue. In contrast, complementary technologies are optional, serving a valuable function but able to be compensated for via the core technology if so needed, or dropped altogether if not functioning or feasible. When an ICT product is the core technology, all of those using it are vulnerable to problems of access, costs or breakdowns. When an ICT product is only a complement, it can be dropped from the learning setting if its use becomes a problem. In terms of *learning with ICT*, web-based environments are frequently becoming core technologies, especially when some of the teachers or trainee teachers are participating at a distance. When ICT prod-ucts are used as complementary technologies for teacher education, these products most typically include email, web resources, databases of elec-tronic teaching resources, as well as individual computer-based learning resources.

Combining these two dimensions, learning *how* to use ICT and learn-ing *via* ICT and ICT as core technology or complementary technology, gives the approach to analysing ICT in teacher training shown in Figure 9.1.

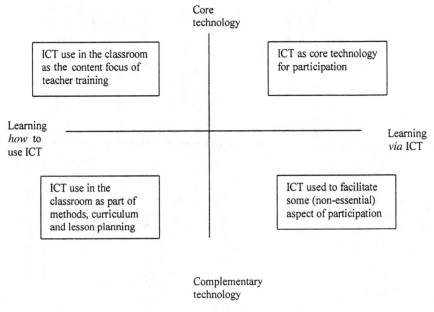

Figure 9.1 Categories for ICT in teacher training

The categories shown in Figure 9.1 can help position the examples of ICT used in teacher training discussed later in this chapter.

The upper-left quadrant 'ICT use in the classroom as the content focus of teacher training' refers to helping teachers gain competence with ICT, for example, with specific software packages or the Internet. The lower-left quadrant includes courses in which ICT use (predominately subject-specific resources or general applications software) plays a part, but not the major part, for example, in courses where teachers learn the method-ology of teaching in their subject areas or focus on students with certain learning characteristics or difficulties. The upper-right quadrant relates to ICT (predominately web environments) as the tool used to support flexible learning for teachers and particularly for specialist or postgradu-ate school- or home-based study for teachers, *just-in-time* professional development including networking with other teachers, mentoring new teachers, and inter-regional or international collaboration. The online learn-ing networks for teachers provided in many parts of the world and shown later in this chapter are examples of teacher learning via ICT as a core technology. The lower-right quadrant includes examples of ICT (pre-dominately email and web) used to bridge theory and practice, support trainee or in-service teachers in their in-school activities, help teachers to manage student assignments, student queries and feedback, facilitate access to resources, and support partnerships between schools, univer-sities, and the larger community.

APPLICATIONS: TRAINING ABOUT ICT USE AND TRAINING VIA ICT USE

ICT as a focus of initial teacher training: the Singapore experience

In 1997, Singapore's Ministry of Education launched the Masterplan for IT in Education to ensure that all students have the knowledge, skills and confidence to compete in a constantly changing technological envir-onment. This Masterplan aimed to train every teacher in the use of ICT for teaching, equip trainee teachers with core ICT teaching skills, and involve institutions of higher learning and industry as partners with schools.

Singapore's only pre-service teacher training institute, the National Institute of Education (NIE), was entrusted with integrating ICT into initial teacher-training programmes. NIE developed and began imple-menting the new ICT plan in 1998, identifying four main areas needing change: curriculum, physical and technological infrastructure, human resource infrastructure, and R&D in the use of ICT in education. For the purposes of this chapter, we focus on how NIE has revised its curriculum to promote ICT use in the classroom by future teachers (Jung in press).

The curriculum was revised to include three kinds of ICT courses for student teachers: basic ICT-skill workshops, a thirty-hour ICT foundation course, and a twenty-six-hour elective course. In addition, 6–12 hours of ICT integration into each curricular subject was recommended. The basic ICT skill workshops, which have to be paid for by students, are provided by external organizations and cover word processing, PowerPoint, Internet literacy, and other technical skills. The thirty-hour ICT foundation course, Instructional Technology, is offered by the Division of Instructional Sciences (DIS) and covers: learning, thinking and the effective use of instructional technologies in the classroom; instructional planning models; selecting, creating, evaluating, and integrating instructional technologies and resource materials; promoting creativity and complex thinking through IT project work activities; and organizing and managing instructional activities with appropriate IT resources in the classroom. The student teachers are required to prepare computer-based micro lessons, and at the end of the course the better lessons are selected, edited and published in CD-ROM and distributed to schools for use by teachers. The twenty-six-hour elective, Message Design and Computer-based Instruction, is provided by DIS and covers the design and production of computer-based instruction.

Besides taking these courses, the NIE Diploma in Education students have five weeks' teaching practice during the first year of their pre-service training and ten weeks during the second, during which time, depending on the school's ICT infrastructure, they are expected to use ICT in their teaching. When interviewed about the new teacher training curriculum, the student teachers agreed that the foundation course provided useful pedagogical strategies for the use of ICT in classroom teaching. In particular, they appreciated being able to download basic information and materials from the Internet. However, they reported that thirty hours of instruction were not enough to gain ICT proficiency, and some wanted more ICT integration in the practice.

ICT as part of teacher training methodology

A number of web-based programmes have been developed for this purpose.

Captured Wisdom <http://www.ncrel.org/cw/> is a US resource developed by the federally funded North Central Technology in Education Consortium for K-12 teachers, school administrators and adult literacy educators. It uses videotape and CD-ROM to help teachers see how technology can be integrated into their work. After viewing video descriptions and demonstrations in these CD-ROMs, teachers' focus groups then discuss the strategies and techniques of classroom management, assessment, etc.

The School Administrators' Technology Integration Resource (SATIR-RITAS) <www.satir-ritas.org> is a bilingual Canadian initiative providing tools and resources to help school administrators successfully integrate the Internet and other ICT into their schools' curriculum.

The Korea National Open University <http://www.knou.ac.kr>, with the support of the Korean government, created a sixty-hour nationwide distance training programme for primary school teachers using cable TV as the core technology and a self-study textbook and two-way video-conferencing as supplementary media. The programme has been delivered twice a year, each time with 1,000 primary school teachers, administrators and school principals participating.

The Shoma Teacher Development Programme <http://www.shoma.co.za/>, a programme supported by various ICT companies and South Africa's national and provincial Departments of Education, uses satellite TV, Internet technology and collaborative lesson planning to support in-service training for underqualified teachers in South Africa. Its primary foci are the South African Government's 2005 Outcomes Based Education programme, teaching methodologies and classroom assessment. Teachers have access to video materials, the Internet, and other learning support through eight training centres, each of which provides a broadcast room, a computer room, and a lesson development room.

ICT as a core technology in teacher education

Websites have been developed for this purpose too.

The Virtual High School (VHS) <http://vhs.concord.org> is a US non-profit organization that facilitates collaboration between participating secondary schools. Students and teachers are expected to attend their VHS NetCourse on a daily basis (or, for students on block schedules, at least three times a week). Participating schools must provide release time for their VHS teacher and a VHS site co-ordinator who acts as a contact for the VHS students and provides technical and administrative support to all local VHS participants. Site co-ordinators are trained in an eight-week online site co-ordinators orientation programme. VHS has developed two graduate-level online professional development courses for teachers, a twenty-six-week teachers learning conference, designed to enable teachers to become online course instructors and course developers; and a fifteen-week NetCourse instructional methodologies programme, designed to provide instruction on the pedagogy, methodology, and moderation skills required to teach an existing NetCourse of VHS.

LearnLink <http://www.aed.org/learnlink> is operated by the Academy for Educational Development (AED), supported by USAID and AED, and has implemented computer-mediated professional development programmes to improve training and support services for teachers in Guatemala, Morocco, Namibia, Uganda and Brazil (Fontaine 2000). The Guatemalan *Proyecto 'Enlace Quiche'* (Quiche Networking Project) uses ICT to train future teachers in Mayan languages to help strengthen cultural identity in indigenous communities. The project focuses on developing culturally appropriate Mayan language instructional materials, including an interactive multimedia system on CD-ROM, and improving teachers' competence in Mayan languages, first and second language education. The *Computer-Assisted Teacher Training Programme (CATT)* in Morocco has provided the pre-service teacher-training colleges in five provinces with multimedia labs and training so that teacher-trainers and trainee primary school teachers can learn about ICT and its application. The project also aims to develop networks between teacher trainees, teacher-trainers, and inspectors. Namibia's *Computer-Assisted Teacher Training (CATT)* project is a part of a wider plan to improve teacher training nationwide. It is concerned with developing computer-assisted teacher-training courses (improving educational quality through project-based learning and training in ICT applications is emphasized rather than technology training *per se*) and constructing a communications network through the Internet and other technologies. The Ugandan *Connectivity for Educator Development (Connect-ED)* project is designed to improve subject knowledge among pre- and in-service primary school teachers through online training. It also aims to increase computer literacy among teachers, provide teacher-training colleges with IT, and facilitate the integration of IT into the classroom. The US-Brazil *Learning Technologies Network (LTNet)* is an Internet-based learning environment and clearing-house on the role of ICT in education and promoting interactive collaboration between teachers in the two countries. LTNet's web-site includes a virtual library for teachers, a SchoolNet program, a help desk, and other interactive features such as email, threaded discussions and live chat, provides networking among teachers, and promotes collaborative projects via virtual exchange environments.

LearnLink's teacher-training activities differ in their target groups, scope, content, materials, methods, and national government involvement but they all partner with local education professionals, train teachers in ICT, establish multimedia centres for educators, build networks of master information teachers, and develop web-sites and/or curriculum materials. These projects are still in their early days and the outcomes are not yet available but it is anticipated that they will increase collaboration and interaction among educators nationally or between countries, and provide institutionalized support for learning technology, greater ICT access, ICT-based curriculum reform, and enhanced pedagogy.

ICT used to facilitate professional development and networking

There are widespread examples of the use of ICTs for this purpose.

Virtual Workplace <http://education.qut.edu.au/vwl/>, created by Queensland University of Technology, Australia, uses video-conferencing and web-based technologies for synchronous and asynchronous interaction between pre- and in-service teachers. It aims to enhance pedagogy in teacher training, student teachers' learning in their undergraduate studies and teaching practice, and teachers' supervision or mentoring of the students.

The European Commission-supported *Telematics for Teacher Training – T3 Project* <http://telematics.ex.ac.uk/T3/>, which ran from 1996 until 1998, aimed to enhance primary and secondary teachers', teacher trainers' and librarians' professional development and encourage teacher-trainers to adopt ICT across Europe. A web-site provided resources for teacher trainers and modelled best practice in site design. Participating universities developed courses on topics such as telematics for teachers of mathematics, while others used telematics for school-based teacher training, tutoring teachers on an MEd programme, and developing a European core curriculum framework for telematics for teacher training.

The *Virtual Teachers Centre* <http://vtc.ngfl.gov.uk> is part of the British National Grid for Learning/BECTA <www.ngfl.gov.uk> Teachers Online project, allowing teachers to link electronically to learn about others' work, create a virtual community of practice, sharing ideas through livechat, and access and share a variety of learning and teaching resources and links to other sites. 'Support Providers' enables teachers to identify resources for professional development, for example, through the ICT Support Network Directory, which provides easy access to ICT provision and training and the New Opportunities Fund (NOF), which provides ICT training for teachers and librarians. 'International Professional Development' helps teachers learn from and contribute to educational ideas and best practice throughout the world.

EduNet <http://www.edunet4u.net/teach/teacher.htm> is an integrated educational Internet service for K-12 students and teachers managed by the Korea Education and Research Information Services (KERIS). It supports the introduction of virtual learning in primary and secondary schools, provides online teacher training, promotes teachers' networking and supports teachers' voluntary clubs by providing self-training materials and various online forums. There are thousands of voluntary teachers' clubs across Korea which aim to help teachers acquire the knowledge and skills needed for the effective use of ICT in teaching and learning. These clubs provide their members with informal professional development opportunities using printed, web and EduNet material and personal contacts.

TINTIN in the Netherlands was established and supported over a four-year period by a curriculum specialist and a specialist in online teacher networking. It provided two teachers' networks, one for teachers of German, the other for teachers of French. These networks used email, listservs and occasionally, face-to-face interaction. The teachers primarily used this network to share information – reflective exchanges occurred rarely – and it was shown that teacher anxiety decreased and productivity increased during the network experience (Moonen and Voogt 2001).

The US *Teachers Network* <http://www.teachnet.org> is a nationwide, non-profit educational organization that identifies and connects teachers exemplifying professionalism and creativity within public school systems, promotes collaboration among educators to improve teaching and student achievement, provides resources to support teachers in their own professional development, and disseminates the work of outstanding classroom teachers.

Other examples include: *TeacherNet UK* <http://www.teachernetuk.org. uk>, which is an independent professional association for teachers and others in education who wish to make effective use of ICT in education; *SchoolNet SA* <http://www.school.za>, a South African organization that supports educators and learners in transforming education through the application of ICT; *SchoolNet* <www.schoolnet.ca>, a bilingual Canadian initiative providing online educators' forums; *Singapore's Clearinghouse* <http://www.moe.edu.sg/iteducation/resources/welcome.htm>, a website created by the Ministry of Education to share ICT resources and lesson plans among teachers; *Swedish Schoolnet* <http://www.skolverket.se/ skolnet/english/>, established in 1994 by the National Agency for Education to stimulate the use of ICT in schools; *Project Lighthouse* in Thailand <http://el.www.media.mit.edu/logo-foundation/pubs/logoupdate/ v7n1/v7n1-lighthouse.html>, designed to help Thai teachers and learners adapt to new technologies and change their traditional teaching and learning methods; *Red Escolar*, or the *Mexican School Net* <http://www. schoolnet.ca/magazine/pdf/fall-2000.pdf>, based on the Canadian model; Portugal's *NONIO Twenty-first Century Programme* <http://www.dapp. min-edu.pt/nonio/nonio.htm>, which provides support from universities, colleges of education, in-service training centres, and teachers' associations for teachers and schools in their use of ICT; and *European Schoolnet* <http://www.eun.org/eun.org2/eun/en/index.html>, which is the framework for co-operation between European ministries of education on ICT in education.

International collaboration in teacher training and ICT

There are still many places in the world where limited resources and ICT infrastructure prohibit teachers from using ICT for their professional development. The following sites developed by international organizations aim to bridge this gap by collaboration in sharing resources and teachers' networking.

Unicom's *Teachers Talking About Learning* <http://www.unicef.org/teachers/> was designed for international collaboration between teachers in developing countries using the Internet and television. It provides access to teacher-training materials and useful links and promotes discussion among teachers.

UNESCO's International Institute for Capacity Building in Africa <http://www.unesco-iicba.org/> has developed an electronic library to support the improvement of mathematics and science teaching in primary schools. Designed for teachers, teacher-trainers, curriculum developers and supervisors, this is available in CD-ROM and online.

The World Bank's World Links for Development (world) programme <http://www.worldbank.org/worldlinks/english/index.html> provides Internet connectivity and training in the use of ICT and other technologies in education for teachers, teacher-trainers and students in developing countries. It also links secondary school students and teachers in developing countries with schools in industrialized countries for the purpose of collaborative learning via the Internet.

The *OECD Centre for Educational Research and Innovation* <http://www.oecd.org/cer/> has promoted educational research and innovation in OECD countries for nearly 30 years. Its activities aim to encourage better links between research, policy innovation and practice, enrich knowledge about educational trends internationally, and involve educational researchers, practitioners and government officials in international discussions.

The USAID/AED *LearnLink* <http://www.aed.org/learnlink>, as shown earlier, uses ICT to strengthen educational systems in support of socio-economic development in developing countries. It uses ICT for teacher training, to link teachers to teachers, and to improve teachers' capacity to access resources to meet their professional needs.

In an international survey of web-based services for teachers, Lai-Kuen and Eastham (2001) identify the common ICT services appearing in all or most of these networks. These are: links to electronic resources, electronic discussion groups, email services, provision of Internet search engines, electronic newsletters or magazines, online directories of links and mailing lists, provision of up-to-date news, promotion and facilitation of collaborative school projects, and online feedback mechanisms. While the examples of these applications above provide some idea of the potential of ICT for teacher training, we still lack firm understanding of its effectiveness in these areas. Therefore, it is important pay close attention to the impact of ICT use in various teacher-training contexts to gain a better understanding of the factors influencing the effectiveness of ICT in teacher training.

ICT USE FOR TEACHER TRAINING: THE IMPLICATIONS

Experience with the use of ICT makes it possible to explore its implications for policy-makers.

Integration of national visions into ICT use for teacher training

The Singaporean National Institute of Education (NIE) successfully integrated the national vision for ICT use in its Masterplan for IT in Education and in the ICT-based environment created in Singapore's teacher training system. The USAID/AED LearnLink project in developing countries is being implemented in close collaboration with the national governments and integrates its activities with the various national educational policies. ICT teacher training programmes seeking to reflect national education policies should:

- incorporate and reflect national visions for education in any ICT training plans for pre-service and in-service teachers;
- include consideration of national policies for telecommunications and human development, and their impact on ICT costs and serving the number of pre-service and in-service teachers;
- develop specific outcomes based on the national vision;
- identify the appropriate means to achieve these outcomes;
- collaborate with national policy makers in developing ICT plans for teacher training.

Implementing cost-saving policies

Most nations have limited resources for teacher training and must make decisions based on cost-effectiveness. The experiences discussed in the preceding sections suggest several cost-saving strategies:

- Maximize use of computer facilities in training centres to lower user contact hour costs through efficient scheduling. Outside training hours, open computer labs to the public for a small fee (as Uganda has planned in the Connect-ED project).

• Share web-based resources and training materials with other training institutions (Jung and Rha 2000).

• Standardize on hardware and software and negotiate best prices with vendors. Complementary peripheral devices can mean savings in hardware costs and free, public-domain software lowers costs. Some vendors include ICT skills training in the purchase price.

• Form partnerships across public and private sectors (inside and outside the country) to share the costs of innovation, infrastructure, and hardware and software systems, collaborate in the recruitment of students and share advanced technical skills.

Investment in teacher-trainer training

Teacher-trainers are unquestionably the key change agents behind adoption and utilization of ICT in pre- and in-service teacher training. The experiences of NIE, VHS, and LearnLink indicate the importance of providing a variety of formal and informal teacher-trainer training so that the teacher-trainers, teachers and trainee teachers can access those methods that suit them best. Experience shows that to enlist staff support and involvement, it is useful to:

• employ a variety of teacher-trainer training methods, ranging from face-to-face workshops to online self-study programmes;

• integrate informal support into the formal teacher-trainer training system so that the less experienced teacher-trainers can obtain timely assistance;

• provide multiple incentives such as workload reduction, recognition and reward in faculty evaluations, increased research allocations to encourage use of ICT in teaching, and compensation for those providing educational or technological assistance to others.

Implementing flexible teacher-training policies

To promote ICT use for teacher training, flexible policies have to be institutionalized within conventional teacher-training institutions in regard to access, curriculum, and teaching and learning processes. Experience in the use of ICT for teacher training suggests the following:

• provide legal incentives and policies for teacher-training institutions to restructure their programmes to include ICT-based teacher training (Jung 2000);

- reduce teachers' workloads and compensate them for their training time costs during ICT-based training programmes;
- acknowledge the teachers' involvement in collaborative work during ICT-based training.

Development of outcomes-oriented, ICT-integrated training curricula

Teacher-training courses must themselves model effective ICT-integrated instructional practices. In NIE's Instructional Technology course, the student teachers must apply what they have learned by producing ICT-based micro lessons which may then be distributed to teachers on CD-ROM. The US VHS programme has developed web-based teacher-training courses to help teachers design and deliver web-based courses. Teacher-training institutions might consider these points in incorporating ICT into their curricula:

- provide short, hands-on ICT foundation courses at the initial stages of pre-service teacher training, courses that relate ICT to the achievement of wider pedagogical objectives;
- provide more advanced ICT courses as electives;
- demonstrate ICT-integrated teaching and learning by using the technology in teacher-training curricula;
- provide opportunities for teachers to produce and disseminate ICT-based instructional materials.

Adopting a systems approach in the change process

In our experience, instructional technologies are not seen merely as complementary educational tools but part of a whole new teaching and learning environment. Reigeluth notes that 'piecemeal change leaves the structure of a system unchanged. In contrast, systemic changes entail modifying the structure of a system, usually in response to new needs' (Reigeluth 1999: 16). Our recommendations for adopting a systematic approach to the change process are as follows:

- identify problems and opportunities in the functions and systems of teacher training in the country, state or province where ICT may be of help. These may include aspects of pre-service training, professional development, campus-based and off-campus support systems, research and development, and policy-making;
- examine the specific needs for structural change in each of these and where ICT can help;

- develop and implement strategies for meeting these needs;
- build a co-ordinating body to support the implementation process and promote its goals.

Base implementation on factors influencing the success of ICT for teacher training

The factors that influence a teacher's or teacher educator's ability to make use of ICT in his or her classroom practice only partly relate to the training that the teacher receives. We use the 4-E model (Collis and Pals 1999; Collis and Moonen 2001) to categorize the factors that influence the use of ICT in a teacher's daily practice. The 4-E model shows that the likelihood of a teacher making use of an ICT application in his/her own teaching is a function of four clusters of variables. These are shown in Table 9.2.

Some of these aspects can be directly influenced by teacher training; others not so, or only indirectly.

For the *Environment* cluster, the readiness of teacher educators and teachers to change and utilize technology in education can be improved via effective teacher training and support. Support from those in leadership positions is likely to increase if some form of ICT training is also made available for them.

For the *Educational effectiveness* cluster, teacher training should focus on examples of new forms of learning experience involving ICT, how ICT can support the curriculum, and how it can help the teachers or trainee teachers in their teaching practice and work in the schools.

For *Ease of use*, teacher training can help teachers increase their computer and network literacy, thus improving their skills in handling ICT in the classroom.

For *Engagement*, teacher training needs to help the trainers and teachers become more self-confident as ICT-using educators, and develop a positive attitude towards managing change, particularly change relating to ICT. Well-managed teacher networks can also help increase positive and self-confident attitudes.

The examples earlier in this chapter illustrate teacher-training strategies relating to one or more of the 4-Es.

When teachers themselves are the learners, making use of ICT to access some or all of their training or professional experiences via an Internet-based teacher network or programme, many of the same factors can also be described in terms of the 4-E model.

For the *Environment* cluster, the teacher should feel supported within his or her professional activities and learning via the network by the school. Support in this case relates to recognition of the time and efforts made by the teacher, provision of technical and educational support, and release time for training.

Table 9.2 Factors influencing an individual's use of a technology innovation in learning-related practice

Cluster	Key sub-factors and indicators
Environment The institution's profile with respect to technology use	*Organizational context* The vision, support, and actual level of use within the institution for technology use for learning-related purposes The readiness to change among the people in the institution when it comes to the use of technology in education
Educational effectiveness Gain from the technology use	*Long-term payoff* Likelihood of long-term tangible benefit for the institution or individual *Short-term payoff* Payoff such as efficiency gains, doing routine tasks associated with learning more quickly *Learning effectiveness* New forms of valuable learning experiences, improved communication, improved capacity to individualize aspects of the learning experience, valuable support to the existing curriculum
Ease of use Ease or difficulty in making use of technology	*Hardware/network* The network is convenient to access, adequate in terms of speed and bandwidth, and reliable. Computer and printer access are convenient *Software* Software associated with the technology is user-friendly, does what the user wishes, and is easy to learn
Engagement Personal engagement about technology use for learning-related purposes	*Self-confidence* Personal orientation towards trying out new ways to carry out learning-related tasks, being interested in new technological developments, and sharing these interests with others *Pleasure with the web* Particular interest in new technologies, currently the web

Sources: Collis and Pals 1999; Collis and Moonen 2001

For the *Educational effectiveness* cluster, the web-site should offer resources and materials that are useful to the teacher, appropriately organized and described, and evaluated by other teachers.

For *Ease of use*, the teacher needs convenient access to a computer with Internet connection at both school and home and with an adequate rate of network connectivity. The interface of any web environment or other software must be designed for ease of use, being consistent, easy to learn and remember, easy to navigate, and easy to find what one wants.

For *Engagement*, teachers can benefit from building a sense of professional community among their peers as they learn from each other.

The examples provided earlier illustrate these characteristics.

FUTURE DEVELOPMENTS

We conclude by discussing several lines of developments, some technical, some social, some institutional, that are likely to have a major impact on ICT for teacher training about technology or via technology.

Future developments related to convergence

A major current characteristic of ICT development is convergence. Convergence can be seen from the micro, meso and macro levels as well as within the technology types themselves (this section is summarized from Collis 2001).

At the micro level, digital data involving a variety of signal types, such as text, audio, and video, are now handled within the same application. The convergence of mass-media communication technologies (radio and television) with telephone technologies and data-network technologies is also well under way. Such convergence of technologies means that ICT will be increasingly ubiquitous in society, and easier to access and use. It will therefore become more of a complementary and even core technology in teacher training.

At the meso level, the convergence between ICT and curriculum in schools will also affect teacher training. ICT applications as tools for learning mathematics, physics, language, environmental education, law, medicine, and other subjects are well established. ICT use will be so common throughout society that specific lessons on how to use the computer or the Internet will rapidly become unnecessary, for teachers and learners alike. What will still be needed is the skill and the wisdom to use ICT efficiently and wisely to enhance learning.

Another form of convergence at the meso level relates to the roles of teacher-trainers, teachers and students. Increasingly students are engaged in activities that were previously the domain of the teacher educator or teacher. They can enter new resources into course web environments, and take on the role of peer evaluators, making use of web-based tools such as shared workspaces. Teachers' and teacher educators' roles are also changing and converging with those of the students. Teachers must seek for, sort through, and evaluate many different resources for use in their lessons. Teacher educators are also supporting and sharing in school-based pre-service and in-service learning activities, rather than lecturing about what should happen in the classroom.

A third convergence at the meso level relates to the learning resources. Increased use of the web does not necessarily mean that books will disappear in favour of digital libraries, but rather that the book will be extended via its associated web-site, by the addition of examples, links to contact persons, and links to the teacher's own resources via a course web-site. The convergence of real-time communication and video on demand is another technical convergence of high significance to teacher education. Teachers and trainee teachers will be able to review their teaching or other performance by accessing video segments via the web-site, and discuss these with their mentors or peers.

At the macro level, convergence is reflected in the ways that teacher development is increasingly provided flexibly, using various forms and mixes of delivery, locations and schedules. The convergence of local and externally provided learning experiences for teachers and teachers in training is only just beginning. Its impact is not yet very much felt. But it will be.

Future developments related to costs and access

Although ICT is becoming more and more pervasive in society, not all teachers have equal ease in accessing and using ICT in their teaching or professional development. Serious differences still exist between countries and regions in terms of computer-access ratios, costs and possibilities for Internet access, and help to support the use of ICT.

There are technological developments that offer promising new opportunities. For example, the use of satellites to transmit digital network data can allow countries with poor telephony infrastructures to leapfrog the need to first update those infrastructures before Internet access can improve. All of the benefits of web technology can be available via local area networks (intranets) where institutional access to the external web is a problem for financial, cultural, or quality-control reasons.

Cost structures to help teachers with the affordability of ICT, for example, in preparing Internet-based lessons from their home computers, are slower to develop as they involve human and institutional change. In some countries and regions, teachers are gaining support for Internet access, but this is still the exception rather than the rule. Teacher educators and teachers will need the same support for home and school use of the networked computer as they expect with respect to the blackboard or overhead projector.

Future developments in teacher training

Teacher training itself will change in its forms and methods, partly as a result of ICT. The flexibility of ICT-learning will lead more and more teachers-in-training to expect flexibility in their courses and course provision. No longer will the local institution be the obvious and automatic choice for their training; they may choose from online generic and specialized courses from locations around the world. The only constraint will be accreditation, forcing the beginning teacher to fulfil some local requirements for teaching certification.

In the field of continuing professional development, we can expect to see a rapid development of what has already started: teachers using online networks to join and collaborate with communities of practice that best suit their development needs and educational visions and regardless of their location. Only language need stand in the way of worldwide virtual professional development communities. However, a common language and common points of reference will still be critical for many teachers and teacher educators, so teacher networks within the same country will also continue to grow in importance (Moonen 2001).

REFERENCES

Collis, B. (2001) 'An overview of information technologies in education', in H. Adelsberger, B. Collis and J. Pawlowski (eds) *Handbook of Information Technology in Education and Training*, Berlin: Springer Verlag, pp. 1–21.

Collis, B. and Moonen, J. (2001) *Flexible Learning in a Digital World: Experiences and Expectations*, London: Kogan Page.

Collis, B. and Pals, N. (1999) 'A model for predicting an individual's use of a telematics application for a learning related purpose', *International Journal of Educational Telecommunications*, 6(1): 63–103.

Fontaine, M. (2000) 'Teacher training with technology: experience in five country programs', *TechKnowLogia*, November/December, pp. 69–71.

Jung, I.S. (2000) 'Korea's experiments with virtual education', *Technical Notes Series*, 5(2). Washington, DC: World Bank.

Jung, I.S. (in press) 'Singapore's approach to preparing new teachers to use technology in the classroom', in J. Capper (ed.) *Case Studies of Innovations in Teacher Training and Technology*, Washington, DC: World Bank.

Jung, I.S. and Rha, I. (2000) 'Effectiveness and cost-effectiveness of online education: a review of literature', *Education Technology*, July/August, pp. 57–60.

Lai-Kuen, K. and Eastham, T.R. (2001) 'Network services', in H. Adelsberger, B. Collis and J. Pawlowski (eds) *Handbook of Information Technology in Education and Training*, Berlin: Springer Verlag, pp. 450–70.

Moonen, B.H. (2001) *Using Teacher Networks to Support the Professional Development of Teachers*, PhD dissertation, Faculty of Educational Science and Technology, University of Twente, Enschede.

Moonen, B.H. and Voogt, J. (2001) 'Teacher inservice training in networks: a strategy of ICT integration', in C. Morales, G. Knezek, R. Christensen and P. Avila (eds) *Impact of New Technologies on Teaching and Learning*, Mexico City: Instituto Latino Americano de la Comunicación Educativa, pp. 137–51.

Reigeluth, C. (1999) 'What is instructional-design theory and how is it changing?' in C. Reigeluth (ed.) *Instructional-design Theories and Models: A New Paradigm of Instructional Theory*, vol. II, Mahwah, NJ: Lawrence Erlbaum Associates, pp. 5–30.

Chapter 10

Evaluation, research and quality

Bernadette Robinson

The quality and effectiveness of distance education as a means of training and developing teachers is much debated and doubted. This points to a need for sound research and evaluation evidence to inform the debate. This chapter summarizes findings so far and appraises the evidence available. It also offers a framework for judging quality and for planning the evaluation of distance education programmes for teacher education.

EVIDENCE SO FAR

Empirical research on the effectiveness of distance education programmes for teachers is sparse (see Chale 1983; Mählck and Temu 1989; Dock *et al.* 1988; Nielsen and Tatto 1991; Murphy and Zhiri 1992; Tatto *et al.* 1991; Perraton 1993; Murphy and Robinson 1996; Bosch 1997; Creed 2001; Perraton *et al.* 2001). This is partly because it is mostly funded separately and in addition to funding the programme itself, usually from donors or agencies external to the provider unless undertaken as an institutional evaluation or quality assurance activity. Some of the more substantial empirical studies (such as Dock *et al.* 1989; Mählck and Temu 1989 and Nielsen and Tatto 1991) were carried out in the 1980s and there is a shortage of more recent ones. This may be due to the amount of effort or resource needed, especially for a comparative study and if attempting to evaluate training effects on a teacher's performance (see Box 10.1). These kinds of studies 'demand intensive work on the ground and a greater commitment to evaluation than many authorities have felt able to give. For the most part, therefore, we have to rely on much more partial evidence' (Robinson 1997: 133). However, without this kind of occasional study, our knowledge about the use and value of distance education for teacher education remains limited. If policy-makers and planners remain reluctant to invest in occasional well-designed evaluation and research, they will lack the informed guidance they need.

Box 10.1   Comparative programme research in Sri Lanka

A rare example of empirical field-based research compared the costs and effectiveness of three different modes of teacher education in Sri Lanka, one of them distance education, one a pre-service programme for young recruits (college of education) and one in-service programme for experienced teachers on a two-year release from schools (teachers college). It used a cross-sectional, quasi-longitudinal design and detailed data on the teachers' backgrounds, previous and current experience and knowledge. It also compared pupils' learning achievement.

The first step was the development of comparative programme profiles. This led on to the task of making each programme's conceptual foundations explicit, through a study of documents, interviews and discussion forums with key staff on programme goals and the means taken to achieve them. A team of about five or six main researchers (from the United States and Sri Lanka) had a year for field-work and a year for preparation of the study, data analysis and reporting. Nearly 200 field-researchers, with experience of teacher evaluation and supervision, were trained for classroom observation tasks using three observational scales developed (on classroom resources and their use, on specific teaching skills and on time distribution). The knowledge, skills and attitudes of the teachers-in-training were measured at three points in time (programme entry, exit and during the programme while teaching in the classroom). A control group of teachers without formal qualifications was used for comparison in terms of background, experience, knowledge and practices.

Analysis of covariance was used across the different programmes and cohorts of teachers to check for similarity in relevant background variables and to compare the different outcome measures (knowledge, skills, attitudes, teaching practices and pupil achievement). In the analysis of classroom observation data, the data were contextualized in terms of teachers' background variables and school context. In analysing pupil achievement data, pupils' and teachers' background and school context was taken into account using multiple regression techniques. The study of programme costs formed a separate set of activities.

There were four main findings from the research;

1   Teacher development made a difference to what the teachers did in the classroom and this positively correlated with pupil achievement.
2   Teachers who participated in a teacher development programme performed better than those who did not (they had better subject and pedagogical knowledge).

> 3   Graduates from the colleges of education and the distance education programmes were stronger in subject matter and pedagogy than those from the teacher colleges.
> 4   The distance education programme was the most cost-effective.
>
> Source: Tatto (forthcoming)

Findings

From the limited evaluation data available, the following broad conclusions can be drawn (some more tentatively than others).

- Distance education programmes for teachers can provide acceptable courses and qualifications on a larger scale than conventional programmes and over a wide geographical area in countries with very differing infrastructures and for a wide range of purposes and learner levels.
- Successful completion rates for award-bearing programmes vary between 50–90 per cent. Examination pass rates tend, on the whole, to be similar to those in conventional programmes (though completion rates tend to be lower). Completion and examination pass rates are affected by internal factors within distance education programmes (for example, deficiencies in the particular learning systems or their management or resource availability) as well as external ones (such as lack of adequate rewards for successful completion or political decisions about the proportion of students to pass in contexts of acute teacher shortages). Where teachers have been promised improved status or pay at the end of the course or where the programme is a higher level one (such as master's degrees which strengthen promotion prospects), completion rates are higher.
- In general, distance education programmes have demonstrated that they are effective in teaching academic subjects, though some subjects, such as science, mathematics or music, need greater elements of face-to-face teaching, interaction with tutors, coaching and practical work. Courses involving the supervision or management of school-based practice present distance education providers with logistical challenges; with them, implementation of local partnerships with schools or institutions is more difficult.
- Teachers on distance education courses have achieved results equivalent to conventionally trained teachers, though with different profiles of strengths and weaknesses (Chale 1983; Mählck and Temu 1989;

Nielsen and Tatto 1993). For example, primary teachers on distance education courses in Sri Lanka did better than their counterparts on conventional courses in language knowledge but less well in language skills and mathematics knowledge and skills (Nielsen and Tatto 1993). This points to a need, found elsewhere too, for programme designs which take full account of subject and learner differences.

- Unqualified serving teachers on distance learning courses for initial qualifications are often rated more highly on classroom teaching than newly qualified college equivalents. However, two studies found that differences disappeared after a few years, with the exception of science teaching, where college-trained teachers continued to perform better (Mählck and Temu 1989; Chale 1993).

- Self-report data by teachers on distance education courses generally rate them useful and relevant to their teaching, especially where no other options are available to them, and commonly report increases in teachers' confidence, knowledge and teaching skills.

- There is relatively little evidence available on the transfer of teachers' learning to teachers' practice, as is also the case with more traditional training programmes.

- Where teachers in developing countries have low educational levels (such as incomplete secondary education) on entry to the distance education programme, they tend to achieve lower pass rates and require more learner support. This has implications for the design and costs of programmes.

Limitations in the evaluation data

The conclusions that can be drawn and substantiated with empirical findings are limited. Most reports are largely descriptive, only sometimes including detailed statistics and often lacking well-evidenced findings on outcomes. A recent review of distance education programmes for teachers in seventeen countries (mainly in Africa and South Asia) illustrates this (Creed 2001): the sources of information include only a handful of empirical studies and these, with few exceptions, tend to be of modest dimension and scope.

While 'the dearth of evaluative literature seems partly to do with the difficulties of assessing a complex and interrelated range of factors related to effectiveness' (Perraton *et al*. 2002: 37), it is also due to inadequacies in practice. Some evaluation activities are restricted by a provider's failure to establish the base-line data and record systems essential in monitoring and evaluating key activities, because of either lack of staff expertise or the day-to-day pressures of implementing programmes. They are seldom planned early enough in programme life to measure achievements or changes. Studies are sometimes too narrow in scope, confined to internal efficiency data alone or to teachers' short-term reactions to the learning materials or media.

Few studies have evaluated the impact of distance education programmes on teachers' working practices or beliefs and fewer still their impact on pupils' learning. What constitutes 'better teaching' often remains impressionalistic or ill-defined, making improvements difficult to identify or measure. Only a few classroom observation studies have been done. In these cases, the purpose has usually been to compare distance-trained teachers' performance with college-trained teachers on a given set of categories (for example, Chale 1983; Mählck and Temu 1989), though one study in Sri Lanka (Dock *et al.* 1988) used in-depth interviews and classroom observation to examine changes in teaching approaches. Tracer studies too are few, though these are needed for judging the longer-term value of the distance education programme.

Conducting comparative studies between distance education and institution-based programmes adds further complexity, because of differences in learner populations, organizational structures and programme content and design. Newly qualified teachers from conventional colleges tend to be younger, with higher entry qualifications, differently motivated (entering teaching as a last resort in some countries) and with less teaching experience than newly qualified serving teachers emerging from distance education courses. Student-teachers on distance education programmes for initial qualifications tend to be older on average, less well qualified academically on entry, often strongly motivated and more experienced as teachers. So 'comparative' studies are not always comparing similar populations of teachers-in-training. For example, research in Uganda (Murphy and Robinson 1996) showed that while the pass rates for college students on an initial training course were higher than for serving teachers taking an equivalent distance education programme, pass rates became more similar when the analysis was based on a comparison of 'like with like' using matched samples.

Although there is much pragmatic experience of distance education programmes and projects for teacher education, the research and evaluation base is relatively small and in need of development. At the same time many of the limitations identified do not belong to distance education alone, as researchers of more traditional teacher education will know. However, some problems arise specifically from the nature of distance education: its scale, distribution of learners, tutors and schools, range of stakeholders and partners responsible for different tasks. This presents a number of logistical and methodological challenges for researchers and perhaps influences their choice of approach and methodology; for example, survey research is more easily managed centrally than qualitative or observational classroom studies.

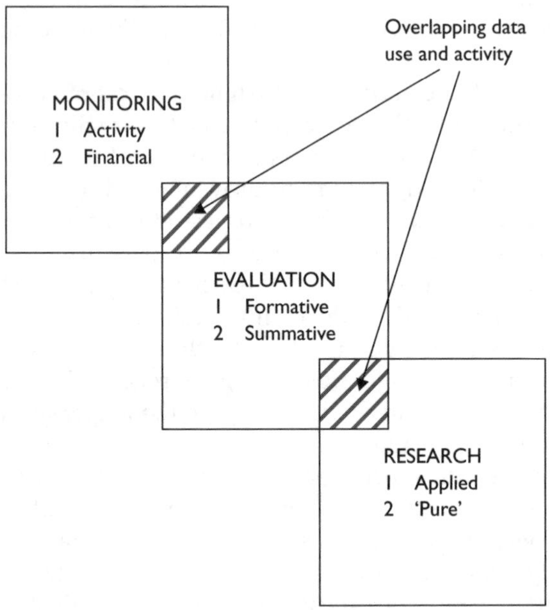

Figure 10.1 The relationship between monitoring, evaluation and research

MONITORING, EVALUATION AND RESEARCH

Monitoring, evaluation and research are overlapping areas to some extent (see Figure 10.1). Some of the activities needed for evaluation depend on the availability of monitoring data. While evaluation places an emphasis on 'utility, relevance, practicality, and meeting the needs of specific decisionmakers', research focuses on 'generalizability, causality and credibility within the research community' (Patton 1986: 15).

The role of student statistics

A starting point for distance education providers wanting to improve evaluation is to review their information bases, especially student records (in this case, teachers in training) and demographic data. A student-records database is a cornerstone of monitoring and evaluation in open and distance education programmes, though its usefulness, together with learner demographic data, is often underestimated. Student statistics can show demographic and educational characteristics, enrolment trends, progress and completion rates (by programmes, courses, subjects and cohorts), the relationship between characteristics and subsequent progress, points of withdrawal and dropout, repetition rates, course-work submission patterns, participation rates, student attainment levels in academic and practical subjects, gender and ethnic group balance and outcomes, sponsorship levels, distribution patterns of students, course preferences and employment characteristics. Unfortunately, records are frequently unreliable, incomplete or out of date, or contain irrelevant information or are little used after data entry. Two key questions in establishing a records system are 'What questions do you want to be able to answer from it?' and 'Given our level of resource, what is feasible?'

Monitoring

Monitoring is the routine checking of progress against a plan to confirm that activities are proceeding as planned or to indicate where variation is occurring and intervention needed. It provides information on the procedures and processes involved in the development and delivery of a programme. This can be used for three purposes: for managing a system, for quality-assurance activities and to support evaluation.

Any activity in a distance learning system can be monitored in some way, for example, student attendance at tutorials, the demographic characteristics and educational levels of each intake of students, the turn-around times for course-work marking by tutors, the quality of tutors' correspondence tuition, cycle times for dealing with complaints or the distribution of materials, the use or comparability of facilities at learning centres or the costs of tutors' travel.

Evaluation

Evaluation is the collection, analysis and interpretation of information, in methodologically sound ways, as the basis for forming judgments about the value of a particular programme, course or project for decision-making purposes. It uses both qualitative and quantitative methods. The nature of an evaluation varies according to its purpose, audience, approach, resources and time available. Evaluation findings feed into quality-assurance and quality-improvement activities.

Teacher education programmes are evaluated for several reasons:

- to measure how far a course or programme has met its objectives;
- to provide information on the cost-efficiency and effectiveness of a programme or particular technology or course component;
- to measure the impact of a programme on teachers' knowledge, understanding, beliefs and skills and on pupils' learning;
- to provide information on the perceptions of a programme's value;
- to compare the efficiency and effectiveness of different delivery modes;

- to give feedback to course providers and to indicate where improvements are needed;
- to provide evidence on quality and efficiency for policy-makers and planners (though whether or not they make use of it is another issue).

The emphasis between these purposes varies but in Bruner's view,

> Evaluation is often viewed as a test of effectiveness – of materials, teaching methods, or whatnot – but this is the least important aspect of it. The most important thing is to provide intelligence on how to improve these things.
>
> (1996: 165)

Approaches to evaluation

There are many different approaches to evaluation and the literature on them is extensive. In choosing how to evaluate a distance education programme for teachers, and what to evaluate, where should one begin? What options are there? Five approaches (not mutually exclusive) are summarized in Table 10.1.

The decision-focused approach in Table 10.1 is of particular relevance to evaluators whose primary audience is planners and policy-makers. This approach has been developed in detail in Stufflebeam et al.'s (1971) CIPP (context, input, process, product) model, a useful one for occasional and in-depth evaluation. This model addresses four aspects of a programme:

- context evaluation: description of the programme, objectives, intended outcomes and measures for judging achievement;
- input evaluation: the programme strategy and inputs;
- process evaluation: the implementation of the programme procedures and strategies;
- product evaluation: the success of the programme (summative evaluation including its longer-term impact).

The CIPP approach can accommodate a variety of quantitative and qualitative data, pays attention to context (a feature of particular relevance to teacher education and distance education programmes) and can incorporate a variety of stakeholder views. An example of its use in evaluating a distance education project for teacher education is given in Box 10.2.

Another type of evaluation, much used in distance education, is Scriven's (1991) formative and summative evaluation. While they tend to be presented as polarities (see Table 10.2 for a summary), in practice

Table 10.1 Five approaches to evaluation

Approach	Emphasis	Focusing issues	Evaluator's role	Specific information needs
Experimental	Research design	What effects result from programme activities and can they be generalized?	Expert/scientist	Outcome measures. Learner characteristics. Variation in treatment. Other influences on learners. Availability of a control group.
Goal-oriented	Goals and objectives	What are the programme's goals and objectives, and how can they be measured?	Measurement specialist	Specific programme objectives. Criterion-referenced outcome measures.
Decision-focused	Decision-making	Which decisions need to be made and what information will be relevant?	Decision support person	Stage of programme development. Cycle of decision-making. Data-gathering and reporting.
User-oriented	Information users or clients	Who are the intended information users and what information will be most useful?	Collaborator	Personal and organizational dynamics. Group information needs. Programme history. Intended uses of information.
Responsive	Personal understanding	Which people have a stake in the programme and what are their points of view?	Counsellor/facilitator	Variation in individual and group perspectives. Stakeholder concerns. Programme history. Variation in measures and sites.

Source: Stecher and Davis 1987: 40, 54

Table 10.2 Formative and summative evaluation in distance education programmes

Areas of difference	Formative evaluation	Summative evaluation
Purpose	Management information. Improvement of remaining programme activities. Meeting reporting requirements. Contribution to later summative evaluation or quality assurance.	Assessment of value overall and in particular respects. Systematic construction of evidence-based conclusions and lessons to guide policy and decision-makers.
Orientation	Action-oriented Focus on processes. May focus on only a component of the learning system.	Conclusion-oriented Focus on effectiveness and outcomes. Focus is on learning system as a whole, as well as components.
Target audience for report	Programme managers and practitioners (materials developers, tutor managers). Institutional committees.	Policy-makers, sponsors or funders, teacher education authorities, the public and researchers.
Focus of data collection	Activities in relation to policy goals, plans and schedules. Nature of implementation (logistics, delivery, co-ordination, learner support, supervision of school practice, staff training and development). Learning achievements, learning processes and use of materials.	Implementation issues and experiences. Output (products and services) and outcome measures (effects). Costs and cost-effectiveness. Overall programme achievement.

Role and nature of evaluators	One part of their role is to establish an evidentiary archive. In-house or internal, limited external input (except perhaps to support evaluation process). Often participatory or practitioner-oriented. May combine local practitioner evaluation plus centralized activities.	Role is to provide overall systematic evaluation in a credible and well-evidenced way. Mixture of internal and external (or independent) evaluators. May place greater focus on external measures or perceptions (i.e. relating to programme context).
Methodology	Combination of quantitative and qualitative approaches. Tends to emphasize the qualitative. Requires construction of a student records database.	Broad combination of quantitative and qualitative approaches, and use of formative evaluations done. Tends to emphasize quantitative and cost aspects because of target audience. Depends for some of its work on the existence of an adequate student records database.
Frequency of data collection	Continuous monitoring plus formative evaluation of key aspects at critical points.	Usually undertaken at the end of a programme, or at some time beyond programme completion. More rarely, impact analysis includes longer-term activities.
Reporting procedures	Informal via discussion groups, internal meetings and circulation of internal reports or memos. Reports may include specific guidelines for new or amended practice in the short term. Evaluator reports to a programme. A collection of items of report.	Formal reports based on a range of source materials. Often includes recommendations for broad action or policy development. Evaluator reports on a programme. Usually a single written report.
Frequency of reporting	Throughout the period of the programme presentation, but especially in the first year.	On completion of programme or as a required evaluation of an ongoing programme (by a sponsor, government department or quality assessment agency).

Source: Scriven 1967; Herman et al. 1987; Patton 1986

Box 10.2   Using the CIPP model in Uganda

The MITEP (Mubende Integrated Teacher Education Project, 1991–5) was designed to upgrade one cohort of about 900 unqualified teachers in two districts of western Uganda (Mubende and Kiboga) through the use of distance education. An evaluation of it took place in 1995, with external funding. It was carried out over seven months with a team of four evaluators, all part-time and giving varying amounts of time to the work. The main evaluation work began shortly before the project finished.

The evaluation approach was based on examining context, input, process and product (the CIPP model), and bringing into the evaluation a wide range of stakeholder views.

Context. The context and role of the project were constructed from project documents, interviews and policy analysis (of government's, donors' and implementers' intentions) together with baseline data on teacher supply, qualifications, needs and information on the previous use of distance education for teacher education in Uganda. Measures for judging achievement were identified from international research and experience in distance education and adapted to be relevant to the evaluation questions being addressed and the resources and skills available.

Input. Quantitative data were gathered to establish broad patterns of information about the project and internal efficiency (completion rates, subject and gender differences in performance and relationships between entry-level qualification and completion rates and costs). Cost data for the distance education and two college-based equivalent programmes were constructed and analysed.

Processes. Project implementation, strategies and outcomes were examined through a combination of quantititative and qualitative data. The rationale for project strategies and development was examined in terms of events and critical incidents which affected implementation. Questionnaires with a mixture of open and closed questions were used with about 200 students, tutors and headteachers to gather information about the learners and the programme and the experience of participation. Qualitative data were gathered through group and individual interviews to pursue aspects of the questionnaire in more depth as well as to construct a picture of the MITEP experience through the eyes of participating teachers, headteachers, personal tutors, seminar and subject tutors, school inspectors, personnel in the Teaching Services Commission and Uganda National Examinations Board, sponsors, students in training at the two conventional colleges and parents of pupils.

Product. Analysis was made of completion and success rates overall, by gender, by subject, by entry-level qualifications, in comparison to the regular college programmes for contemporary cohorts of students and in relation to project aims and objectives. Perceptions and judgments of the project's value to different stakeholders were analysed and summarized in several ways. Project strengths and weaknesses were analysed on the basis of the evidence and conclusions used to construct lessons for other projects in process. Cost data were produced on the cost per successful completer and cost comparisons with conventional colleges.

Problems in carrying out the evaluation included shortness of time for the amount of work needed, an underestimation of the work involved, the timing of the evaluation (coinciding with the project's closure), lack of an established and up-to-date student records database, partial and unreliable registration data, the need to construct retrospectively data which should have been readily available as management information, lack of formative evaluation data in project archives and too heavy a representation of internal project staff on the evaluation team, opening up the risk of bias. Like many evaluations, time and resources did not permit systematic observation of teachers at work in classrooms and the more limited instrument (a list of criteria with rankings) used nationally for assessing teachers' performance as part of the final teaching examinations was used as a rather uninformative proxy.

Source: Robinson *et al.* 1995

there is overlap between the categories. Formative evaluation can also serve some summative functions for particular components or stages and feeds into summative evaluation. Formative evaluation has improvement as its primary goal and can be considered as a form of quality assurance, whereas summative evaluation is undertaken to determine the overall effectiveness of a programme and may be viewed as a form of quality control.

Planning evaluation

Evaluation plans need to be built into project or programme activities from the start. This happens much less than it should, except where evaluation activities are part of a standard approach in large institutions, like open universities. Evaluation plans need to focus on three key aspects: the questions or issues to be addressed, the procedures to be used, and the resources needed to carry out the activities. Evaluators also need to distinguish between routine monitoring and evaluation activities and occasional ones.

Routine information management activities include statistical analyses from the database: demographic analyses; student progress and performance information; enrolment and completion rates; examination results; dropout rates; course-work submission rates; and grade profiles.

Regular monitoring activities include take-up of learner support services; tutorial attendance; use of learning centres, monitoring of correspondence tuition or tutors' work; mentoring activities in school-based training; course feedback; and staff development provision for field staff and tutors.

Occasional studies are likely to focus on the use and value of materials and media; tracer studies of teachers' employment and careers; comparative studies with other teacher education programmes; assessment of the relevance of programmes and materials to teacher education standards or teachers' needs, in-depth studies of some routine activity (for example, assessment of course-work or use by trainee-teachers of activities in course materials); or the evaluation and costs of electronic discussion groups in supporting school-based training programmes.

Between them, these activities can generate a variety of information for programme providers and planners (see Table 10.3 for the range of sources available to programme providers).

Table 10.3 Five criteria for judging teacher education by distance education

Criteria	Indicators
Effort (extent or reach)	Student numbers participating. The reach or coverage of the distance education system (facilities and services), geographically and in terms of meeting teachers' needs. Composition of student population (rural/urban, disadvantaged groups, gender balance, ethnic minority teachers). Accessibility and affordability by learners.
Performance (effects: output, outcomes and impact)	Achievement of stated programme and course goals. Completion and dropout rates. Examination entry and success rates, overall and by subjects. Assessment of practical teaching skills. Learning gains in knowledge and understanding of academic subjects, school curricula and pedagogy. Improvements in pupils' learning achievement. Course work submission rates and grades. Comparisons with conventional alternatives. Evidence of changes in teaching practices, professional attitudes and beliefs.

Table 10.3 (continued)

Criteria	Indicators
	Acceptance of qualifications by employers, peers, professional associations and other educational institutions for entry to further study.
	Equivalence in pay-scales and levels for teachers trained by distance and traditional modes.
	Reputation and status of programme and individuals trained through it.
	Extent of integration with 'mainstream' teacher education and relative status.
	Influence on teacher education in general (use of distance education materials in conventional system, extent of participation in the programme by conventional teacher-trainers, as tutors, assessors, mentors, co-ordinators, supervisors of students' teaching; participation in staff development activities).
Adequacy (impact relative to needs)	Strategic role, scale and contribution to supply and quality of teachers overall.
	Contribution to improving the qualification levels and quality of the teaching force, teacher supply and individual teachers' career development.
	Extent to which the needs overall and of sub-groups within the teacher population are met (ethnic minority teachers, educational levels, rural/urban, language needs, regional differences of social context and environment).
	Relevance to teachers' schools and contexts of work.
	Appropriateness of media and technology choices to the conditions of participating teachers.
	Extent and quality of materials and services to support teachers' learning.
Efficiency	Cost per student and per successful student.
	Reliability of the delivery and administrative systems.
	Appropriate deployment of resources (human, financial, technical, facilities, equipment) and their management.
	Comparisons with other providers.
	Employment rates of completers (and in the longer term, length of time in post).
Process	Identification of strengths and weaknesses and reasons for success and failure.
	Quality of the teaching and learning system (materials, media use, learner support, advisory services, provision for interaction with others, assessment, supervision of practical work, administrative services, staff training and management).
	Quality of learning experience and outcomes.
	The system and mechanisms for managing quality and standards (quality assurance).

Source: McAnany 1975: 238

QUALITY

Monitoring and evaluation are integral parts of the management of quality and quality assurance. One task for evaluators is to map, prioritize and co-ordinate their activities within the array of options open to them.

Judgments about the quality of distance education programmes for teachers come from many sources and may coincide or vary because they are based on different criteria of quality. For example, academic subject specialists may judge the quality of learning materials on the subject content while student-teachers may focus on the extent to which the materials are relevant and useful for their particular teaching situations. Policy-makers and economists may judge on the basis of cost-effectiveness or cost-savings or on a programme's ability to increase teacher supply within a more rapid time-scale.

Some distance education programmes for initial teacher training work to at least two sets of quality standards: national standards, sometimes highly specified (as are those provided by the Teacher Training Agency in Britain), and internal institutional standards, with varying degrees of definition. Other programmes work to internal standards alone (audited or not, as the case may be) or set their own quality-assurance standards and procedures and are subject to the standards set for the national teacher education examinations at the end of programmes. Quality standards for continuing professional development often tend to be less explicit.

However, one issue affects conventional and distance teacher education programmes alike. The quality of teachers is mostly judged by the qualifications they have. Yet some of these bear little relation to the quality of teaching or to the use of training programmes to engender better teaching. Teachers often obtain qualifications by choosing the easiest subjects to pass, and for serving teachers, these may bear no relation to the subjects they teach. The type of assessment chosen also may fail to engage with the kinds of learning needed by teachers, for example, teachers' qualifications through distance education programmes in Indonesia have generally been awarded on the basis of only multiple-choice questions addressing mainly the lower levels of cognitive performance. So completion rates as a measure of programme quality may lose some of their value when the curriculum and form of assessment are taken into account. The quality of teacher education programmes varies widely, whether they are delivered conventionally or through distance learning.

One framework for judging the quality of a distance education programme for teacher education is given in Figure 10.2. This also maps the focus and kinds of evaluation data needed. As can be seen (and like the CIPP model), it accommodates a range of sources, a mixture of the factual and the less tangible effects and a variety of quantitative and qualitative data and approaches to permit triangulation of findings.

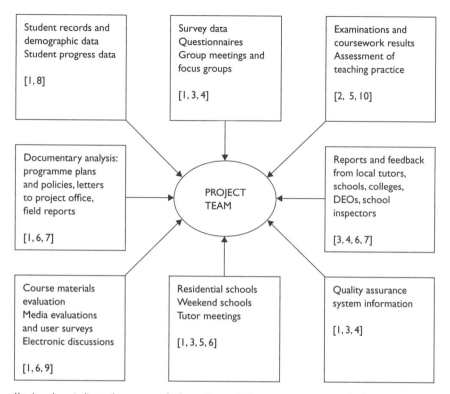

Figure 10.2 Sources of evaluation data (formative and summative) for providers of a teacher education programme

Key (numbers indicate the sources of information available to programme providers)

1   Project team providing the programme
2   Institution or parent body responsible for the programme
3   Part-time tutors
4   Headteachers and senior teachers (mentors)
5   Staff from teacher-training institutions, acting as lecturers or part-time tutors or course-work assessors
6   Students (teachers in training)
7   District eduction officers and school inspectors
8   Regional co-ordinating tutors
9   External assessors
10 External national examination board or teacher training standards authority

CONCLUSIONS

More and better evaluation and research is needed on the use and effects of distance education for both initial teacher training and continuing professional development. The latter especially, whether provided in traditional forms or through distance education, receives little evaluation attention. It is often difficult to say with certainty what effects an in-service continuing professional development programme has had.

The capacity of those undertaking evaluations, especially practitioners whose primary role is not evaluation, needs strengthening in most cases. Evaluators need to be skilled in the use of both quantitative and qualitative approaches and to take a practical approach which allows for integration of methods within a single study rather than struggling to remain within a particular evaluation paradigm. As Patton (1990) recommends, methodological appropriateness should be used as the primary criterion for judging methodological quality, since different methods are appropriate for different situations.

Even with soundly conducted evaluations, a persistent problem remains. However good the evaluation findings and reports are, getting the information into decision-makers' orbit and processes often presents a major obstacle. This problem applies to the use of evaluation not only by the teaching institution but also by national decision-making bodies. Many small-scale, useful studies do not see the light of day beyond the confines of their institution or even a department within it. Better dissemination of what is available or what is in progress and dialogue about it would help to strengthen the current knowledge and conceptual basis of distance education for teacher education.

REFERENCES

Bosch, A. (1997) 'Interactive radio instruction: 23 years of improving educational quality', *Education and Technology Technical Notes Series*, 2(1), Washington, DC: World Bank. <http://worldbank.org/education/digitaldivide>

Bruner, J.S. (1996) *Towards a Theory of Instruction*, Cambridge, Mass.: Harvard University Press.

Chale, E.M. (1993) 'Tanzania's distance-teaching programme', in Perraton, H., *Distance Education for Teacher Training*, London: Routledge.

Creed, C. (2001) *The Use of Distance Education for Teachers*, Cambridge: International Research Foundation for Open Learning (IRFOL) (reported to Department for International Development).

Dock, A.W., Duncan, W.A. and Kotalawala, E.M. (1988) *Training Teachers through Distance Methods: An Evaluation of a Sri Lankan Programme*, Education Division Document 40, Stockholm: Swedish International Development Authority (SIDA).

Herman, J.L., Morris, L.L. and Fitz-Gibbon, C.T. (1987) *Evaluator's Handbook*, Newbury Park, Cal.: Sage.

Mählck, L. and Temu, E.B. (1989) *Distance versus College Trained Primary School Teachers: A Case Study from Tanzania*, Paris: International Institute for Educational Planning.

McAnany, E.G. (1975) 'Radio schools in non-formal education: an evaluation perspective', in T.A. La Belle (ed.) *Educational Alternatives in Latin America*, Los Angeles: UCLA Latin America Center Publications, University of California.

Murphy, P. and Robinson, B. (1996) *Costs and Effectiveness of Distance Education and College-based Initial Teacher Training in Uganda: A Comparative Study*, internal research report, Washington, DC: World Bank.

Murphy, P. and Zhiri, A. (eds) (1992) *Distance Education in Anglophone Africa*, EDI Development Policy Case Series, Analytical Case Studies, 9, Washington, DC: World Bank.

Nielsen, D. and Tatto, M.T. (1991) *The Cost-effectiveness of Distance Education for Teacher Training*, BRIDGES Research Report Series, 9, Cambridge, Mass.: Harvard Institute for International Development.

Nielsen, H.D. and Tatto, M.T. (1993) 'Teacher upgrading in Sri Lanka and Indonesia', in H. Perraton, *Distance Education for Teacher Training*, London: Routledge, pp. 95–135.

Patton, M.Q. (1986) *Utilization-focused Evaluation*, 2nd edn, Newbury Park, Cal.: Sage.

Patton, M.Q. (1990) *Qualitative research and evaluation methods*, Newbury Park, Cal.: Sage.

Perraton, H. (1993) *Distance education for teacher training*, London: Routledge.

Perraton, H., Robinson, B. and Creed, C. (2001) *Teacher Education through Distance Learning: Technology, Curriculum, Evaluation, Cost*. Paris: UNESCO.

Perraton, H., Creed, C. and Robinson, B. (2002) *Teacher Education Guidelines: Using Open and Distance Learning*, Paris: UNESCO.

Robinson, B. (1997) 'Distance education for primary teacher training in developing countries', in J. Lynch, C. Modgil and S. Modgil (eds) *Innovations in Delivering Primary Education*, London: Cassell Education. Available at <http://wbln0018.worldbank.org/hdnet/hddocs.nsf/>

Robinson, B., Tuwangye, E., Serugga, S. and Pennels, J. (1995) *Report of an Evaluation of Mubende Integrated Teacher Education Project (MITEP)*, Cambridge: ActionAid-Uganda and International Extension College.

Scriven, M. (1967) 'The methodology of evaluation', in R.W. Tyler, R.M. Gagné and M. Scriven (eds.) *Perspectives of Curriculum Evaluation*, Chicago: Rand McNally, 39–83.

Scriven, M. (1991) *Evaluation Thesaurus*, 4th edn, Newbury Park, Cal.: Sage.

Stecher, B.M. and Davis, W.A. (1987) *How to Focus an Evaluation*, Newbury Park, Cal.: Sage.

Stufflebeam, D.L., Foley, W.J., Gephart, W.J., Guba, E.G., Hammond, R.L., Merriman, H.O., and Provus, M.M. (1971) *Educational Evaluation and Decision Making*, Itasca, Ill.: Peacock.

Tatto, M.T. (forthcoming) 'The value and feasibility of evaluation research on teacher development: contrasting experiences in Sri Lanka and Mexico', *International Journal of Educational Development*.

Tatto, M.T., Nielsen, H.D., Cummings, W.C., Kularatna, N.G. and Dharmadasa, D.H. (1991) *Comparing the Effects and Costs of Different Approaches for Educating Primary School Teachers: The Case of Sri Lanka*, BRIDGES Research Report Series, 10, Cambridge, Mass.: Harvard Institute for International Development.

Chapter 11

The costs of distance education for training teachers

João Batista Oliveira and François Orivel

Education budgets in both rich and poor countries face resource scarcity. In those countries where the number of children is decreasing, teacher salaries and improved conditions of work such as smaller class sizes require more expenditure per pupil. But the budgets for these must compete with other societal demands, including those of an increasingly older and politically powerful population. In those countries where the number of children is still increasing – it is estimated that the next thirty years will see an additional billion children in the developing world – millions of teachers will be needed. Hence the need for planners and decision-makers to identify cost-effective alternatives for teacher education and training and for deploying adequately trained teachers in schools.

Teacher training paradigms are also changing and more educational technologies are being used in formal and informal teacher development settings. These settings are also changing, becoming more open to – or even dependent on – the use of information and communications technologies. So far, it has often been considered sufficient to train teachers through conventional, face-to-face methods. This is now increasingly questioned in a world where, in addition to technological progress, demographic and economic factors require new models of teaching and learning and new ways of organizing schools in response to rapidly changing circumstances. This new educational era therefore calls for substantial changes in the ways in which teachers are educated and for them then to be constantly upgraded in their knowledge and skills. Understanding the costs and the effectiveness of alternatives for training teachers is therefore no longer simply an academic exercise or a question of conducting a search for cheaper alternatives: it becomes imperative to determine the most effective ways of deploying scarce funds for the accomplishment of affordable but high-quality teacher education.

It is curious to note that in spite of their increasing importance, cost-effectiveness studies are becoming rarer in the literature. There are several possible explanations for this. There may be a feeling that the issue is resolved, that the cost-effectiveness of distance education and educational media is well established and such studies may now find no room in the educational journals. International organizations that funded such studies in the 1970s and 1980s may feel that they have made their contribution to establishing the reputation and worth of distance education, and see no need for further investments in expensive cost studies. The analysis of cost became standard practice in the launching and evaluation of large-scale projects and distance learning institutions, but increasingly calculations of this kind have been treated as sensitive information which is not in the public domain. Also, the diversity and complexity of the ways in which distance education is conceived and delivered make generic studies quickly obsolete and direct comparisons more difficult and less useful. Or it may be that although cost studies are being increasingly used, they are just not published. However, it is often the case that many providers of distance education do not know what their programmes cost.

This chapter aims to contribute to the work of researchers, practitioners and decision-makers in distance teacher education in three ways. First, it offers renewed reasons for undertaking case studies in costings and highlights the validity of standard concepts and methodologies. Second, it considers case studies of teacher-training situations in terms of costs. Third, it analyses how the specific characteristics of distance teacher training can and should be analysed through cost studies. It should be read as an encouragement for planners and providers of distance education to conduct more cost studies of their programmes and thoroughly examine the alternatives before embarking on projects demanding substantial resources.

In this chapter we use terminologies similar to those used in other parts of this book in examining initial teacher training, whether undertaken pre-service or in-service, and continuing professional development for those already qualified or those unqualified but practising as teachers. And the term 'distance education' is used to characterize any programmes with a distance component – correspondence, self-study, videotapes, open broadcast, computers, Internet or computer interactions – as the major form of instructional delivery. The advent of new information and communications technologies and the increasing use of technology-based instruction in conventional education is blurring the frontiers between distance, technology-based and conventional education. Conversely, it is increasingly difficult to design and operate a successful distance education programme or system based totally on distance components. This is particularly true of the practical components of initial teacher training. The term distance education is therefore used even where examples refer to programmes and systems using a mix of methods and technologies.

WHY DO COST STUDIES?

Economists, planners, decision-makers or practitioners do cost studies for a number of reasons: to understand the cost structure of distance or technology-based projects; to improve the efficiency of such projects; to establish financing or cost-recovery strategies to help finance such projects; to analyse trade-offs of different technologies or inputs that might be used in given projects; or to compare different forms of teacher training. However, the original and most important reason for cost-effectiveness studies remains unchanged: to lead to a more efficient use of educational resources. Overall, as Levin (1983: 15) puts it:

> the case for using cost-effectiveness analysis is that is integrates the results of activities with their costs in such a way that one can select those activities that provide the best educational results for any given costs or that provide any given level of educational results for the least cost.

Different purposes require different methodologies and lead to different uses of results – so there is no single methodology or standard way to conduct a cost study. For example, to determine whether face-to-face instruction is more cost-effective than television-based teacher training requires a different methodology from that needed to determine which of these delivery systems minimizes dropout rates. The basic concepts of such analysis have been summarized elsewhere (UNESCO 1977; Levin 1983) and remain unchanged. The next section provides a summary of these basic concepts as they apply to distance teacher training.

BASIC CONCEPTS IN CONTEXT

One does not need to be a professional economist to understand the basic concepts necessary to perform cost analysis. This section summarizes these concepts using questions relevant to understanding the cost structures of teacher-training projects.

Total cost: how much does it cost?

The *total cost* of any undertaking must be estimated before rational decisions can be taken about its implementation. If the total – or even the initial cost – is too high for the available resources, the project is not feasible. The concept of cost implies sacrifice: the cost of doing something corresponds to the sacrifice of not doing other things with the money. Cost is always related to opportunities forgone.

Table 11.1 Major cost components of face-to-face and distance learning

Face-to-face	Distance learning
• Personnel	• Personnel
• Facilities	• Equipment
• Equipment	• Materials
• Materials	• Other
• Other	• Facilities

As the term implies, total cost includes all of the costs involved in a project – regardless of who is paying. A common mistake is to confuse cost with expenditure or cash disbursements made by the institution running the project. These may only be part of the total cost. A thorough analysis must identify the costs of all relevant resources employed, translated in money terms, and regardless of whether or not the money was actually or directly spent. This cost may, for example, include the construction or use (rental) of a building or the paid or unpaid time of any permanent or casual staff or volunteer workers. It also includes the time people spend studying (as opposed to working), as well as the individual's costs of transportation, lodging and book or other materials purchases.

To identify the total cost the analysis must identify the major components of the project. Table 11.1 illustrates, in order of relative importance, the major cost components of face-to-face and distance learning. The order of importance reflects the authors' experience with a number of projects, but this order may differ in individual cases. A major cost in many countries may be related to transport and accommodation of students if they have to travel to a training centre. Travel costs of this kind increase the cost of conventional education and may suggest the need for technology- and distance-based approaches.

In distance education projects, another useful breakdown involves separating the costs of production and delivery. Production usually comprises such items as facilities, equipment, personnel, maintenance and supplies. Personnel may be further broken down into categories of personnel responsible for the management, administration, content development, teaching and learning, delivery and infrastructure and learner support. Delivery may be categorized by functions such as tutors, graders, counsellors, and managers. The level of detail required depends on the importance of the items – personnel, for example, typically represents from 50 to 80 per cent of the cost of a project, and this cost must be carefully detailed. If supplies or the reproduction of materials represent less than 10 or 5 per cent, gross estimates of sub-items may be acceptable.

Again, a complete study must include all costs – including those borne by the participants. Such costs may also include interest paid on loans and other financial charges. Total cost, however, does not give the full picture. It is only a first step for further analysis: is the project cost-effective? To answer this question one needs to know about average and unit cost.

Average and unit cost: how much does a student cost?

This is an important question for managers and cost-analysts in both face-to-face and distance education. In face-to-face instruction, the usual, practical, but incomplete way to arrive at an *average cost* is to divide the annual expenditure by the number of students enrolled in any given year. This is obviously inadequate, because annual expenditure typically refers to recurrent costs, namely, those that are repeated to implement a project or programme. These *recurrent costs* are typically to do with personnel, phone bills, supplies and materials.

From a cost perspective, recurrent costs typically refer to students attending a course during a given year, while investment costs refer to costs incurred in bringing benefits to the students over a longer period – for example, the costs of producing texts, tapes and other materials. Such investments can be *amortized* – that is, annualized over relatively long periods of time. For example, an educational television programme produced to help teachers can be reused for several years and a building constructed or converted to provide a local teachers' centre may last for many years. The costs of production should therefore be divided according to the numbers of students in the various years the programme will be delivered.

To calculate the *unit costs* one must first define what the unit is – for example, the course offered, the number of graduates, or the number of graduates who actually become teachers. Finally, unit costs must also take into account the average number of products or units produced over a certain number of years – projects may start small and grow over time.

Major differences exist in the cost of face-to-face as opposed to distance education projects. One lies in the concept of fixed and variable costs.

Fixed and variable costs: when the number of students matters

Fixed costs are what one must spend regardless of the number of students. *Variable costs* depend on the number of students. In face-to-face instruction the most obvious fixed costs are those of the buildings and furnishings. These may be expensive to buy or hire, but they last a long time and, if intensively used, tend to represent a relatively minor cost over time – typically 6 to 8 per cent of the total costs. Cost studies that ignore this element tend therefore to underestimate unit cost by this amount. But in general, personnel is considered a variable cost: if there are students, teachers are hired, if there are no students, no teachers are needed. The most typical variable cost in face-to-face instruction is personnel – the more students, the more the need for personnel. One could add that teacher training is in itself a fixed cost. It costs the same to train a teacher who decides to quit the teaching profession after a short period and has only benefited a limited number of student cohorts as it does to train a teacher who will teach for forty years and educate forty cohorts. But on the whole, the usual equation for face-to-face instruction is relatively low fixed costs and relatively high variable costs. Since the number of teachers in general is relative to the number of students, there are not many economies of scale to be achieved: the average costs of teaching 40 or 4,000 students are not very different. There may be economies of scale associated with using buildings, libraries, or management personnel, but they are relatively minor, as will be clear by a comparison with distance education.

In distance education, in general there is a large initial investment in the production of materials that sometimes require expensive and sophisticated production facilities and operations. When dedicated distance-teaching institutions are set up, as happened when the various national open universities were being established, there can also be a huge investment in buildings and equipment. However, the cost of the equipment is coming down (although it may still be virtually unaffordable in some poorer countries), the variety and quality of the production tools is increasing and, as these migrate to the desktop, most production jobs can now be carried out on personal computers and by teaching staff who have been appropriately trained rather than by computer or media specialists. The size of equipment is also reducing, which means that it requires less space. And most of the distance education projects are now based on existing institutions and therefore do not require costly investment in new dedicated accommodation or equipment. However, where information and communications facilities and infrastructure are not in place, establishing such systems for an entire project, or equipping institutions and schools with a complex new technology may not be a wise decision. The educational use of technologies should ride on the back of available technologies, and not vice versa, particularly in countries where infrastructures are severely limited.

Assuming that the necessary infrastructure is in place, the costs of delivering the programmes by post, mail, broadcasting or electronic means are variable and tend to be relatively cheap. The cost of delivering self-study material can be reduced to the cost of buying and mailing, broadcasting or downloading the reading materials. Thus, copies of the same instructional material can be used by one, ten, one thousand or one million students at relatively little extra cost, thus providing significant economies of scale. If the programme is also supported by correspondence, tutoring, paper grading, computer chat, virtual or actual meetings, workshops and laboratory sessions, then of course the recurrent delivery costs will increase.

Nowadays, the convergence in the use of technologies in both face-to-face and distance education is changing the basis for comparison: face-to-face education is becoming increasingly technology-intensive, and distance education makes use of face-to-face meetings and tutorial support. In school-based initial teacher training, the practical components – teaching practice, language teaching and laboratory and fieldwork – require face-to-face contact and individual supervision. Thus distance education programmes are becoming more sensitive to the variable costs and face-to-face programmes are becoming more sensitive to the fixed costs.

Shadow price: what if I do not know the price?

Let us take a typical case: an existing building has been recycled as a teachers'centre. This building has no other apparent use or purpose. Should it be costed? The answer is 'yes' – everything has a price. If we do not know the price or even if the price has been paid or amortized in the past, one must estimate what it would cost to buy or rent a similar facility. Or alternatively, what we would lose if we used this building for educational purposes rather than renting it out. There is nothing free in the world of costing. Someone is paying for it: usually the taxpayer. So there is need to cost everything from old buildings to voluntary work.

Marginal cost: what if I add something?

The term *marginal cost* has many meanings and uses. To calculate the marginal costs one asks: what additional or incremental services will be needed in order to provide something new, or add someone new (for example an additional student)? Consider case 1: we can accommodate two new students in a classroom with thirty others. In this case, the marginal cost of adding two new students is close to zero. But now consider case 2: the classroom cannot accommodate two additional students – for example, because of regulations (e.g. no more than thirty students per class) or because of a lack of space. In this second case, two new students would trigger the opening of a new class – and the marginal cost of these two new students would be equal to the cost of opening a new class. By comparison, the marginal cost of two extra students studying by correspondence would be low – the cost of buying and shipping two new sets of materials. The marginal cost is equal to the variable cost, which means that every additional student is less costly than the average student because she or he does not generate any new fixed cost. Hence the occurrence of economies of scale.

Opportunity cost: study or work?

In costing teacher-training programmes, an important consideration is the use of time. Training young people to become teachers or training existing teachers or working adults to become teachers always entails forgone earnings or *opportunity cost*. The real question here is 'Who bears the cost?'

Who pays may be an important consideration in the design of programmes for initial training or continuing education. The implications are various. For example, the number of years a teacher stays in employment after graduation will affect the period and rate of return of the training investment, both to the government and to the individual. Whether the teachers or trainees are studying in their own time or they have been granted paid leave of absence for their studies has different cost implications. There may also be equity considerations. Some countries provide free initial training for young trainee teachers but charge fees to existing teachers working towards formal qualifications. This is the case, for example, in China. Systems which provide for initial teacher training in full-time residential or external courses are often obliged to provide public funding for trainees who cannot themselves bear the earnings forgone. These examples illustrate differences in cost-sharing beween students engaged in full-time face-to-face programmes and those taking distance education or part-time face-to-face programmes while remaining in their teaching positions or other jobs. Whether met by the employer or the teacher, the opportunity cost is an important ingredient in costing education programmes and deciding on the most appropriate and cost-effective strategies and techniques. Teachers or trainee teachers engaged in part-time and/or distance education programmes who are still in employment may be more capable of supporting themselves and temporarily reducing their earnings.

Cost or expenditure?

Very often decision-makers consider as costs only items that affect their own budget or direct expenditures made by their own institution or ministry. One of the reasons is that, in some circumstances, other costs are paid for by external donors or in kind, as when using existing installations, equipment or personnel. In some circumstances, deciding to undertake a distance learning project in spite of higher costs may be justified, or acceptable, given that the other non-computed costs are donated and will not burden existing budgets. But this is not the equivalent of saying that the goods and services donated are cost-free. If it is decided to omit some costs from the computation, special attention then needs to be given to the future implications of what originally appear as donations, such as replacement of equipment and parts, or the training and payment of technical personnel.

So far we have dealt with cost concepts. We turn now to the issues of effectiveness and cost-effectiveness.

EFFECTIVENESS

Effectiveness is related to effects, results or outcomes. Effects are related to objectives such as mastering the contents of a discipline, the methodologies for teaching or showing proficiency in teaching children in specific situations. Outcomes are not measured in monetary terms – they are measured on their own merits, for example, in testing scores of teachers or their students, the number of students reached, the employment of the graduates, etc.

A major challenge in comparing alternatives is agreeing on the *performance indicators*. One might agree that what a teacher knows about calculus or multi-grade teaching can be equally measured, regardless of whether he or she learned this at a distance or in class. One may argue that the effect of face-to-face instruction is different from that of distance education – because of the contact with teachers, opportunities for collaboration, etc. But one may also argue that distance education develops self-study, or that a broadcast or videotaped lecture or lesson demonstration benefits all of the teachers, while face-to-face instruction or observation could only benefit the select or favoured few. These examples illustrate the point that effects are never fully comparable and alternatives are never identical. Effectiveness measures always reflect a compromise on what the most important effects should be. In practice, and given the expectations and requirements of teacher training, it is again often the case that some combination of face-to-face and group and technology-based and individualized methodologies may be most useful and most cost-effective.

COST-EFFECTIVENESS

Cost-effectiveness refers to the relative worth of an alternative to reach comparable effects, for example, face-to-face versus distance education.

Cost studies merely identify the cost components of a given project. Cost-effectiveness studies compare the relative costs, the costs to produce a given outcome, or effect. To determine cost-effectiveness one must:

- determine what is being compared, and then establish and collect a measure of effectiveness;
- determine what alternatives are being considered or compared;
- obtain information about the costs of each alternative;
- combine the cost and effectiveness data into a cost-effectiveness (C/E) ratio. This ratio shows the amount of effectiveness that can be obtained for an estimated cost, and allows the decision-maker to choose among the least costly alternatives.

How cost-effectiveness studies can inform decisions

Decisions often have to be made as to whether to provide training face-to-face on campus or through some form of off-campus self-study. Here the number of trainees is often the critical consideration. Distance education entails higher fixed costs and lower marginal costs. What needs to be identified is the 'break-even point' – the minimum number of students for economies of scale to obtain. The break-even point depends upon three factors: choice of media, the availability of resources and the production costs.

The choice of media is significant as the fixed costs of media vary. For example, printed materials and radio programmes or audio-cassettes tend to generate lower fixed costs than similar programmes employing television or video-cassettes. Lower fixed costs yield a lower break-even point, i.e., fewer students are required to make the distance learning more cost-effective.

The availability of resources will vary widely. If the production facilities for, say, television and video production already exist, one may only need to factor in the cost of time and space, as opposed to that of building facilities and training production crews. The marginal costs become lower, thus lowering the threshold at which distance education breaks even. The same is true of telecommunication facilities. For example, in south Morocco an underutilized network of optical cable set up by government created a low-cost opportunity for distance education. The same principle applies when the students already have access to the necessary television sets or computers. The costs will still be there and borne by the students – the fixed costs are the same – but the break-even point becomes much lower because the infrastructure and equipment are available.

Production cost may vary from very little – for example when one uses existing materials – to many thousands of dollars – for example, to produce one hour of learning by means of an interactive computer program or high production standard television or video programme. The Arizona Learning System has demonstrated that the cost of developing a three-unit Internet course varies from US$6,000 to US$1 million according to type of content (Rumble 2001). However, there is no evidence that, of itself, highly sophisticated production yields better educational results. Higher production costs raise the break-even point, requiring many more students to make distance learning alternatives cost-effective. If the number of students is very high, it may be worth investing in instructional materials to ensure a high level of quality and uniformity. If the number of students is very low it is inadvisable to commit major resources to sophisticated production.

Experience shows that cost forecasts often underestimate the real costs of implementation by a factor of two to one. Therefore, to be convincing, proposals for distance education projects should show that they can achieve unit costs of between 35 and 50 per cent less than those for conventional, face-to-face, means.

WHAT PRACTICE TELLS US

Thus far we have discussed the ways in which the costs of distance education are constructed and calculated. They provide the planners and providers of teacher education with the tools for making some analysis of their programmes. But what does the actual practice of using distance education tell us about costs and cost-effectiveness? And what conclusions can be drawn from these findings? This section reviews some of the cost issues confronting planners and decision-makers in applying distance education to the various types, phases and levels of teacher training.

There is abundant evidence in the literature about the effectiveness of distance and media-based education for most cognitive outcomes and for many other outcomes typically expected from schools. There is also documented evidence about the cost-effectiveness of distance education programmes for the various levels and types of education (see for example, UNESCO 1977; Dhanarajan et al. 1994; Rumble 1999) including teacher training (Stromquist and Basile 1999). The worldwide explosion of distance and mediated education in both the public and private sectors and for both formal and non-formal education and training is witness to this fact. The arguments and data will not be reviewed here in detail, but Table 11.2 presents a summary of the evidence compiled by Perraton (2000). The issue therefore is not to demonstrate or prove that teachers and student teachers can learn at a distance, but which issues and distance learning alternatives one must consider in designing national, regional or local teacher education programmes.

Table 11.2 Cost and effects of some teacher education projects

Country, project, date	GNP per capita at time of study		Student numbers	Average cost (constant 1998 US$)	Educational and cost impact
	US$ (For dates shown)	US$ (1998)			
Tanzania Teacher Training at a Distance 1979–84	310 (1982)	524	15,000 p.a. 45,000 total	1,863 per student p.a. 7,316 per graduate	Effects comparable to conventional education; cost about half conventional education
Brazil Logos II 1976–81	1,650 (1978)	4,125	24,400	211 per student p.a. 741 per graduate	80% pass rate; costs lower than alternative
Sri Lanka 1984–8	410 (1986)	610	c.5,000	116 per student p.a.	Cost 1/6–1/3 of alternative; more effective than alternative for some subjects but less effective for others
Indonesia 1985–8	530 (1986)	788	c.5,000	805 per student p.a.	Cost about 60% of equivalent; more effective than alternative in languages but less so in mathematics
Nepal Radio Education Teacher Training Basic teacher-training course 1978–80	130 (1979)	292	3,000	196 per student p.a.	Cost slightly lower than alternative; completion rate 83%, pass rate 57%; no evidence that less effective than alternative
Nigeria National Teachers' Institute 1978–89	730 (1984)	1,145	20,327	79 per student p.a.	Cost probably lower than regular colleges; completion rate estimated 42%, pass rate estimated 27%, both rates higher than those of regular colleges

Table 11.2 (continued)

Country, project, date	GNP per capita at time of study		Student numbers	Average cost (constant 1998 US$)	Educational and cost impact
	US$ (For dates shown)	US$ (1998)			
Pakistan Primary Teacher Orientation Course 1976–	330 (1981)	592	83,658 total enrolment 31,674 completed	107–49 per successful completer	Cost per Allama Iqbal Open University graduate 45–70% of conventional university
Kenya in-service teacher training 1968–77	180 (1972)	661	790	806 per subject equivalent p.a.	Cost relatively high; favourable effect on access
Kenya University of Nairobi BEd 1986–90	370 (1988)	510	515	1,096 per student p.a.	Cost thought to be lower than cost of residential equivalent
Nigeria Correspondence and Open Studies Institute University of Lagos 1980–88	730 (1984)	1,145	2,000	345 per full-time student equivalent 1,304 per graduate	If opportunity costs are omitted then cost per graduate slightly lower than residential campus cost
Uganda Northern Integrated Teacher Education Project 1993–97	240 (1995)	257	2,750	2,000 per successful student	Lower cost than equivalent

Source: Perraton 2000: table 6.5

Alternative delivery modes for teacher training

Distance education has been used worldwide to address various types, phases and levels of teacher training. Open universities have offered training for initial and further qualifications for teachers. Educational and public-service television have been used to offer open, narrowcast and interactive programmes dedicated to teachers and teaching. Radio and interactive radio have also been used to address the various and increasing challenges of professional teacher development. The interactive capabilities of the Internet, the web and computers have created a whole new array of formal and informal possibilities for teachers to access information, receive training and interact with their colleagues.

This experience makes it possible to address two questions, about when to choose distance education and about the use of cost-effectiveness studies in planning its use. The first question is: How do we decide whether distance education is likely to be the appropriate choice?

Consider the following situations in which distance education could be a suitable, cost-effective alternative:

- Teachers or trainee teachers are widely scattered. It would be costly to pay for their travel and accommodation and their classes would need to be suspended or merged with others if they were to leave their schools to attend training.
- Teachers or trainee teachers live and work in rural areas. Bringing them to teacher-training institutions or to other training centres in the major cities or towns for two or more years would make their return to their home towns more unlikely and leave schools short of teachers.
- There are not many good-quality trainers of teachers available to staff the many school and training programmes.
- There is a very large number of teachers to be trained within a short timescale and even if the financial and other resources were available, there is no time to create sufficient number of places in conventional teacher-training institutions.
- A university has an existing (campus-based) specialist programme for teachers and wishes to extend the scope of student recruitment and make it more widely available, perhaps internationally through distance education since teachers have difficulty in finding the funding for a full-time residential course and in leaving their families and jobs.

Such situations may arise when educational reforms extend schooling to new areas, extend educational provision in existing areas or extend the entry age or number of years of schooling. They may also be caused

Box 11.1   Logos II, an in-service programme for Brazilian teachers

Project Logos II was implemented in Brazil in the late 1960s and operated until the late 1980s. It offered a distance learning opportunity for serving primary school teachers without qualifications, most of whom had not even completed the (four years) of primary schooling and were teaching in rural and remote areas where there were no teacher-training institutions or centres. The teachers could take the course modules without leaving their jobs. They could study at their own pace and follow one or more disciplines at a time according to their background, motivations, time availability and ability to pass the exams. They could also participate in monthly evaluations and meetings in regional centres. The course was based on printed materials and there were tests for each of its modules. The teachers were required to apply their new knowledge directly in their classrooms and thus test and learn from their own experiences. The examinations were competency-based. The fixed costs included the preparation of the study units (booklets) and the administrative costs (worktime, travel, and the regional offices) incurred by the Ministry of Education and Culture and CETEB, a private educational organization hired to co-ordinate and implement Logos II. The variable costs were the printing of the booklets and the operation of the project offices/teaching centres (in addition to the regional centres in each state that were treated as fixed costs). Cost-effectiveness studies demonstrated that the cost per graduate was significantly lower than any conceivable face-to-face alternative. Allowing for repeaters and dropouts, the cost of training a teacher by conventional means could be ten times the cost of a participant obtaining a diploma through Logos II. Evaluation showed that the level of the teachers' competencies improved dramatically.

Source: Oliveira and Orivel 1993

by social and political crises (including war) or demographic changes or arise as a consequence of introducing new subjects, new textbooks, new approaches, or new languages of instruction. Such developments may warrant not only initial teacher training (sometimes large-scale emergency training) or retraining of qualified teachers. Many countries use distance education in such circumstances. The costs and effectiveness are always relative to particular situations and dependent on the actual conditions of implementation. The success rates vary, depending upon the motivations, prior learning and capacacities of the teachers or trainees, the adequacy and appropriateness of the content and methodologies, media, infrastructure and technology, the availability or experience of the instructors, and how the budgets and resources line up against the extent of change and the number of teachers to be trained. There have also been missed opportunities, with negative consequences for education. For example, in Madagascar and Guinea during the 1980s, governments decided to revert to French as the medium of instruction. The existing teachers were not competent enough in French to adjust rapidly to the reform and thus not able to provide quality teaching and learning. Moreover, the decision to adopt face-to-face training methods limited the training and retraining to a few teachers; in Madagascar, private schools quickly recruited the few available French-speaking teachers.

The last situation listed above relates more to decision-making by institutional planners who have to consider the comparative costs of offering programmes in one or both of two modes (campus-based traditional forms and distance education, perhaps using ICT). Information on cost comparisons for teacher education programmes of this kind is scarce, but what is available suggests three things: a providing institution may choose to adopt distance education delivery for reasons other than cost-saving; it is not necessarily less costly for the providing institution to use distance education and ICT since the necessary staff time is usually underestimated; it may cost the same as campus-based courses but distribute the costs differently; a programme to train teachers through the use of ICT in Chile, for example, had higher fixed costs, for software development, than a comparable face-to-face programme, but lower variable costs, so that the total cost per student for the two approaches was much the same (Perraton *et al.* 2001: 12).

The second question follows after it has been decided to use distance education for teacher training: How can cost-effectiveness studies help select the best alternative? The issue here is less one of cost-effectiveness than of input mix. The factors with greatest impact on costs are production, choice of medium, delivery, and support services.

In providing the learning packages or other resources for the teacher training, the first major decision, which crucially affects production costs, is whether to develop, translate, buy or adapt the materials. Each of these options has implications for the costs, speed of implementation, quality of what is offered and appropriateness and adequacy of the materials for the specific needs and learning environments. Sometimes, as the Hong Kong experience cited in Box 11.2 demonstrates, identifying what already exists and then adapting this provides for a quicker start-up and learning from experience.

Box 11.2   Utilizing existing materials

The Open University of Hong Kong got off to a flying start by using existing high-quality learning material from other countries. These were also utilized for the teacher education programmes, even though the systems and cultural context were different from the United Kingdom, where materials were first developed and applied. Eventually, the level of adaptation and supplementation needed in courses for Chinese-speaking Hong Kong students became so great that the OUHK produced its own programme material in Chinese and specific to the Hong Kong context.

Source: Murphy and Fung 1999: 193

Depending on the needs, target groups and other circumstances, distance education may also be able to use or adapt commercially produced material. This was the case with Posgrad, a programme designed to upgrade the content knowledge of college teachers in Brazil in the early 1980s, which used the same textbooks as those used by the graduate schools, thus decreasing the need for investing in production of materials and consequently lowering fixed costs. The Enlaces project in Chile, by contrast, involved the actual participants in the teacher-training programme in developing and testing teaching and learning materials for their classrooms and pupils, and this materials development process was a key and integral part of their professional development.

A second critical decision is whether to produce the print, audiovisual or web- or computer-based materials in-house or outsource the production – a practice increasingly being adopted in many countries. Such an approach also avoids the high fixed costs of setting up complex production facilities and teams (Orivel 1976). It also means that the most appropriate, effective and efficient individuals or agencies are contracted for particular jobs and dispensed with or not rehired if they do not perform well.

Until fairly recently, the choice of medium for distance education revolved around print, audio and video, and the delivery options were usually limited to correspondence, radio or television. For some developing countries, these are still the only options. Setting up the infrastructure, facilities and staffing to produce technologically sophisticated programmes could involve substantial investment – and this still holds true in some circumstances. However, the new information and communications technologies dramatically change the cost structures of producing distance education programmes. At the same time, while the costs of equipment for production and distribution may have gone down sophistication has gone up, requiring both more sophisticated equipment and more highly skilled personnel to operate it. Some distance education costs much less than it did in the past, and today's distance education content developers are often able to produce the necessary material within their own office with a minimum of external technical support. This does not, however, necessarily apply to poorer countries where the costs of physical structure, telecommunications and equipment are still a major issue.

In considering the costs of delivery of programmes, as of the media within them, the choice needs to fit the national level of technological development. Delivery facilities and infrastructure are becoming increasingly available, flexible and affordable, but it is important to bear in mind that this is not universally so. The utilization of educational technology should follow and not precede infrastructure and technological development, so that access to the delivery systems is only a marginal cost. There are still many communities without power supply or telecommunications links and economies where even radios and their batteries and telecommunications costs are unaffordable. It is not by chance that the cheapest telecommunications costs are to be found in the most developed countries, such as the United States. This happens because of the huge size of the markets and the severe competition, features that are still rare in many developed countries.

As noted earlier, delivery itself is becoming more flexible and sophisticated and many educational and training programmes now blend uses of mediated and face-to-face instruction both on-campus and off-campus. Some aspects of teacher education require the physical presence of a tutor or mentor, and for the teacher's activities to be supervised and coached, so that they cannot be fully replaced by distance education techniques. There are, however, some situations in which the technologies can help practice through, for example, videos of classroom practice, feedback on teachers' performance through video-recorded micro-teaching, and feedback from colleagues using sophisticated but relatively cheap computer interactive media. The example of Capacitar in Box 11.3 illustrates how video-tapes can be used to help teachers identify positive role models of teaching and learn through imitation and feedback.

Support services are an important determinant of cost, with wide variations in the level and type of support provided to the learner. For the most part support services entail variable costs, but some services may have fixed costs for items such as buying or renting equipment or hiring or installing computer systems for student records. The trend is to increase the level of student support and consequently to increase the variable costs.

Box 11.3   Using video recordings and peer learning to develop teaching competencies

Capacitar is a professional development course for serving teachers which has been implemented since 1997 throughout schools in Brazil. It focuses on the development of teaching skills in disciplines such as languages, mathematics, natural and social sciences. The programme comprises forty-eight taped lessons, twelve in each subject. For each lesson, the teachers first read about the contents of the lesson and individually prepare themselves using the printed guidelines. The teachers then form themselves into groups to watch a twenty-minute video-recording of an actual class, showing how specific strategies and skills are used to teach the different disciplines. After analysing and discussing what they saw on the tape, the teachers then individually prepare different lessons, applying the ideas demonstrated in the video-tape. After collectively discussing and revising their individual lesson plans, each teacher teaches the topic by these means to a class of children, observed by a colleague who gives her or him detailed feedback.

The costs of producing these video-tapes is relatively high, at US$10,000. But the costs of delivery are very low because the printed materials and copies of the videos can be used by large numbers of teachers across the nation, and in both schools and teacher-training institutions. No tutors are required. An evaluation of this programme (ISCR 1998) showed that 100 per cent of teachers used what they learned in the tapes within one week of viewing each programme.

Source: ISCR 1998

At one extreme, with variable costs at the low end, correspodence education is used by itself with no interaction with students. This has, however, become a less usual approach as distance education has been incorporating other support services typical of face-to-face teaching such as careful marking of assignments, offering various different forms of tuition, providing opportunities for interaction with tutors and other students, laboratory sessions, and short residential courses (see Box 11.4). Inevitably these elements increase costs, so that it is necessary to demonstrate, in each case, the effectiveness of an additional service. It is, however, often necessary in initial teacher training to include supervised teaching practice, even though this increases variable costs, which must be budgeted for.

Box 11.4 Support for distance teacher education in Bahia, Brazil

Teacher training is a major component of a large-scale five-year project in Brazil's Bahia province, involving more than a million fifth- to eighth-grade students and over 30,000 teachers. Teachers do not have the formal teaching qualifications, experience or understanding to implement the student-centred curriculum.

Instruction for the teachers is delivered through print, using commercially available textbooks, supplemented by guidelines for individual study and assignment specifications. Teachers submit their assignments by mail, fax or email. Tutors email comments on these papers within twenty-four hours. Additional support services include answers to individual questions, virtual scheduled and unscheduled chat sessions and conferencing and one or two days of face-to-face meetings per year.

There are two relatively important cost components in this programme – purchasing, delivering and installing computers in each of the municipalities and meeting the costs of tutors – each student represents about one hour of tutoring per student per month, or one-and-a-half tutor-days per enrolled student per year. This means that a full-time tutor could supervise 120–150 students per year. The costs of communication, including the Internet costs, are practically irrelevant in Brazil, amounting to less than 0.5 per cent of the total project cost.

This case illustrates several cost issues. One is the low fixed costs, given the decision to use commercially available textbooks. The second is the variable cost of tutors, who are only paid according to the number of hours they work grading students' papers. This is a strategic use of the Internet to motivate the teachers to use a new technology and thus become able to use it for teaching purposes as well.

Source: Oliveira 2001

CONCLUSIONS

Distance learning and media-based instruction are becoming a normal part of the set of tools available for the initial and continuing professional development of teachers. All over the world, universities, distance-teaching institutions, ministries of education, teacher-training institutions, and schools are using these technologies to improve the quality of teachers and teaching. The effectiveness of such programmes will always depend upon the relevance and quality of course content, the materials and the tuition – there is nothing intrinsically good or bad about distance learning or technology to make them more or less effective than face-to-face instruction. And the cost-effectiveness of any programme will always be a function of decisions about costs of its various components, as well as of the choice and adequacy of the media for the country, the existing infrastucture, and the circumstances under which the programme is implemented.

Over the last few years, technologies have been seen as important not only in relation to issues of cost and economies of scale, but also because they can provide flexibility in education and training, in much the same way as information technology applied to production has created new flexibility for manufacturing. It is now possible to conceive and deliver instruction in a variety of ways and modes, to the same or different people, using the same or different languages or media. New technologies have created a new concept – economies of *scope* – in addition to the conventional concept of economies of scale. Information technologies now make it possible to create cost-effective, individualized, even interactive programmes for small numbers of teachers. It may require more complex management, but it may also yield increased effectiveness as well as flexibility.

One consequence of this flexibility is that there can now be educational by-products. Older models of distance education did not often enough foster the multi-usage of materials, whether in print or as tapes, or in other formats. The convergence of face-to-face and distance or technology-based education forces producers of programmes to think about the multiple users of materials and multiple ways of using them. The effect of this is to increase the number of users and so to lower the break-even point. In teacher education, a particular concern is the transfer of materials across contexts – be they different countries or regions, different subject matters or different school situations.

Finally, it is timely to highlight a comment made at the outset of this book and recurring in other chapters: that new models and new realities of teaching require new modes of teacher training. Teachers need to learn how to become independent learners and to deal with the new information and teaching technologies. Besides filling important economic functions where resources and time are scarce, or where distance is a barrier, distance learning and technology-based programmes may help form a generation of teachers better equipped to deal with the challenges of teaching in an information society.

REFERENCES

Dhanarajan, G., Ip, P.K., Yuen, K.S. and Swales, C. (1994) *Economics of Distance Education: Recent Experience*, Hong Kong: Open Learning Institute Press.

ISCR (1998) *Avaliação do Programa Capacitar*, Belo Horizonte: ISCR-Instituto Internacional de Avaliação Sérgio Costa Ribeiro (mimeo).

Levin, H. (1983) *Cost Effectiveness: A Primer*, Beverly Hills, Cal.: Sage.

Murphy, D. and Fung, Y. (1999) 'The Open University of Hong Kong', in Harry, K. (ed.) *Higher Education through Open and Distance Learning*, London: Routledge, pp. 190–98.

Oliveira (2001) 'Novas evidências sobre o impacto de programas de recuperação do fluxo escolar', *Ensaio*, 9(32): 305–42, julho a setembro.

Oliveira, J.-B. and Orivel, F. (1993) 'Logos II – an in-service programme for Brazilian teachers', in H. Perraton (ed.) *Distance Education for Teacher Training*, London: Routledge.

Orivel, F. (1976) *Cost Analysis of Educational Television in the Ivory Coast*, Washington, DC: Academy of Educational Development.

Perraton, H. (2000) *Open and Distance Learning in the Developing World*, London: Routledge.

Perraton, H., Robinson, B. and Creed, C. (2001) *Teacher Education through Distance Learning: Technology, Curriculum, Evaluation, Cost*. Paris: UNESCO.

Rumble, G. (1999) *The Costs and Economics of Open and Distance Learning*, London: Kogan Page.

—— (2001) *The Costs and Costing of Networked Learning*, Milton Keynes: Open University.

Stromquist, N.P. and Basile, L. (1999) *Politics of Educational Innovations in Developing Countries*, London: Falmer Press.

UNESCO (1977, 1980) *The Economics of New Educational Media: Present Status of Research and Trends*, vols. I and II, Paris: UNESCO.

Chapter 12

Conclusions

Bernadette Robinson and Colin Latchem

Enough evidence and experience are available to show that open and distance education can be a viable, effective and even cost-effective way of providing initial training and continuing professional development for teachers, if well planned, adequately resourced and competently managed. The range of use is wide, as the preceding chapters show. The role it has played within teacher education systems has varied from the essential (in enabling countries to reach some of their development goals) to the supplementary (offering more teachers more learning opportunities while they continue to teach). The interest of policy-makers, planners, international organizations and educational institutions in its potential is matched by growth in its varied use as illustrated in this book. It is clear from the experience reported in this book and from recent research sponsored by UNESCO, carried out by the International Research Foundation for Open Learning and summarized in Perraton *et al.* (2001), that distance education has been used to solve a variety of problems in teacher supply and quality, often on a large scale. It has produced larger numbers of qualified teachers faster than conventional college programmes, acted as a vehicle for school-based professional development, used limited resources (budgets, facilities, people) in more productive ways, created high-quality learning resources and opened up pathways to career development for working teachers, headteachers and teacher-trainers.

However, not all programmes have been of good quality. Sometimes they have lacked one or more of the necessary key ingredients: adequate resourcing, policy support, well-informed planning, efficient management and co-ordination, well-designed and relevant learning materials, skilled human resources for the different roles needed, good alignment and integration with teacher education generally, and well-functioning partnerships in implementing programmes which involve school practice.

The preceding chapters have illustrated the achievements and limitations of distance education for teacher education as well as some of the problems and issues. Together, they have provided answers to the questions raised in Chapter 1, about the role and capability of distance education for teacher preparation and development, as well as highlighting aspects where we need to extend our knowledge about it. In this final chapter, we focus on two key issues important for the future development of distance education for teacher education, its legitimacy and appropriate use; we also identify areas for further research and conclude with some guidelines for planners.

ESTABLISHING LEGITIMACY

Establishing the legitimacy of distance education has been a persistent problem, especially in contexts where there is a legacy of poor-quality commercial correspondence provision with profit as its main goal. However, legitimacy for open and distance education can be claimed on five grounds:

- evidence from public-sector open universities and dual-mode universities providing both on-campus and distance courses, that students can achieve similar results in course-work and examinations;
- demonstration of distance education's ability to provide worthwhile learning opportunities and formal and informal recognition of the value of the outcomes by employers, peers and communities;
- provision for dialogue and social interaction in good-quality programmes, through the ways learning materials are constructed (incorporating a variety of viewpoints and opening the way for discussion), and through local or regional group meetings, contact with tutors or mentors and the use of interactive media (such as electronic conferencing);
- the visible products, the learning materials (open for peer and public scrutiny in ways that campus-based class teaching is not) and the graduates or beneficiaries of a programme (the teachers and what they have learnt);
- legitimacy by association, where teacher educators and specialists from the regular colleges and universities contribute to the learning materials and act as summer-school teachers or local tutors or where conventional institutions act as partners in programme provision, combining periods of self-study with institution-based training.

An interesting side-effect of questioning the legitimacy of distance education has been to focus new attention on the, often variable, quality of traditional and institution-based provision for comparison.

How can distance education providers strengthen the credibility and legitimacy of their teacher education programmes? Mechanisms used include:

- establishing internal quality-assurance procedures and external validation;
- setting up advisory panels with representatives from national and provincial education authorities, professional bodies and associations for teacher training, examinations boards, school inspectors, teachers, headteachers;
- involving a wide range of participation and perspectives in programme and materials development (teacher education specialists from traditional universities or colleges or provincial services, school inspectors, headteachers and teachers in a variety of roles);
- using appropriate, fair and monitored assessment strategies, with external involvement and conforming to any regulatory requirements (though conformity has also in some cases restricted the amount of innovation and improvement possible);
- negotiating recognition of the distance education qualifications so that they earn equivalent status and salary to those of conventional programmes or enable entry to other programmes of study;
- conducting research on the performance of teachers trained through distance education and disseminating findings from this;
- ensuring representation of the distance education providers on national and local committees for teacher education and other decision-making and professional bodies.

USING DISTANCE EDUCATION APPROPRIATELY FOR TEACHER EDUCATION

Though general education, subject knowledge, knowledge of school curricula, pedagogy, practical classroom management and skill development all come under the heading of teacher education, they place different demands on teacher education providers. Can distance education meet these equally well? What is it good for? What kinds of teacher education require a combination of approaches?

Experience has shown that distance education can do much to raise the levels of teachers' general education, both through structured distance learning courses and through the use of mass media (especially in information-poor rural areas). However, teachers with low educational levels (for example, below secondary-school completion in some developing countries) are more likely to drop out or fail on teacher-training programmes. Where programmes have relaxed their entry qualifications to take in teacher-trainees with low educational levels like these, the failure rates of this sub-group have been higher than those with higher levels of general education. Two strategies are possible to avoid this, if trainees with higher levels of education are not available.

One is the provision of stronger elements of learner support and face-to-face interaction with tutors for trainees with low educational levels, especially for 'difficult' subjects like mathematics or science. The second is the use of bridging or preparatory courses to bring these learners to levels of competence and confidence which enable them to complete the distance learning programmes as successfully as better-qualified entrants.

In terms of academic subjects, distance education has been reasonably successful in helping teachers to develop good understanding of the subject domain or discipline they will teach, if designed to discourage rote learning. The significance of this is that without good understanding of the subject domain, training in teaching methods will not by itself solve pupils' learning problems or improve the quality of teaching. Developing practical skills through distance education presents more challenges, though there is evidence from other fields of training, as well as from teacher education, that in combination with other approaches, distance education can be effective in helping teachers to manage the complex activity of teaching. Developing skills in teaching requires a mixture of information, support for the development of understanding, guided observation, opportunities for experiment, practice, feedback, reflection and re-planning. Some of this learning can be assisted through the use of different media, such as video or audio, but skill development needs practice over time, feedback, coaching and interaction on an individual basis. So the supervision and support of school experience is more problematic for distance education providers, though they can provide a process and system for supporting the local partners or mentors in schools who supervise trainee-teachers, and in some cases support mentors' development too. The capabilities and limitations of distance education for teacher education are summarized in Table 12.1, following Joyce and Showers' (1988) model of teacher development.

IMPROVING TEACHERS' PRACTICE

Though there is a considerable literature on in-service training in general, it is not very helpful in indicating the effectiveness of particular approaches or strategies for specific purposes. Many accounts are anecdotal or reflections by practitioners (useful but not sufficient by themselves) or do not stand up to scrutiny as credible evaluations. Many studies report on particular aspects of training rather than providing a comprehensive evaluation of the training process and its outcomes. The methods of evaluating provision tend to be narrow and short-term. The situation has not changed much since Greenland (1984) found that, although half of the sixty in-service teacher education activities he examined in West Africa

Table 12.1 The capability of distance education for teacher education

Functions	Distance education's capability to provide them
Provides information and subject content	• can provide materials for wide and rapid dissemination; • can create good-quality learning materials explaining new theory and techniques, and illustrate them, using print and other media; • can draw on 'best experts' or 'best practitioners' to contribute to materials, and provide a wide variety of ideas and techniques; • can present new ideas and raise awareness
Demonstrations of their application	• can demonstrate through print (case studies, examples of teachers' work) and through audio and video materials; can illustrate teachers and children at work in a variety of classrooms and in discussion with each other; can include 'teachers' voices' and their real concerns in the materials; • can show a wider range of practice and contexts than a teacher would otherwise have access to
Practice by the teacher	• can support a teacher's practice by structuring teaching activities in self-study texts and guiding the teacher through them; offers some support for reflective practice, especially if linked to peer-group meetings and tutor support; • can set course assignments which link theory to practice and give students feedback on them; • can organise practical sessions at local centres with other teachers, in partnership with local agents; • cannot observe individual teacher's practice in schools; needs local partners; • cannot easily negotiate local access to particular schools for special practice or observation sessions, without local partners
Feedback to the teacher	• can provide feedback on written work and reports of practice; • cannot provide feedback on actual practice to individual teachers; other agents, including group activities, are needed for this
Coaching over time	• can assist coaching activities through providing support materials to develop the concepts, theory and attitude changes which underpin practice; • can provide support materials and guidance in good practice for local agents (tutors, mentors); • cannot provide individual diagnosis, feedback, coaching or counselling without local agents or the use of new interactive technologies (such as two-way video)

Source: Robinson 1997: 130

had undertaken some form of evaluation, the predominant methods were written questionnaires or question-and-answer sessions at the end of courses, relying heavily on self-report. This is still commonly found. Follow-up visits to schools and systematic observation continue to be rare in evaluating the impact of continuing professional development programmes. The kind of follow-up and ongoing support needed to bring about enduring change is usually labour-intensive and difficult to resource in terms of personnel and finances.

Another factor in achieving change and improvement in teaching is the social dimension. Schools are social systems. New teaching methods tend to become established only when they have been proven in practice and adopted by a critical mass of teachers who, together, reinforce each other's beliefs, reduce the risks of innovation and eventually change the culture of teaching. Shared goals, a supportive headteacher and a collaborative atmosphere are needed for this. Where distance education programmes aiming to improve practice are undertaken by a lone teacher in a school, change is more difficult to establish, however good the programmes are. The implication here is that distance education planners need to plan beyond delivery, seeing materials and programme delivery as a launchpad for further teacher activity rather than as the endpoint of the process. More focus needs to be placed on the contexts of use when designing programmes.

In relation to professional development in general, different outcomes follow from different kinds of provision and some are more critical than others in achieving lasting changes. The process is also complex, since the outcomes are interdependent and together affect practice. Kinder and Harland (1991) illustrate this through a hierarchical framework of outcomes from different kinds of inservice continuing professional development (see Figure 12.1). Though it was constructed from a study of primary science education, this kind of framework offers a basis for both empirical investigation and planning. Kinder and Harland suggest that sustained impact and change in teaching practice are not achieved equally well from all outcomes and in fact are rarely achieved if value congruence is absent. In this model, first-order outcomes depend on second- and third-order outcomes, but the latter by themselves are unlikely to result in lasting impact, the ultimate goal. The implications of this for distance education planners are that they need to attend to more than information delivery in providing programmes. They need to do three things: align the intended outcomes closely with the input or kinds of programmes appropriate for different levels and cells, and the balance among them; determine which of these inputs or programmes they can best provide and how and over what period of time to achieve the particular outcomes; and identify which are best done in collaboration with local partners. So designing programmes for teacher education involves

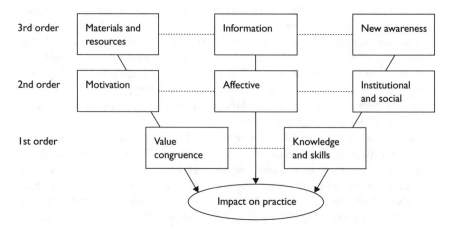

Figure 12.1 A framework for outcomes of in-service professional development programmes (Kinder and Harland 1991)

more than mapping curriculum content and chopping it into manageable
slices for consumption by teachers through self-study.

A further issue in changing teachers' practice is that of relevance. Distance education's capacity to offer high-quality standardized programmes
and materials brings both benefits and disadvantages. On the one hand
this can provide a unified approach to teacher education, much valued in
some countries (for example, China) trying to achieve common national
standards. On the other hand, where changes in practice are involved,
standardization can reduce the relevance of materials and programmes
to local contexts with their own situation-specific characteristics. Ways of
accommodating local variation need to be found, particularly when planning large-scale programmes, since change is most likely to be achieved
through starting where the teachers are, in terms of their knowledge,
skills, conditions, beliefs, practices and languages. Teachers are most likely
to adopt those new practices which are most congruent with their existing roles, values and practices, so change is incremental and evolution-
ary. Attempts at introducing radical change rapidly have often failed. In
large countries or large-scale programmes, the degree of change demanded
of teachers will vary according to their contexts – a point sometimes
ignored by planners.

AN AGENDA FOR RESEARCH

Although the research and evaluation base of distance education in general
has grown over the last decade, we still need more and better research on

its use for teacher education. At least five main aspects are of relevance to planners and in need of attention.

First are the costs, of teacher education in general and through distance education. This continues to be a neglected area. Some of the data are not available even to providers themselves because they have not been recorded at all or have been recorded in ways which make analysis difficult. Some costs are known but confidential since they are a sensitive topic. Better understanding of what to cost and how to analyse costs is needed. Without knowing costs, policy-makers and planners are on uncertain ground.

Second, we need more comprehensive information on efficiency rates (enrolment, participation, completion and success rates). It is sometimes surprisingly difficult to get data on these basic aspects (see Perraton and Creed 2000; Creed 2001; Perraton et al. 2001). In some cases, the data exist but are not easily accessible or used much as management information. Where teachers participate in less formal, unstructured programmes, other appropriate measures are needed to find out what the participation rates are and what they signify in terms of effects and impact. For example, the claim that over 50 per cent of primary teachers in a country participated in a programme says little, without some information about the degree and nature of participation, the kind of activities involved, the learning that resulted and its effects on classroom practice. In many cases, claims like these lack firm evidence to substantiate them.

Third, we need to know more about effectiveness and the impact of programmes on teaching and learning, especially for continuing professional development programmes. This is often lacking for conventional provision too. We need to know more about the benefits and drawbacks of different options and outcomes in deploying resources for initial training and continuing professional development.

Fourth, we need to find out more about the policy environment of distance education for teacher education. This varies widely between countries. Although some have distance education as a strategic tool within their policy and plans for training teachers, other make little mention of it, even when it is used. Because new training needs demand new solutions, there is a need to pay greater attention to the policy aspect in developing alternative options like distance education. In some countries the policy aspect is limiting the scope of distance education for teacher education.

Fifth, we need to develop better evaluation of teacher education through distance education, to go beyond the descriptive to the analytic. Building evaluation capacity into the implementation of programmes would help achieve this goal. We also need to find better ways of disseminating what we already know or getting studies done. International agencies such as the Commonwealth of Learning, UNESCO and the World Bank are contributing to this through publications and websites, though more dissemination activity and exchange is needed.

In addition, we need more and better research on the issues common to all teacher education providers, whether through distance or traditional modes, for example, on how to turn knowledge about teaching methods into improved practice, or how to distinguish between in-service activities which have only a short-term impact and those which are likely to generate lasting change, and which kind of teacher development policies are most productive in improving the quality of teaching, and at what costs.

GUIDELINES FOR PLANNERS

We conclude with a starting point for planners. This is based on UNESCO's guidelines (Perraton *et al.* 2002) on using open and distance learning for teacher education and a fuller set can be found there.

- Make sure that open and distance education is the right solution to the problem. If the problem is really one about deployment and utilization of teachers rather than the need for more trained teachers, then distance education may be the wrong solution. Model some scenarios of the implications, especially financial, of successful programmes.
- Work within the relevant policy framework so that the programme fits its national context and, where appropriate, its regional or international one. There may be several sets of policies to attend to, for example, in the use of communications media or information and communication technologies in schools or regulations governing the provision of initial training or continuing professional development.
- Establish baseline data on the extent and profile of needs and the nature of the target audience. Define the scale of provision needed and the timescale and budgets available.
- Identify through wide consultation the role that the distance education provision will play, and in relation to the teacher education system overall, and set up consultative and collaborative mechanisms.
- Decide what learning outcomes are intended, which media are appropriate, affordable and accessible to learners. Ensure that choices are based on sound information.
- Identify clearly the purpose and intended outcomes of the training and the resources, people and partners, from whatever sources, needed to make it work.
- If choosing information and communication technologies as a main component of the programme, construct data on the real costs of use (costs of consumables, support and training) and build this into programme plans and budgets.

- Assess what kinds of partnerships would make practical work possible and the resources needed to support them.
- Ensure that the programmes meet the regulatory requirements for recognition so that teachers are not left at a disadvantage on completion.
- Plan an appropriate quality-assurance framework or adapt an existing one to fit the requirements of a distance education programme, to ensure good practice and credibility.
- Decide what it is you want to know about the programme and its outcomes when it is operational and when it is completed, and plan monitoring and evaluation activities as part of programme planning.

REFERENCES

Creed, C. (2001) *The Use of Distance Education for Teachers*, Cambridge: International Research Foundation for Open Learning (report to Department for International Development).

Greenland, J. (1984) 'Inset policy and provision in Africa in the early 1980s: where do we go from here?' in U. Bude and J. Greenland (eds) *West African Approaches to Primary School Teachers*, German Foundation for International Development, Bonn: Deutsche Stiftung für Internationale Entwicklung (DSE).

Joyce, B. and Showers, B. (1988) *Student Achievement through Staff Development*, New York and London: Longman.

Kinder, K. and Harland, J. (1991) *The Impact of Inset: The Case of Primary Science*, Windsor: National Foundation for Educational Research.

Perraton, H. and Creed, C. (2000) *Applying New Technologies and Cost-effective Delivery Systems in Basic Education*, Paris: UNESCO.

Perraton, H., Creed, C. and Robinson, B. (2002) *Teacher Education Guidelines: Using Open and Distance Learning*, Paris: UNESCO.

Perraton, H., Robinson, B. and Creed, C. (2001) *Teacher Education through Distance Learning: Technology, Curriculum, Evaluation, Cost.* Paris: UNESCO.

Robinson, B. (1997) 'Distance education for primary teacher training in developing countries', in J. Lynch, C. Modgil and S. Modgil (eds) *Innovations in Delivering Primary Education*, London: Cassell Education, pp. 122–38. Available at <http://wbln0018.worldbank.org/hdnet/hddocs.nsf/>

Index